teaching, learning and intersecting identities in higher education

Questions about the Purpose(s) of Colleges & Universities

Norman K. Denzin and Shirley R. Steinberg
General Editors

Vol. 21

The Higher Ed series is part of the Peter Lang Education list.
Every volume is peer reviewed and meets
the highest quality standards for content and production.

PETER LANG
New York • Washington, D.C./Baltimore • Bern
Frankfurt • Berlin • Brussels • Vienna • Oxford

teaching, learning and intersecting identities in higher education

EDITED BY SUSAN M. PLINER & CERRI A. BANKS

PETER LANG
New York • Washington, D.C./Baltimore • Bern
Frankfurt • Berlin • Brussels • Vienna • Oxford

Library of Congress Cataloging-in-Publication Data

Teaching, learning and intersecting identities in
higher education / Edited by Susan M. Pliner, Cerri A. Banks.
pages cm. — (Higher Ed; vol. 21)
Includes bibliographical references and index.
1. Education, Higher—Sociological aspects—United States.
2. Educational sociology—United States.
I. Pliner, Susan M., editor of compilation.
II. Banks, Cerri A., editor of compilation.
LC191.94.T43   306.43/0973—dc23   2012016214
ISBN 978-1-4331-1314-7 (hardcover)
ISBN 978-1-4331-1313-0 (paperback)
ISBN 978-1-4539-0846-4 (e-book) (print)
ISSN 1523-9551

Bibliographic information published by Die Deutsche Nationalbibliothek.
Die Deutsche Nationalbibliothek lists this publication in the "Deutsche
Nationalbibliografie"; detailed bibliographic data is available
on the Internet at http://dnb.d-nb.de/.

The paper in this book meets the guidelines for permanence and durability
of the Committee on Production Guidelines for Book Longevity
of the Council of Library Resources.

© 2012 Peter Lang Publishing, Inc., New York
29 Broadway, 18th floor, New York, NY 10006
www.peterlang.com

Printed in the United States of America

To my family, whose support, compromise, and love has made this entire project possible. To David, for his ability to always make me laugh, his enduring belief in me and for balancing out my intensity. And, to Lily, whose presence in my life generates boundless joy and love. May Lily, like me, find ways to surprise herself throughout her life's journey and continue to encourage us both with her mantra, "Never give up".

—Susan

To all of my nieces, nephews, and godchildren—you inspire me to help make the world a better place! With this project and through others I will continue the work to help schooling systems see and value your beauty, strength, and intellect. Be proud to be who you are because who you are is *magnificent*.

—Auntie Cerri

Contents

Introduction

Cerri A. Banks and Susan M. Pliner

In higher education in the United States, there is a need for literature that discusses teaching and learning as integrated and synergistic practices that are informed by intersecting identities and the resulting institutional power dynamics between educators and students. Historically colleges and universities in the United States have relegated conversations and scholarship about best educational practices to education departments and programs that prepare students to be K–12 educators. Dialogues about pedagogical theory and identity generally occurred in foundational education programs that situated higher education in historical, sociological, and philosophical frameworks. While we agree that some disciplines lend themselves to conversations about education and identity more than others, we are pleased to see an increased focus on best practices of teaching and learning across a range of disciplines. We argue that in today's complex world, institutions of higher education must pay attention to the ways intersecting identities and inequitable structures of privilege and disadvantage enter all educational settings regardless of unique disciplinary perspectives. By acknowledging these obstacles, colleges and universities can use this information in the practices of teaching and learning.

The contributors to this text represent various disciplines and approaches to this topic. This interdisciplinary approach facilitates our suggestion that ideas related to teaching and learning should not follow traditional models that separate teachers, students, and disciplines, but rather these ideas should traverse the messy terrains where they overlap. There is institutional power connected to particular identities, and these power relationships are reconstituted and reinforced in all U.S. institutions including higher education (Banks, 2009). For example, being able bodied carries particular social, economic, and political privileges in the United States. These privileges (e.g., access, perceived competence, being seen as normal and most desirable) are bestowed on those who are able-bodied even when they are not wanted or deserved (Kendall, 2006; McIntosh, 1988; Rothenberg, 2008; Wildman,

1996). The resulting power relationships evidenced in the dominance held by the able-bodied over those who are labeled "disabled" is re-created in everyday language, media, legal systems, and schools (Howard, 1999).

Intersectionality, Teaching, and Learning

Dill and Zambrana (2009) described intersectionality as "an innovative and emerging field of study that provides a critical analytic lens to interrogate racial, ethnic, class, ability, age, sexuality, and gender disparities and to contest existing ways of looking at these structures of inequality, transforming knowledges as well as the social institution in which they have found themselves" (p. 1). The theory of intersectionality stems from the work of feminist scholars of color whose contributions to academia include the understanding of race, class, and gender as well as other markers of identity as "simultaneous and overlapping spheres of inequality" that impact daily life on both individual and systemic levels (Brewer, 1999; Collins, 1998, 2000; Crenshaw, 1993). In other words, intersectionality forces us to recognize that features of identity are not equal. The interplay of these features creates specific lived experiences, both privileged and not, that inform both the institution of higher education and the individuals operating within the system.

Academic scholarship that is inclusive of the tenets of intersectionality has taken many forms. Most often the concept is taken up in the language of race, class, and gender, leading to what Collins (2009) described as a preoccupation with "personal identity narratives." She states:

> In recent years, intersectional analyses have far too often turned inward, to the level of personal identity narratives, in part, because intersectionality can be grasped far more easily, when constructing one's own autobiography. This stress on identity narratives, especially individual identity narratives, does provide an important contribution to fleshing out our understandings of how people experience and construct identities within intersecting systems of power. Yet this turning inward also reflects the shift within American society away from social structural analysis of social problems. (p. ix)

This book is an attempt to address the conundrum that Collins (2009) presents. Rather than focus solely on individual narratives we will use narrative as one part of a larger social structural analysis of inequality in higher education and highlight the ways an intersectional lens applied to teaching and learning works to mitigate that inequality. While much has been written that captures the features of intersectionality, the concept is not often presented in its purest form; it is often reduced to the language of *race, class, gender*. In addition, credit is not always given to Black women feminists like Kimberle Crenshaw, Rose Brewer, and Patricia Hill Collins who led the charge to make discourse about identity more inclusive and others who joined them, like Assata Zerai and Rae Banks (2002) who persisted in developing the theory of intersectionality as a core curricular theoretical consideration, the way other groundbreaking concepts are attributed to the scholars who presented them.

As editors we speculate that there are two explanations for this problem. First, Black women feminists continue to be systemically undervalued in an academy that places them and their scholarship at the margins. Second, intersectional analysis requires engaging all features of identity including and going beyond race, class, and gender. This generates thinking about individual roles in both privilege and oppression simultaneously, that is, not just the ways we are impacted negatively by inequality but also how our privilege perpetuates inequality (Wildman, 1996). This is a difficult analysis and it is not surprising that there is resistance. For example, colleges and universities that maintain strong connections with religious organizations may espouse principles of inclusive excellence and social justice, like racial equity, but still maintain a patriarchal and sexist approach to gender and a homophobic stance on sexuality. Intersectionality recognizes that the lived consequences of some social identities are often more severe than others but pushes each one of us as individuals and collectively to move past the focus on hierarchies based on individual identity markers. Instead, the theory calls for analysis that is structural and that makes visible the ways identity markers are layered and complicated.

We recognize that one theoretical framework alone will not account for the challenges that occur in teaching and learning as institutions of higher education work to challenge inequity. We will draw upon other perspectives in this conversation, but we believe that an intersectional approach effectively draws attention to the ways these complexities inform policy and practice. Intersectionality is a useful and necessary tool that facilitates equity in higher education. To that end, we have decided in this text to center the concept of intersectionality as a framework that infiltrates the complicated layers of teaching and learning. Each of our contributors uses this concept as they present their discussions of pedagogy, personal exploration, curricular choices, and scholarship.

Intersectionality and Shifting Contexts in Higher Education

The historical context of higher education in the United States is steeped in issues of social equity and identity (Bowen, Kurzweil, & Tobin, 2005; Davis, 2006; Peters-Davis & Shultz, 2005; Rury, 2009). Multicultural education, social justice education, sociology, social psychology, and women's studies have addressed these issues as they relate to teaching and learning in varying ways (Ayers, Quinn, & Stovall, 2009; Newman, 2007; Nicholson, 1997; Nieto & Bode, 2007; Steele, 2010). These disciplines, which are represented by some of the contributors in this text, are most often referenced when issues of identity, culture, power, and difference become salient in higher education discourses. The nature of higher education as discipline specific leads some scholars to feel that content that addresses difference is not relevant to their area of study or to what happens in their classroom. We take the stance that it is relevant, and the impact of intersecting identities and the resulting power dynamics inform every curricular and co-curricular educational space, including: (a) majors and courses offered and how students make decisions about pursuing them; (b) what knowledge is valued in the classroom and how that becomes evident; (c) who is represented in the classroom and who is not, both numerically and in curricula; (d) how varied levels of status and legitimacy are assigned to markers of identity; (e) who has access to particular co-curricular opportunities; and (f) what kinds of interactions exist between faculty, staff, and students in the classroom and in other campus spaces. This necessitates scholarship that shows the ways this content informs disciplines less often thought of as relevant to the discussion. We have accepted this charge and through our contributors include the ways the concept of intersectionality informs academic disciplines like mathematics, legal studies, writing and rhetoric, English, communication studies, anthropology, and sociology.

As our world becomes more connected and complex as evidenced by the ongoing discourses of inclusion and exclusion in higher education, and as students and educators grapple with the complexities of their own identities and those of others, an interdisciplinary approach facilitates the development of expanded strategies for teaching and learning. These strategies enhance institutional relationships in ways that support attempts to build upon differences and create authentic and more equitable learning spaces. In addition, employers are expressing a growing desire to hire college graduates who have skills that include a global perspective, the ability to work within and across differences, a critical and analytical worldview, and the ability to engage in difficult dialogues (Smith, 2009). As educators and scholars our attention and commitment to this matter are simply intellectually sound, academically practical, and ethically responsible.

In recent years, academic scholars have highlighted the ways institutions and processes in higher education operate in broad contexts (e.g., social, political, and economic) and in response to large educational discourses (e.g., access, equity, and assessment) (Giroux & Giroux, 2004; Golden, 2006; Sacks, 2007). As a result, academic anthologies examining the intersections of race, class, and gender and other markers of identity have become vital texts in interdisciplinary approaches to social equity (Adams, Bell, & Griffin, 2007; Ferber, Jiménez, O'Reilly Herrera, & Samuels, 2009; Johnson, 2006; Heldke & O'Connor, 2004; Ore, 2009; Rosenblum & Travis, 2008; Rothenberg, 2010). These texts have explored the following broad themes: (a) theorizing privilege and oppression, (b) socially constructing difference, (c) maintaining and dismantling systems of inequality, and (d) building alliances and social activism. These texts most often begin with historical approaches; delve into social realities of oppression, as in economics, health care, the legal system, education, and media; and conclude with a discussion of ally work. That these texts are organized in this way reflects a movement in recent years in disciplines that study the social context of oppression and power, from acknowledging and recognizing cultural differences between groups to an examination of the larger institutional forces at play in a multicultural society. Even with this shift, these texts most often analyze identities separately or discuss the intersections between two or three identities. Rarely is there an explicit discussion of intersectionality.

In this text our goal as editors is to discuss the intersections of identity in the most inclusive and expansive way possible. We mean to include race, class, gender, sexuality, ability (including age), religion, and any other feature of identity impacted by privilege and oppression. We take the stance that privilege and oppression happen simultaneously (Wildman, 1996), so for example, homophobia based on religious beliefs should not be shielded by analyses that only examine race and gender, even if the analyses consider race and gender intersectionally.

Teaching, Learning, and Intersecting Identities in Higher Education draws upon the principles underlying these cited anthologies and it is different in three important ways: (a) this text focuses on pedagogy and learning, (b) it is explicitly interdisciplinary, and (c) it includes faculty and student voices writing in dialogue.

Challenges to Teaching and Learning with an Intersectional Approach

The institution of education is informed by socially constructed master narratives (i.e., ideologies) that serve as guidelines for practice and policy. For example, the ideal of a democratic society includes the narrative that every member of the society should be educated, at least in principle. The claim is that the realization of this ideal guarantees access, power, and privilege—this is often called the "myth of meritocracy." The myth is that anyone who tries can achieve this level of success. In reality, the benefits of economic, social, and political prosperity—the American Dream—are reserved for those who receive the highest degrees from colleges and universities. Access to this level of education is typically limited to those who have money, high standardized test scores, family legacy, and extensive political and economic networks (Langston, 2000; Shipler, 2005).

Socially constructed master narratives also create obstacles to teaching and learning intersectionally. These narratives about negotiating difference can inform the ideals and behaviors of both teachers and students in the classroom and in other educational settings. Most of us who have experience teaching about identity, power, oppression, and related concepts have likely experienced a certain amount of resistance from our students and sometimes from our colleagues. Likewise, many of us have stories of students and colleagues who, after considerable struggle with these ideas, really seemed to "get it." What follows is a discussion of the types of challenges created when master narratives infiltrate the teaching and learning process.

Master narratives that minimize difference

The master narratives that minimize difference are socially constructed. They infiltrate classroom environments whether that is the intention of the instructor and students or not. Many of the narratives are well meaning and are attempts to alleviate stigma, find points of connection, and create the impression that one is unbiased. Individuals may accomplish this at some level, but minimizing difference makes it difficult to address the societal inequalities that are functioning in classrooms and other educational spaces. These systemic outcomes cannot be mitigated unless we recognize the major ways difference informs histories, biographies, and societies (Mills, 1959). For example, the ideology of *color blindness* (and we would add ability blindness, sexuality blindness, etc.) is a popular social discourse. This is the idea that one person can look at another person without seeing visible biological identity markers. We know that if one has vision, this is impossible. Someone looking at the contributors of this text would at least see variances in gender and race. The interactions between the observer and the contributors would be informed by all of the things connected to what we have been instructed to believe (and what we have accepted as true) about gender and race. When individuals claim color blindness, what they mean is that they try not to judge, be prejudiced towards, or behave in discriminatory ways based on biological identity features. Scholars who study difference have shown that if an educator does not "see" who is in the classroom, and students do not "see" each other, then they cannot prepare for or address the complex interactions that can occur when one is teaching and learning in a diverse group (Howard, 1999).

Another way individuals try to find points of connection across differences is through the ideology of *sameness*. This plays out in multiple ways. For example, at times it is useful for individuals to look for and focus on commonalities in the lived experiences of themselves and others (Gaertner & Dovidio, 2009). This pursuit of sameness can lead to the use of stereotypes, broad generalizations, and assumed familiarity in the classroom, resulting in awkward interactions, conflict, and other obstacles to learning. Intersectionality teaches us that differences occur between and within groups. This lens pushes students and teachers to recognize that sharing identity markers does not automatically mean sharing perspectives. In addition, teachers and students should also understand that because they have had particular identity-related experiences does not mean that they fully understand the perspective of others. For example, a white student who has been situated as a racially numeric minority at an event does not fully understand the lives of people of color from this instance. In addition, a faculty member who has spent significant time studying a cultural group or phenomenon may be an academic expert but should not assume that this proficiency makes them experts about the lived experiences of students who may belong to that group. It can be said that having these interactions may provide these individuals with sensitivity and a sensibility about issues of difference, but what is most important is that they do not allow this knowledge or experience to lead to assumptions of familiarity and sameness that block the ability to address the consequences of inequity.

The narrative about difference that paints one person or group as always a perpetrator and another person or group as always a victim also presents challenges to teaching and learning with intersectional approaches. One of the features of intersectionality involves the movement away from binary ways of thinking, like good and bad, to more complex interplays. When placing blame or claiming to be a victim, it is difficult to see one's own privilege at work. An intersectional approach tells us that this dualistic way of thinking needs to be replaced by the more complex "multiplicative" thinking that allows one to recognize that most people experience privilege and disadvantage simultaneously (Brewer, 1999).

Master narratives' impact on emotion and behavior in the classroom

In the classroom, teachers and students may not initiate or participate in identity-related discussions about difference and power because of conscious or unconscious feelings of *guilt and shame*. This guilt and shame stem from having an inadequate understanding of these topics from their family histories and prejudices and because of limited experiences and interactions across boundaries of difference. In order to avoid personal discomfort, students and teachers may restrict conversations about difference to accounts of personal experiences as a way to resist talking about the potency of racism, sexism, classism, ableism, homophobia, and the like. For example, a student may say about the child of their housekeeper, "We are like siblings." Likewise, a teacher might say, "One of my closest friends is gay." These personal statements may be true, but on their own, they minimize the systemic and intersectional nature of social class inequity and homophobia. Students who believe they have not had similarly positive experiences with difference may sit silent during this type of personal discussion, thinking they have nothing to contribute or feeling shame connected to a negative encounter they may have had.

When engaging difficult topics, guilt and shame can be paralyzing. Centering personal experiences can stifle the development of academic knowledge about difference, like intersectionality, that can not only help students and teachers negotiate personal experiences and interactions, but that, more importantly, gives them the language and critical thinking skills that allow them to address systemic issues of power and privilege (Harper & Quaye, 2009). Personal experiences situated in systemic analyses can provide important anecdotal references that can support talk about difference, but they should not be the center of the interactions. It is important that teachers and students get past each of these obstacles in order for authentic teaching and learning to occur.

Behaviors that minimize difference are at times used to mask limited understandings and show resistance. For example, faculty may choose to completely avoid content that has to do with diversity even if it is relevant to their curriculum. When they do address this content students may act out by refusing to participate in class discussions or activities, being absent on days when that content will be covered, or dropping the course altogether. In addition, during discussions of difference teachers and students at times will focus on lessons of vocabulary and political correctness (e.g., saying the right thing), which is a way to avoid the risk and responsibility that come with dialogue about larger social, economic, and political implications of inequity.

We have outlined some of the master narratives that infiltrate attempts at teaching and learning intersectionally. In this text the contributors will discuss the wide range of ways master narratives appear in classrooms across the disciplines and at different kinds of institutions. The authors use the concept of intersectionality to focus on the similar and divergent identities and experiences of marginalized and privileged groups. They analyze the ways inequality and power infiltrate the classroom experience and provide suggestions to address these obstacles. Since doing so requires more than just a sense of social justice, it is our belief that the application of the theory of intersectionality to teaching and learning creates new social knowledge with a goal of social change.

Outline of the Book

As mentioned, the editors and contributors to this text represent a range of social identities, academic disciplines, and relationships to the concept of intersectionality. One of the things we all agree upon is the significance of utilizing this conceptual space in our teaching and learning, particularly as we engage in increasingly diverse classrooms. As editors we asked the contributors to think about the role of intersectionality in their teaching and learning in multiple ways. This text reflects those thought processes.

Some of the chapters in this text are authored by scholars across disciplines who focus on their own identity work. These chapters include reflections on difficult situations in the classroom and the authors' attempts to include intersectionality in their scholarship and teaching and their efforts to understand how it impacts student learning. Other chapters represent a dialogue between scholars and their students. These coauthored chapters involve reflections on the ways intersectionality has informed the teacher-student relationship, including student expressions about the impact of intersectionality on their learning.

Khuram Hussain explores the ways his move towards teaching history through an intersectional lens better prepares students to interpret the voices of the past. He argues that student stories need to interact with the stories of historical change agents. This interaction can facilitate students making connections between personal transformations and structural change and develop skills necessary to engage authentically with lessons of educational history.

Kim Case, Angela Miller, and Shaprie Bambacigno Jackson discuss student discomfort with confronting multiple forms of oppression in a course that on the surface only deals with gender. They describe their collaborative work to revamp the course Psychology of Gender, Race, and Sexuality to include intersectionality at theoretical and applied levels.

Leah Wing examines the ways educators should utilize an intersectional discourse to enhance models of conflict resolution education. She argues that the absence of this discourse reinforces master narratives that hide institutionalized privilege being reinforced in the classroom.

Anna Creadick, Jalisa Whitley, Patrice Thomas, Amber Jackson, Katy Wolf, Martin Quigley, and Reina Apraez present their experiences in a first-year seminar entitled Seeing Whiteness. As part of their dialogue they seek to understand whether the process of isolating whiteness for critical examination serves the purpose of "dismantling its power" or "reinforces" it.

Linda McCarthy and Laura Larson argue that a pedagogy of intersectionality is useful to help sociology students on a diverse community college campus expand their understanding of marginalization to include ways privilege and oppression occur simultaneously.

Neeta Bhasin presents a rhetorical perspective of intersectionality and discusses how she and her students examine socially constructed identity categories that are mapped onto or transformed into features of situated ideology and identity as they become interactionally activated and relevant. She further argues that social identity can thus be viewed as something that people "do" rather than what they "are."

Lesley Bogad, Ibilolia Holder, Juanita Montes de Oca, Andres Ramirez, and Chris Susi discuss the advanced learning and leadership initiative for educational diversity (A.L.L.I.E.D.). This program was developed for future teachers who self-identify as members of historically underrepresented groups to come together for the complicated work of intersectional coalition building.

Jennifer Esposito and Alison Happel situate their conversation in the context of the Obama presidency and highlight the ways intersectional approaches to scholarship and pedagogy can provide educators and students with ways to challenge notions like "color blindness" and "meritocracy" in what many are calling a "post-racial society."

Susan Pliner, Cerri Banks, and Ashley Tapscott focus on their experiences as teachers and learners as they integrate intersectionality into their pedagogy to create transformative learning environments.

Jennifer Bowen responds to stereotypes about gender and race in mathematics and the sciences. She explains that in a class where power, inequality, and social justice are not inherent contextual topics it is imperative that the instructor has a deep understanding of the intersectional lives of the students in the classroom and the ways power dynamics related to identity impact their ability to learn mathematics.

Julia Johnson, Mary González, Cris Ray, Jessica Hager, Diana Leon, Sally Spalding, and Tiffany Brigham discuss education as a practice of freedom as defined by Freire. They engage in dialogue about "intersectional differences" that have impacted their educational experiences and their relationships with others within the context of higher education.

Liz Braun provides a glimpse into the ways institutions of higher education can promote a more expansive approach to "diversity" by using an intersectional framework. She argues that without an intersectional lens, institutions engage in policy and practice that narrowly construct the student experience. She proposes changes to traditional diversity initiatives by providing suggestions to enhance programmatic approaches.

References

Adams, M., Bell, L. A., & Griffin, P. (Eds.). (2007). *Teaching for diversity and social justice* (2nd ed.). New York: Routledge.

Ayers, W., Quinn, T., & Stovall, D. (Eds.). (2009). *Handbook of social justice in education.* New York: Routledge.

Banks, C. A. (2009). *Black women undergraduates, cultural capital, and college success.* New York: Peter Lang.

Bowen, W. G., Kurzweil, M. A., & Tobin, E. M. (2005). *Equity and excellence in American higher education.* Charlottesville: University of Virginia Press.

Brewer, R. M. (1999). Theorizing race, class, and gender: The new scholarship of black feminist intellectuals and black women's labor. *Race, Class, and Gender,* 6(2), 29–47.

Collins, P. H. (1998). *Fighting words: Black women and the search for justice.* Minneapolis: University of Minnesota Press.

Collins, P. H. (2000). *Black feminist thought: Knowledge, consciousness, and the politics of empowerment* (rev. ed.). New York: Routledge.

Collins, P. H. (2009). Foreword: Emerging intersections—building knowledge and transforming institutions. In B. T. Dill & R. E. Zambrana (Eds.), *Emerging intersections: Race, class, and gender in theory, policy, and practice* (pp. vii–xiv). New Brunswick, NJ: Rutgers University Press.

Crenshaw, K. (1993). Mapping the margins: Intersectionality, identity politics, and violence against women. *Stanford Law Review,* 43, 1241–1299.

Davis, L. J. (Ed.). (2006). *The disability studies reader* (2nd ed.). New York: Routledge.

Dill, B. T., & Zambrana, R. E. (2009). Critical thinking about inequality: An emerging lens. In B. T. Dill & R. E. Zambrana (Eds.), *Emerging intersections: Race, class, and gender in theory, policy, and practice* (pp. 1–21). New Brunswick, NJ: Rutgers University Press.

Ferber, A., Jiménez, C. M., O'Reilly Herrera, A., & Samuels, D. R. (Eds.). (2009). *The matrix reader: Examining the dynamics of oppression and privilege.* New York: McGraw-Hill.

Gaertner, S. L., & Dovidio, J. F. (2009). A common ingroup identity: A categorization-based approach for reducing intergroup bias. In T. D. Nelson (Ed.), *Handbook of prejudice, stereotyping, and discrimination* (pp. 489–505). New York: Psychology Press.

Giroux, H. A., & Giroux, S. S. (2004). *Take back higher education: Race, youth, and the crisis of democracy in the post-civil rights era.* New York: Palgrave Macmillan.

Golden, D. (2006). *The price of admission: How America's ruling class buys its way into elite colleges– and who gets left outside the gates.* New York: Crown Publishers.

Harper, S. R., & Quaye, S. J. (Eds.). (2009). *Student engagement in higher education: Theoretical perspectives and practical approaches for diverse populations.* New York: Routledge.

Heldke, L., & O'Connor, P. (Eds.). (2004). *Oppression, privilege, and resistance: Theoretical perspectives on racism, sexism, and heterosexism.* New York: McGraw-Hill.

Howard, G. R. (1999). *We can't teach what we don't know: White teachers, multiracial schools.* New York: Teachers College Press.

Johnson, A. G. (2006). *Privilege, power, and difference* (2nd ed.). Boston: McGraw-Hill.

Kendall, F. E. (2006). *Understanding white privilege: Creating pathways to authentic relationships across race.* New York: Routledge.

Langston, D. (2000). Tired of playing Monopoly? In M. Adams, W. J. Blumenfeld, R. Castañeda, H. W. Hackman, M. L. Peters, & X. Zúñiga (Eds.), *Readings for diversity and social justice: An anthology on racism, anti-Semitism, sexism, heterosexism, ableism, and classism* (pp. 397–402). New York: Routledge.

McIntosh, P. (1988). *White privilege and male privilege: A personal account of coming to see correspondences through work in women's studies* (Working Paper No. 189). Wellesley, MA: Wellesley Centers for Women.

Mills, C. W. (1959). *The sociological imagination.* New York: Oxford University Press.

Newman, D. M. (2007). *Identities and inequalities: Exploring the intersections of race, class, gender, and sexuality.* New York: McGraw-Hill.

Nicholson, L. (Ed.). (1997). *The second wave: A reader in feminist theory.* New York: Routledge.

Nieto, S., & Bode, P. (2007). *Affirming diversity: The sociopolitical context of multicultural education* (5th ed.). New York: Allyn & Bacon.

Ore, T. E. (Ed.). (2009). *The social construction of difference and inequality: Race, class, gender, and sexuality* (4th ed.). New York: McGraw-Hill.

Peters-Davis, N., & Shultz, J. (Eds.). (2005). *Challenges of multicultural education: Teaching and taking diversity courses.* Boulder, CO: Paradigm Publishers.

Rosenblum, K. E., & Travis, T. C. (Eds.). (2008). *The meaning of difference: American constructions of race, sex and gender, social class, sexual orientation, and disability* (5th ed.). New York: McGraw-Hill.

Rothenberg, P. S. (Ed.). (2008). *White privilege: Essential readings on the other side of racism* (3rd ed.). New York: Worth Publishers.

Rothenberg, P. S. (Ed.). (2010). *Race, class, and gender in the United States* (8ᵗʰ ed.). New York: Worth Publishers.

Rury, J. L. (2009). *Education and social change: Contours in the history of American schooling* (3ʳᵈ ed.). New York: Routledge.

Sacks, P. (2007). *Tearing down the gates: Confronting the class divide in American education.* Berkeley: University of California Press.

Shipler, D. K. (2005). *The working poor: Invisible in America.* New York: Vintage Books.

Smith, D. G. (2009). *Diversity's promise for higher education: Making it work.* Baltimore, MD: The Johns Hopkins University Press.

Steele, C. M. (2010). *Whistling Vivaldi: And other clues to how stereotypes affect us.* New York: W. W. Norton & Co.

Wildman, S. M. (1996). *Privilege revealed: How invisible preference undermines America.* New York: New York University Press.

Zerai, A., & Banks, R. (2002). *Dehumanizing discourse, anti-drug law, and policy in America: A "crack mother's" nightmare.* Burlington, VT: Ashgate.

Integrating Intersectionality, Transforming Learning

Khuram Hussain

Introduction

My work as a professor of education is dedicated to supporting student inquiry into the experiences of people who are discriminately targeted by racist, classist, and sexist U.S. school policies and programs. The courses I teach on education history are rooted in an exploration of the innovative ideas and dynamic actions of historically underrepresented school reformers and change agents. Yet, like many history teachers, my courses compartmentalized the social identities of oppressed historical actors.

This chapter will explore my movement towards teaching education history through an intersectional lens and its transformative potential. I argue that employing intersectionality gives students a more accurate understanding of the historical dynamics of school reform movements and supports educators committed to promoting critical and authentic inquiry into the foundations of education. Furthermore, seeing history in terms of intersectionality helps students recognize the complexity of reform movements that promote social justice while also reinforcing certain social privileges.

Chapter Outline

The chapter begins by staging intersectionality within the context of educational historiography. Typically, education historians conceptualize racism, classism, and sexism as separate forces. However an emerging body of scholarship demonstrates the transformative possibilities of an intersectional approach for historical inquiry. Next, I illustrate my movement to incorporate intersectionality into my teaching. This section shows how an intersectional approach can facilitate intimate and dynamic student inquiry into the character of their schooling experiences through storytelling. This section also demonstrates how histories that treat race, class, and gender together can prepare students to recognize the complexity of reform movements that forward an agenda for justice *and* reinforce privileged social positions. This recognition helps students relinquish uncritically accepted master narratives and begin to identify intricate and multidimensional narratives (Hall, 2005). The chapter concludes with a reflection on future possibilities for employing intersectionality as a means of promoting authentic curriculum, cultivating substantive and sustained student interaction, and developing a student-centered classroom.

Intersections in the History of Education

Traditional historians of education have undermined the role of schooling in reproducing sexism, classism, and racism (Graves, Glander, & Shea, 2001; Katz, 1987). In the seminal work *Education in the Forming of American Society*, Bernard Bailyn (1960) argues that traditional American education history is written outside the rigors of mainstream American history and is primarily written for professional educators, not for students of history. Traditional histories are skewed to present a glorified image of American public schooling as engines of social uplift and opportunity. Michael Katz (1987) adds that these histories consist of simplistic narratives on the triumph of "benevolence and democracy" in public schools.

On the heels of Bailyn, a new generation of scholars rejected the claim that public schooling is a vehicle of opportunity. They reframed the story of American education by arguing that schooling functioned to systemically reproduce social inequality (Bowles & Gintis, 1976; Greer, 1972; Kaestle, 1983; Karier, Violas, & Spring, 1973; Katz, 1968; Katznelson & Weir, 1985; Tyack, 1974; Weinberg, 1977). Their historical inquiry provides new insight into the marginalization of nondominant peoples in schools and the dynamics of power and oppression in schooling. A particular interest of these scholars is the function of schooling in reinforcing classism (Cohen & Lazerson, 1973; Katz, 1971; Tyack, 1974) as well as racism and ethnocentrism (Greer, 1972; Kaestle, 1983; Karier, Violas, & Spring, 1973; Tyack, 1974).

Since the 1970s, a growing number of historians are making critical inquiries into race, class, and gender oppression in the context of education (Altenbaugh, 1992; Blount, 2005; Fultz, 1996; Perkins, 1993; Adams, 1995). Scholars of color have added to the ranks of these historians (Anderson, 1988; San Miguel, 2001; Spring, 1997; Szasz, 1999; Walker, 1996). Yet even historians of education who critically examine race, class, and gender tend to treat these social categories separately, isolating systems of power and oppression that could otherwise be examined as a nexus. When multiple categories are addressed as intersecting, they are often framed within particular historic contexts but conceptualized as separate forces.

Rubén Donato and Marvin Lazerson (2000) assert that "[i]ntersections of experience among communities of color have the potential to improve research and teaching" (p. 8). Their argument about communities of color can be extended to include the experiences of people across multiple social identities. Moreover, if history teachers fully present the complex and significant interplay between the historic function of schooling and the multiple social locations of historical actors, then students can witness a richly integrated view of how schooling has functioned in the lives of people over time and the complex role schooling plays in their own lives.

This richly integrated view of history is typified in recent education histories that interrogate multiple social disparities. For example, in *Gender, Race, and the National Education Association*, Wayne Urban (2000) traces the interweaving relationship of gender, race, and social class in his century-long history of the National Education Association (NEA). Taking an intersectional approach allows Urban to illustrate the common and diverging social class challenges of Black and white female teachers in their effort to win opportunities through the NEA. Specifically, the interlocking relationship between racism and sexism was a salient feature in the lives of Black female teachers who shared in the struggle against exclusionary gendered practices, but repeatedly had their grievances on racial inequity undermined by white NEA representatives.

Works by Jack Dougherty (2004) and Davison Douglas (2005) interrogate the dynamics of intra-racial social class disparity among Black school reformers confronted by white supremacy in northern school reform efforts. Their studies demonstrate that recognizing racism is a necessary but insufficient factor for understanding the complex trajectory of Black school reform struggles. This is exemplified by the 1940s debate over whether Blacks would fight for equitable resources in separate schools or for school desegregation. The debate was largely across class lines with middle-class professionals supporting desegregation and working-class Blacks vying to protect Black teachers and paraprofessional positions in segregated schools. This historical event can be understood through the tenet of intersectionality that social class differences are both between and within racial identity markers.

Recent histories serve as an encouraging indication of the possible directions for utilizing intersectionality in the study of education history. One of the most powerful contributions of recent histories is their disruption of unified narratives of race and gender. Master narratives function to subsume complex forms of gender and race oppression into simplified story arcs that reinforce the legitimacy of the most privileged members of society and maintain false divisions among the oppressed (Hall, 2005). Histories that examine the intersectional matrix of race-class-gender break apart the smooth surface of master narratives and unearth a complex and uneven terrain of multiple narratives on movements for equality and opportunity.

An intersectional approach to history assists students in deconstructing uncritically accepted master narratives. For instance, most of my students start out believing that school desegregation was the result of a handful of heroic men like Thurgood Marshall, who represented the interests and aspirations of all Black Americans. When students dig into the intersection of race, class and gender during the struggle for school desegregation between the 1930s and 1970s, they uncover discontent among working-class Blacks regarding the racial desegregation of schools. In contrast to working-class Blacks, the NAACP, which was predominantly middle class, aggressively advocated desegregation (Douglas, 2005). Added to this was the realignment of female Black teachers behind integration, which helped shape the trajectory of grassroots Black support for school desegregation (Dougherty, 1998).

Throughout our study of more than a century of schooling history, my students consider the respective intersectional dynamics within Native, Chicano/a, Black, and immigrant schooling experiences. Students explore readings that treat race, class, and gender together, thereby moving beyond popular narratives towards a more accurate understanding of how and why reform movements emerge and whom they serve. This approach provides students with a richer sense of the significance of school policies. It also provides them with new questions and considerations for addressing issues of social justice and schooling.

A Move from Singularity to Intersectionality

I did not come to an intersectional approach initially or automatically but through reflection and classroom experimentation. The theoretical framework for examining multiple subordinate group identities initially emerged in women's and ethnic studies (Dill & Zambrana, 2009). My graduate studies prepared me to identify and evaluate intersections of race, class, and gender as compounding forces but not to utilize intersectionality as a primary analytical tool. Like many historians, I examine the compounding oppression of racism, classism, and sexism within particular historic contexts but tend to conceptualize these as separate forces. Over the past three years, my interactions with colleagues at our small liberal arts college helped me reexamine this tendency.

Originally, I developed my history of education course with the explicit aim of highlighting the relationship between social identity and school policy. My students trace 19th- and 20th-century schooling policy through the perspectives of people of color, the working class and working poor, and women of every group. Students discover how people face oppressive policies and practices and find creative ways to speak truth to the powerful and win important victories through school reform. My students often find inspiration in the everyday actions of historical figures who stand up, speak up, and get things done. "Why haven't I ever heard of this person?" is a common reflection in student writing. For many students, this is the first time they learn about the role of local community organizers in fomenting serious school reform.

In its original formulation, students would first examine social class through the experiences of 19th-century European immigrants and then move to an analysis of race and ethnicity through the study of Native, Black and Latina/o communities, and then gender through the study of boys' and girls' education. While intersection was addressed in each section, primary conceptual consideration focused on elements of privilege and oppression within one social identity at a time.

During my first year of teaching, I began to rethink my approach after I was invited by my colleagues to guest lecture in their co-taught course Race, Class, and Gender. In preparation for my lecture, I reviewed my colleagues' weekly reading assignment from David Newman's *Identities and Inequalities: Exploring the Intersections of Race, Class, Gender, and Sexuality* (2005). Newman identifies elements of socialization within each social identity and then moves into examples of intersectionality within schooling contexts. The chapter assigned that week focused on schools and socialization.

As I read his chapter, I considered what his ideas might have to do with my work as a professor of education history. I was struck by the degree of connection between Newman's contemporary sociological analysis of identity oppression and the dynamics of identity oppression in the history of schooling. One of Newman's salient assertions is that socioeconomic status works in tandem with racial domination and gender inequality to shape the socialization of children. While he is describing contemporary society, he could easily be remarking on the experiences of working-class girls of color a century ago.

For instance, James Anderson (1988) and Donald Spivey (1978) describe the concerted effort of the post-bellum Southern white planter class and Northern white industrialists to develop Southern vocational schooling for newly freed Blacks in order to enforce class-caste domination. The race and class oppression of working-class Blacks was compounded for women of color through gender oppression. Tera Hunter's (1997) study of Southern Black women domestic workers reveals how these women were not only tracked towards low-paying jobs, but their schooling was also intended to reform their "low culture" tendencies.

Both middle-class Blacks and middle-class whites singled out female Black domestic workers for attending dance halls in their leisure time, despite the fact that Black men attended the dance halls as well. Middle-class Blacks feared these women would bring shame and disgrace to the Black race. Middle-class whites feared these women would expose their white children and wives to immorality and vice. Both the Black and white middle class argued that schooling could help reform working-class Black women by teaching them subservience and dutiful service.

The distinctions in educational socialization between working-class Black women and men are as crucial for historians to appreciate as they are for scholars of contemporary educational problems. Newman's approach to intersectionality provides a useful framework for addressing the differentiated consequences of early school policy and the complex challenges faced by oppressed people seeking voice and recognition. In preparation for the guest lecture, I reflected on how I could integrate an intersectional approach into my lesson.

For the lesson I prompted students to examine the intersection of race, class, and gender in the history of Native schooling. Despite their lack of extensive background in Native schooling history, and my lack of background in teaching through an intersectional lens, the students engaged with complex, overlapping, and compounding forms of oppression. Student comments and reflections demonstrated their capacity to interpret single historical events from multiple vantage points of race, class, and gender. Furthermore, they drew parallels between gender and racial oppression in the 19th century and schoolchildren's experiences today. This discussion was catapulted by the personal stories and observations of several students who brought in examples of the intersection of race, gender, and class in their own lives in order to connect to our historical inquiry.

Integrating Intersectionality

During the following semester I reorganized my history courses to more intentionally highlight intersecting identities. I integrated elements of intersectionality into several sections of the course. This was done in part by adding different readings. For example, I originally focused on the scholarship of Michael Katz (1968, 1995) to introduce the early role of schools in enforcing social class hierarchy. I now add Carl Kaestle's *Pillars of the Republic* (1983), which illuminates the early vision of white middle-class Protestant male reformers who aimed to construct a schooling system that reflected their values of capitalism, republicanism, Protestantism, and white, middle-class gender norms.

An intersectional approach is relatively new to history of education scholarship. Therefore, my task is often one of cobbling together relevant readings and accepting the reality that some areas of educational scholarship lend themselves more to intersectional analysis, especially histories of Black American education and women's education. Local histories by Jack Dougherty (2004) and David Cecelski (1995) provide students with insight into the matrix of historical forces that guided Black social movements to achieve educational equality. Dougherty in particular weaves the intersections of race, class, and gender into his analysis of grassroots liberation struggles in Milwaukee between the 1930s and 1990s. Jackie Blount's *Fit to Teach* (2005) provides students with a view of the complex intersection of gender, social class, and sexuality. Blount reveals that 1950s female teachers were beginning to fill administrative ranks before they were halted and systemically excluded, largely through the combined use of homophobic and sexist gender role stereotypes.

While Dougherty and Blount illustrate intersectionality throughout their respective works, most of my course readings do not. Therefore, to help anchor intersectionality in our ongoing study of education history, I encourage students to explore intersectionality in their own lives. The journey into this process is among the most important and most challenging for making intersectionality a meaningful and productive concept for students.

Utilizing Personal Identity Narratives

Telling stories allows people to situate their experiences and identity within a wider world with meaningful coherence (Blum-Kulka, 1993; Schiffrin, 1996). Personal stories play an important role in dialogue-based educational programs that are dedicated to addressing racism, classism, and sexism. In higher education, courses on multiculturalism, diversity workshops, and intergroup dialogues on race, class, and gender commonly include personal identity narratives in order to foster deeper student understanding of issues of privilege and oppression (Enberg, 2004; Srivastava & Francis, 2006).

These stories bring a deeply significant and critical knowledge to student dialogues about difference. Without personal stories, even well-intended dialogues about race, class, and gender can result in misunderstandings and a failure to understand how others represent issues. Linda Flower (2003) observes that even common terms and expressions can have profoundly different meanings, based on experience:

> For behind the words we use in common lie strikingly different life experiences that instantiate a concept (such as "police-enforced") with different flesh and blood realities. Such experiences may allow you, for instance, to make sense of that concept with an image of your own son, in his stocking cap and braids . . . who was recently harassed by police on his way to the corner store. As an inner city resident you may instantiate that concept of police-enforced curfew with the visceral feeling of what "no recourse" means in a confrontation with authority. (p. 38)

According to Flower, individuals automatically *enact* certain concepts based on life histories of encounter. These experiences serve as the grounding for certain presumptions. Individuals that have no familiarity with these experiences often fail to appreciate or imagine differing conceptualizations.

Courses and workshops that are committed to anti-racism, anti-classism, and anti-sexism use participant storytelling to get at these "different life experiences." Storytelling becomes a way to build knowledge and initiate a critical examination of social inequality. Moreover, the goal of storytelling is not simply to disclose student experiences and feelings but to co-develop a new and sustained understanding of social relations (Srivastava & Francis, 2006).

In my classroom, the sharing of personal stories is an important way of promoting understanding among students and intimately involving them in course content. This approach has been particularly helpful in buttressing students' engagement with controversial educational issues that carry different meanings for members of privileged and oppressed social identities. Educational issues such as the "achievement gap," standardized testing, "cultural deficiency," and tracking often carry a personal significance for students. This significance is rooted in their experience with (or ignorance of) racism and classism.

Without a discussion of personal experiences, students may not recognize the different meanings that issues like tracking represent. College-tracked students often describe how they benefited from tracking because it ensured that school resources would be allocated to provide them with AP classes and SAT prep, along with guidance to support their college preparation. Students in non-college tracks or trade school tracks often describe how tracking represented fewer resources, lower expectations, and classrooms where discipline, not teaching, was the primary function of their teachers.

Personal experiences often point to truths that guide an individual's interpretation of issues (Flower, 2003). Sharing experiences is crucial for classroom dialogues because it serves to substantiate student conceptualizations of issues from both privileged and oppressed perspectives.

From the first day of class onward, my students and I engage in an exploration of our schooling biographies to spark awareness about the intimate and dynamic character of our experiences with schooling. My approach to student storytelling is pedagogically grounded in the strategies of contemporary intergroup dialogue work. According to many practitioners and scholars of intergroup dialogue, their work is designed to facilitate shared meaning around issues of injustice, in a safe space, where all participants speak and learn from one another (Nagda & Zuniga, 2002). The structure of intergroup dialogue typically begins with sharing experiences and building trust before moving into direct conversations about structural inequality. Therefore, I focus first on promoting positive and respectful student-to-student interactions and establish ground rules for difficult conversations about difference.

Students are asked to self-identify their race, class, and gender. We then move into dialogues on aspects of their identity that are difficult to experience in school and those that are easy or even advantageous. While students are free to share only what they are comfortable sharing, they are encouraged to listen deeply and open themselves up to understand the experiences of others.

As individuals share and discuss their most salient experiences with difference in schooling, I introduce them to concepts of privilege and structural oppression.

Students are guided to operationalize privilege and oppression in the context of one another's stories. In hearing and sharing stories, students often begin to recognize privileges that they were not fully aware of. Early in the semester a female student of color shared a story that left many of her classmates in total surprise:

> Oddly enough I never felt inferior before college and at this place I have felt inferior. It is just subtle enough to feel; your skin color and bank account are important and one is constantly reminded of it. In a way it keeps people in their place.

Students who share stories of exclusion in schooling are often well versed in the oppressive actions taken against them and are encouraged to explore their educational mistreatment within a matrix of power and privilege.

The students receive prompts to identify intersectional points where they were both privileged and oppressed or doubly privileged or doubly oppressed. For example, during a recent class on school segregation students shared their stories about the relationship between neighborhood and school segregation.

During a class on the consequences of residential segregation for racial inequality, a white, female working-class student shared her story of growing up in housing projects. Initially she asserted that "inequality is primarily about social class . . . it's about economics." After intense class dialogue, particularly with consideration to the lives of students of color who grew up in housing projects, she and other students began to recognize in tandem the oppression she faced because of her social class *and* the privilege afforded by her racial identity.

Many of the stories of their classmates stay with students throughout the semester and anchor their consideration of historical actors confronted with racist, classist, or sexist conditions. In addition, the practice of seeing intersectionality in their own schooling experiences better prepares them to notice intersectionality within historical moments and examine its significance.

At the beginning of each new section of the course, we return to stories about ourselves to ground our historical inquiry. For instance, to introduce the Protestant, capitalist ideology of 19th-century middle-class public school advocates, students are asked to examine their experience with the notion of American meritocracy, a central tenet of the Protestant middle class. The myth of American meritocracy can be understood as the belief that everyone, regardless of social class, can anticipate economic success through their own hard work and virtuous actions (Hochschild, 1995).

The students share stories of how the meaning of merit was framed in their family and school life. Through discussion, students have the opportunity to see how social class informs the meaning of meritocracy for their classmates. As they listen to one another, students begin to observe that middle-class and upper-class students have a different belief in meritocracy than their working-class counterparts. For example, middle-class students tend to see Advanced Placement courses and college-bound programs as being populated with students who "deserved to be there because of hard work." These discussions often revolve around intersecting identities, such as how social class and immigration status can inform how students experienced the middle-class myth of meritocracy in their upbringing.

Students carry these stories with them in their critique of 19th-century school reform rhetoric. As they examine the historical ideas and attitudes of white, middle-class reformers who claim "universal" goals for education, students draw a parallel with current formulations of school policy that claim to have a common purpose but emerge from the minds of white, male, Christian, middle-class policy makers. In a recent classroom discussion on the homogeneity of early school reformers, students asserted that even if today's policy makers were committed to anti-racist, anti-classist, and anti-sexist school reform, their efforts would invariably reproduce inequality unless people of color, working-class people, persons with disabilities, and women were represented at all levels of reform.

What was remarkable about the discussion was that students drew on earlier explorations of their experiences with schooling to illustrate their position. For example, several students noted that their concept of meritocracy was so deeply influenced by their middle- or upper-class upbringing that they might miss how the concept could be seen as negative or oppressive.

Personal stories also serve to anchor intersectionality in student analysis of education history. The most transformative example of this has been the intersection of race and class. During my first year of teaching educational history, students often discussed social class inequity in a way that avoided direct discussion of institutional racism and white privilege. Students maintained that the mistreatment of Black Americans had more to do with classism than racism. Other students, who I suspect were more comfortable talking about classism than racism, would often jump on board with the students who argued that classism trumps racism. While such student positions lead to fruitful conversation, they also indicate that there is a missing component in the framing of race and class.

While I never frame race and class as mutually exclusive, the original design of my course treated them at separate points in the syllabus, which limits a full view of how they interact. Thus I was not providing students with the adequate context to evaluate how white supremacy interacts with social class inequality. Moreover, students were not getting a full sense of the pervasive role of white supremacy in characterizing social class in America. Throughout American history, racism separates the Black and white middle class (Frazier, 1993) and divides working-class Blacks and whites (Ignatiev & Garvey, 1996; Roediger, 1991). Without an understanding of the dialectical relationship between race and class, my students are left with a disjointed sense of historical forces.

Since I started to introduce texts that address intersectionality, in tandem with personal identity narratives, students have approached the dynamics of racism and classism with greater nuance. Personal identity narratives about classism and racism in conjunction with readings and class discussions on white privilege and class privilege present my students with a more multidimensional terrain of historical social forces. Hearing and sharing experiences where both racism and classism impact the lives of fellow students serve as a profound lesson in the power of compounded oppression. In turn, students rarely try to trump racism with classism anymore, and when they do there are now voices in the classroom that point out the race-class nexus.

Furthermore, I am thrilled to find students identifying and even seeking out race-class dynamics in historical contexts. Recently my students discussed the 1950s effort of the NAACP to get working-class Blacks to join in desegregation lawsuits. Students raised the issue of social class disparities between the NAACP's Legal Defense Fund and their potential clients. During their conversation, they compared the differing interests of middle-class Blacks and working-class Blacks in dismantling segregation.

A conversation of this nature did not happen the first time I taught my courses, wherein my students tended to isolate race and class. I believe that the joint strategy of including personal identity narratives and historical scholarship that explores intersectionality makes my students better historians. As a teacher this is exciting because intersectionality represents a vital analytical framework for the study of social history, and my journey towards it has just begun!

Challenges and Limitations

While narratives have the capacity of supporting critical inquiry, they can also subvert equitable dialogue, invalidate the experiences of underrepresented people, or become a distracting preoccupation. Recognizing these issues is essential for appropriately engaging with personal identity narratives as well as acknowledging their limitations.

In their qualitative study of 12 anti-racist workshops, Sarita Srivastava and Margot Francis (2006) find that many white participants reinforced dominant conceptions of race and gender, which serve to perpetuate racial inequity. A frequent problem they identify is white denial and dismissal of stories of racism, underscoring the inequitable context within which such experiences are shared. Ilsa Govan and Caprice Hollins (2010) argue that even well-intended whites invalidate the experiences of people of color by telling them that they are misinterpreting their own experiences: "It might sound like, 'That wasn't racism, Mr. Wilson is like that with everyone,' or, 'When I go shopping I'm followed, too,' or, 'I know Mr. Wilson pretty well and I just don't think that's what he meant'" (p. 3).

While I would like to think that my students are especially enlightened, they are also susceptible to denying the experiences of oppressed people. To preempt this thorny challenge, I employ an intersectional approach to class dialogue along with readings on privilege and oppression. Intersectionality can serve as an important resource for getting students to see past their initial denial of the experiences of others. The fact that students and I do not just talk about racism, classism, or sexism, but about all of them and how they interact with one another, provides multiple entry points for students to personally understand power and privilege. Intersectionality has the unique quality of being distributive in its assessment of power structures, while letting no element within the matrix of oppression "off the hook." Therefore, when students discuss oppression in its multiple dimensions, they see how it has impacted their classmates and themselves in different ways. Most students come to recognize a dimension of both privilege and oppression in their own life or the life of someone they care about.

Yet even as I employ intersectionality in these dialogues, I am confronted by the problem of trying to get students to have equitable conversations in an unequal society. Responsible dialogues on difference must address the reality that we are not having these conversations in a power vacuum but that our encounters are between social identities that are structurally unequal in our society. This is especially concerning given the evidence that underrepresented students are exposed to a greater range of harmful outcomes during personal identity dialogues (Ellsworth, 1989; Razack, 1993; Srivastava & Francis, 2006).

This problem is even more salient given our numerical disparity in student diversity. Aside from gender parity, my class numbers tip heavily towards majority group identities in terms of race and class. While my student body is not homogenous, its diversity ratio is comparable or representative of campus demographics at liberal arts colleges nationwide. Any college classroom that does not fully represent our society's richness of diversity is at a loss, so it is especially tragic when diversity is at the heart of a class's academic inquiry. Students of many backgrounds have expressed to me their frustration at the irony of discussing the historic struggle for educational inclusion and access in a room largely consisting of people that have traditionally enjoyed both. We also discuss the challenges faced by students from non-majority group identities, who can potentially feel an even greater pressure to "speak for their group" in unevenly represented classrooms.

The challenges and limitations to authentic and equitable dialogue are not going away anytime soon. However, they stand as stark reminders of how deeply intertwined personal identity narratives are to historic structural forces. Helping students make the connection between their experiences and structures of privilege and oppression can transform their understanding of social relations. Embedding intersectionality into the connection between experience and structure provides students with a fuller view of the character of inequality and a new way of interpreting the historic forces that have shaped our world.

Coinciding with these student dialogues are readings that expose students to the voices of underrepresented peoples. These readings bear witness to the undergirding of privilege and oppression in the cultural and political web of American schooling. Given the limitations of dialogue, these readings do not only reinforce student discussions of identity; at times they provide substantive talking points the student don't or can't raise. This is particularly true when it comes to the issue of productive educational alternatives that underrepresented people develop.

Woven into many of the course readings is the vast world of schooling alternatives promoted by oppressed communities and change agents. My students learn about 1930s socialist Sunday schools and labor colleges that arose in response to public schooling's classist and sexist indoctrination of working-class children (Teitelbaum & Reese, 1983). They also learn about the 1960s Native school control movement, which emerged in response to the brutal legacy of cultural assimilation in public schools. These schools developed the aim of providing children access to discover indigenous ways of knowing and living with modern contexts (Adams, 1995; Szasz, 1999). Students also explore the 1970s Black and Latino/a community control movement. Arising out of organized protest, the New York City community control movement led to an unprecedented community governance structure that allowed for parental and community control of curriculum and hiring in several demonstration schools (Stulberg, 2008).

These alternative schooling models throw light on the systemic inequities of public schooling and demonstrate how the oppressed can envision and develop anti-racist, anti-classist, pedagogical and curricular programs. Sarita Srivastava and Margot Francis (2006) argue that dialogues on difference are substantially limited without a focus on marginalized thinkers and programs. Such a focus moves beyond *what* oppressed people know into an exploration of *how* they know. Exploring how oppressed people conceptualize and make change can lead to recognition of their creative capacities and a curiosity about how change agents make sense of their world.

It is especially important for students to witness these creative actors because the work of recognizing privilege and oppression can leave students overwhelmed and hopeless. Even successful group dialogues about experiences with racism, classism, and sexism do not necessarily inspire students with a renewed sense of creative possibility for school reform. More often, they see the depth and complexity of the problems confronting our society and education system as endemic. Yet an appreciation for the problems alone does not provide students with a sense of agency and will to approach current educational problems differently.

Furthermore, it is important for students to have an energetic sense of possibility to activate their work as critical and creative thinkers. Antonio

Gramsci (1993) famously confronted hopelessness in the face of social inequality by synthesizing hopelessness and possibility: "I'm a pessimist because of intelligence, but an optimist because of will" (p. 229). This kind of synthesis is what I aspire that every student realize. I want my students to participate in a critical engagement with historical and current problems while sustaining their own sense of possibility for affecting current problems.

Students' stories need to interact with the stories of historical change agents, which in turn may help transform their sense of possibility and set them on a new trajectory for their future stories about themselves. For example, when we study the arguments of 1970s advocates for cultural relevance in curriculum, we also share the stories of underrepresented classmates who often feel silenced or misrepresented in their classes. Many of my students from privileged backgrounds began to personally recognize the value and necessity of marginalized voices, not only historically but also in our classroom itself. This illustrates the promise of possible connections students can make between personal transformations and structural change. Moreover, through storytelling students critically address and rethink their assumptions about each other and evaluate the cultural forces that instilled that assumption in them. In turn, students can be directed to reflect on how their capacity for personal transformation presents us with hope for wider transformations.

On Moving Forward

My movement towards integrating intersectionality into my history classes is just beginning. Looking ahead I see new possibilities for employing intersectionality as a means of promoting authentic curriculum, cultivating substantive and sustained student interaction, and developing a student-centered classroom.

First and foremost, I anticipate building more space and structure into my course for student stories. This will require me to give up several classes that could be used to introduce the course's historical content and methods of historical analysis. However this is a crucial step in order to responsibly infuse the course with meaningful student experience. The stories students share are at times powerful and emotional and require processing. Other stories are deeply embedded with assumptions of others, which need to be unpacked alongside comments that invalidate the experiences of others. In addition, there are students who resist seeing structural privileges as fundamentally different from circumstantial advantages, which keeps them from acknowledging how they experience privilege. All of these issues need to be addressed and students should have a sense of ownership over the process; therefore they need to be brought in as co-creators of class expectations and rules for dialogue.

Students need time and space to learn from one another in meaningful and important ways. In order to support my students' movement towards doing substantive dialogue work, I hope to offer historical and interdisciplinary readings that provide more of a framework to help students engage with historical texts and with one another through an intersectional lens. A text like Newman's (2005) is promising for this purpose.

Providing a framework and presenting greater opportunity for students to discover the intersectional dynamics of power and privilege give them a chance to develop analytical and communication skills to effectively engage with the lessons of educational history. They can likewise take their intersectional analyses beyond the particular scope of history towards a shared rethinking of the wider project of social justice education.

References

Adams, D. W. (1995). *Education for extinction: American Indians and the boarding school experience 1875–1928*. Lawrence: University Press of Kansas.

Altenbaugh, R. (1992). *The teacher's voice: A social history of teaching in twentieth century America*. New York: Routledge.

Anderson, J. (1988). *The education of blacks in the South, 1860–1935*. Chapel Hill: University of North Carolina Press.

Bailyn, B. (1960). *Education in the forming of American society: Needs and opportunity for study*. New York: Vintage Books.

Blount, J. M. (2005). *Fit to teach: Same-sex desire, gender, and school work in the twentieth century*. Albany: State University of New York Press.

Blum-Kulka, S. (1993). You gotta know how to tell a story: Telling, tales, and tellers in American and Israeli narrative events at dinner. *Language in Society, 22*, 361–402.

Bowles, S., & Gintis, H. (1976). *Schooling in capitalist America: Educational reform and the contradictions of economic life*. New York: Basic Books.

Cecelski, D. (1995). *Along freedom road: Hyde county, North Carolina, and the fate of black schools in the South*. Chapel Hill: University of **North Carolina** Press.

Cohen, D., & Lazerson, M. (1973). *Education in American history: Readings on the social issues*. New York: Praeger.

Dill, T. B., & Zambrana, R. (Eds.). (2009). *Emerging intersections: Race, class, and gender in theory, policy, and practice*. New Brunswick, NJ: Rutgers University Press.

Donato, R., & Lazerson, M. (2000). New directions in American educational history: Problems and prospects. *Educational Researcher, 29*, 1–15.

Dougherty, J. (1998). That's when we were marching for jobs: Black teachers and the early civil rights movement in Milwaukee. *History of Education Quarterly*, 38, 121–141.

Dougherty, J. (2004). *More than one struggle: The evolution of black school reform in Milwaukee*. Chapel Hill: University of North Carolina Press.

Douglas, D. (2005). *Jim Crow moves North: The battle over northern school segregation, 1865–1954*. New York: Cambridge University Press.

Ellsworth, E. (1989). Why doesn't this feel empowering? Working through the repressive myths of critical pedagogy. *Harvard Educational Review*, 59(3), 297–324.

Enberg, M. E. (2004). Improving intergroup relations in higher education: A critical examination of the influence of educational interventions on racial bias. *Review of Educational Research*, Winter 74: 4, 473–524.

Flower, L. (2003). Talking across difference: Intercultural rhetoric and the search for situated knowledge. *College Composition and Communication*, 55, 38–68.

Frazier, F. (1993). *The Negro family in Chicago*. Chicago: University of Chicago Press.

Fultz, M. (1996). Teacher training and African American education in the south, 1900–1940. *Journal of Negro Education*, 64, 196–201.

Govan, L., & Hollins, C. (2010). Understanding and dismantling privilege. *Common Expressions*, 1, 1–13.

Gramsci, A. (1993). *Letters from prison* (Vol. 1). New York: Columbia University Press.

Greer, C. (1972). *The great school legend: A revisionist interpretation of American public education*. New York: Basic Books.

Hall, J. D. (2005). The long civil rights movement and the political uses of the past. *Journal of American History*, 91: 4, 1233–1263.

Hochschild, J. (1995). *Facing up to the American dream: Race, class, and the soul of the nation*. Princeton: Princeton University Press.

Hunter, T. (1997). *To 'joy my freedom: Southern black women's lives and labors after the Civil War*. Cambridge: Harvard University Press.

Ignatiev, N., & Garvey, J. (1996). *Race traitor*. New York: Routledge.

Kaestle, C. (1983). *Pillars of the republic: Common schools and American society, 1780–1860*. New York: Hill and Wang.

Karier, C., Violas, P., & Spring, J. (1973). *Roots of crisis: American education in the twentieth century*. Chicago: Rand McNally.

Katz, M. (1968). *The irony of early school reform: Educational innovation in mid-nineteenth-century Massachusetts*. Cambridge: Harvard University Press.

Katz, M. (1971). *Class, bureaucracy, and schools: The illusion of educational change in America*. New York: Praeger Publishers.

Katz, M. (1987). *Reconstructing American education*. Cambridge: Harvard University Press.

Katz, M. (1995). *Improving poor people: The welfare state, the "underclass," and urban schools as history*. Princeton: Princeton University Press.

Katznelzon, I. & Weir, M. (1985). *Schooling for all: Class, race, and the decline of the democratic ideal*. New York: Basic Books.

Newman, D. (2005). *Identities and inequalities: Exploring the intersections of race, class, gender, and sexuality*. New York: McGraw-Hill.

Perkins, L. M. (1993). The role of education in the development of black feminist thought, 1860–1920. *History of Education Quarterly, 22,* 265–275.

Razack, S. (*1993*). Story-telling for social change. *Gender and Education, 5,* 55–70.

Roediger, D. (1991). *The wages of whiteness.* New York: Verso.

San Miguel, G. (2001). *"Let all of them take heed": Mexican Americans and the campaign for educational equality in Texas, 1910–1981.* College Station: Texas A&M University Press.

Schiffrin, D. (1996). Narrative as self-portrait: Sociolinguistic constructions of identity. *Language in Society, 2,* 167–203.

Spivey, D. (1978). *Schooling for the new slavery: Black industrial education, 1868–1915.* Westport, CT: Greenwood.

Spring, J. (1997). *Deculturalization and the struggle for equality: A brief history of the education of dominated cultures in the United States.* New York: McGraw-Hill.

Srivastava, S., & Francis, M. (2006). The problem of 'authentic experience': Storytelling in anti-racist and anti-homophobic education." *Critical Sociology, 32:* 2–3, 275–307 (Special Anti-racism issue).

Stulberg, L. (2008). *Race, schools, and hope: African Americans and school choice after Brown.* New York: Teachers College Press.

Szasz, M. (1999). *Education and the American Indian: The road to self determination since 1928.* Albuquerque: University of New Mexico Press.

Teitelbaum, K., & Reese, W. J. (1983). American socialist pedagogy and experimentation in the Progressive Era: The socialist Sunday school. *History of Education Quarterly, 23,* 429–454.

Tyack, D. (1974). *The one best system: A history of American urban education.* Cambridge: Harvard University Press.

Urban, W. J. (2000). *Gender, race, and the National Education Association: Professionalism and its limitations.* New York: RoutledgeFalmer.

Walker, V. S. (1996). *Their highest potential: An African American school community in the segregated south.* Chapel Hill: University of North Carolina Press.

Weinberg, M. (1977). *A chance to learn: A history of race and education in the United States.* New York: Cambridge University Press.

"We Talk about Race Too Much in This Class!"

Complicating the Essentialized Woman through Intersectional Pedagogy

Kim A. Case, Angela R. Miller, and Shaprie Bambacigno Jackson

In the spring semester of 2001, I (Kim) experienced excitement mixed with anxiety in preparation to teach my first Psychology of Women course as a graduate student at the University of Cincinnati. Given my interests in whiteness[1] studies and LGBT issues, I made a conscious decision to infuse race and sexuality into the curriculum for the course. After a good dose of feminist theory and learning about standard women's studies topics such as body image and domestic violence, we would dive into racism and white privilege, collectively considering how intersections of racial and gendered systems of oppression alter women's experiences. Already expecting that our discussion of whiteness and racism would need some special pedagogical attention, I reserved a large classroom so that students could sit in a circle and deconstruct race and white privilege for the two class meetings each week. My naïve expectations aside, the events that transpired just two days before the planned discussions derailed any chance of a calm, collaborative learning experience.

On April 7 that spring, white Cincinnati police officer Steven Roach shot and killed Timothy Thomas, an unarmed African American man running to avoid arrest for several misdemeanor offenses. The resulting race riots, violence, and citywide curfews left many students confused, scared, defensive, and hostile. By the time we arrived at our designated circle of learning that week, racial tensions had escalated to racial hostility and aggression. Although I tried to facilitate the academic discussion (as if the racial climate could be checked at the door), a white woman in the class exclaimed, "I'm sorry, but they are attacking us in the streets. They are ALL animals!" in reference to people of color. Clearly, my attempt to incorporate intersections into this gender-focused course immediately derailed. By the end of the course, the written comments on my student evaluations not only charged that I was "racist against white people" but also questioned the legitimacy of covering racism in a course that "should" focus solely on women. This experience introduced me to the difficulties associated with emphasizing intersections and challenging cultural norms defining the category "woman." In the years since that incident, my pedagogical identity continued to chase the possibility of complicating the paradigms students bring into the classroom.

In this chapter, we describe a student-instructor collaboration that attempted to transform a graduate-level women's studies course. The original iteration of the course, Psychology of Women, perpetuated consistent learning obstacles as student expectations and assumptions collided with pedagogical learning objectives. Although I taught the original course with my own pedagogical goals for teaching and learning about intersectionality, or the ways in which race, class, sexuality, and nation interact with and inform gender, I never felt satisfied that these learning objectives were met. With the aim of redesigning the course to clearly focus on intersectionality, students (enrolled for the upcoming semester) and I came together to create a new framework for the course. Through this co-intentional process, a new course emerged that effectively integrates student voices, instructor experiences, and shared learning goals. The chapter provides reflections on the theoretical contributions of the intersectional framework on the collaborative course redesign inspired by feminist pedagogical practices (Fisher, 2001; Sinacore & Boatwright, 2005) as well as a narrative of student and faculty experiences as the new course unfolded.

"We Talk about Race Too Much in This Class!"

Within the field of psychology, the catalogue typically includes diversity courses focusing on "women" (gender) or "cross-cultural" issues (race or ethnicity). Not only do these limited options neglect a laundry list of social identities and oppressive systems, they also reinforce a hegemonic cognitive schema that marks clear boundaries between gender and race. Outdated and narrow, these curricular practices legitimize and perpetuate rigid categorization of social groups and identities by consistently dividing them into separate courses. If an instructor covers both gender and race within one course, the practice of separating them on the syllabus as part 1 and part 2 of the course remains quite common. In this context, how will students identify a space for discussing the social reality for women of color? Beyond race and gender, psychology programs, as well as many more behavioral science disciplines, only rarely offer courses on sexual orientation, socioeconomic status, international perspectives, transgender issues, or identities involving immigrant status, disability, or religion. An intersectional analysis of such course offerings highlights the need for integrated courses that address various forms of social identity and oppression within one course.

As course readings, assignments, and discussions call cultural assumptions into question, student reactions often include negative evaluations of the learning environment. Students enrolled in my courses commonly expressed confusion as to why the course required them to wrestle with race, sexual orientation, ability, socioeconomic factors, transgender issues, and the experiences of women living around the world. Students entered the course assuming that the category "woman" described only white, heterosexual, middle-class, Christian, U.S. citizens. These invisible and unacknowledged expectations reflected student acceptance and endorsement of what Audre Lorde (1984) identified as the mythical norm. For example, a student felt the course "had an LGBT agenda to push." Although the course curriculum emphasized materials about gender equality, feminist values, and social activism for women's rights, students never complained about a "female agenda." When a course included lesbian and trans-women guest speakers and course materials by women that challenged heteronormativity, many students managed to define these women as something outside the boundaries of "woman." Many students attend the first class session with diversity course schemas that promote strict categorical boundaries and essentialism.[2] Student views that course coverage should be limited to only one aspect of oppression at a time often create conflict due to the widening gap between instructor and student expectations. For example, many students assume the category "woman" and the category "Native American" are mutually exclusive. Therefore, they conclude that a class about "women" or "gender" should not require students to understand how race affects the lives of Indigenous women. Educators must reflect methodically on innovative pedagogical strategies for addressing student assumptions and resistance in order to bring intersectionality to the forefront of diversity courses and the broader curriculum.

Weaving Instructor Identity into the Fabric of Learning

Critical reflection on the part of the feminist educator requires careful consideration of how power dynamics impacts interactions with students in the classroom and during student-faculty collaborative work for change (Enns

& Forrest, 2005). As instructors consider possible avenues for introducing students to the complexity of intersections in terms of both identity and the real-world impact of oppressive systems, reflection on one's personal social location in the matrix of domination[3] (Collins, 1990) and privilege allows purposeful consideration of potential areas of weakness. In other words, my effectiveness as a teacher is strongly connected to my willingness and ability to consider how my own privileged identities might prevent me from creating an inclusive learning environment that promotes voices from traditionally marginalized groups (Sanchez-Casal & MacDonald, 2002). As someone who aspires to behave as an ally in the classroom (Neumann, 2009), I am aware of my own privileged identities (white, gender-conforming, heterosexual, able-bodied, U.S. citizen). These identities threaten to re-create and validate hegemonic knowledge in the classroom if not carefully counterbalanced by intersectional curriculum that highlights not only the experiences of women of color but also lesbian, bisexual, transgender, disabled, and transnational voices. Given my particular social location, I must consciously make an effort to not only include but also emphasize written, works by women from social locations that challenge my role as oppressor in the classroom. If instructors aim to serve as effective allies to marginalized students, we must "deal honestly with our values, assumptions, and emotional reactions to oppression issues" (Bell, Washington, Weinstein, & Love, 2003, p. 464). Effective intersectional pedagogy must include reflections on the process of developing ourselves as allies in the classroom and address privilege and power relations as a central driving force (Dill & Zambrana, 2009). More important, sharing these reflections with other educators will bring the pedagogical ally development process into the teaching commons (Huber & Hutchings, 2005) and normalize such discussions.

Complicating the Essentialized "Woman"

More than two decades ago, bell hooks (1984) and Kimberle Crenshaw (1989) argued that individuals occupy unique social locations based on combined characteristics, such as race, sexuality, nation, class, ability, and gender. Crenshaw (1989) introduced the term "intersectionality" to explain that complex identities sharply contrast with categorical generalizations as they experience unique real-life situations based on simultaneous and multiple characteristics. Therefore, deeper understanding of the reality of people's lives requires scholars to avoid focusing on a single characteristic to define entire groups (Dill & Zambrana, 2009). An intersectional theoretical framework allows scholars to examine these social locations in relationship to disadvantage or privilege (Cole, 2009). Patricia Hill Collins's (1990) explanation of the "matrix of domination" also provides a conceptual structure to aid current understanding of the various social locations that result from complex identities in both privileged and oppressed groups. More recently, scholars call for an intersectional focus to transform higher education (Berger & Guidroz, 2009) and institutionalize intersectionality (Fitts, 2009).

Dill (2009) points out "intersectional analysis is marginal in all of the mainstream disciplines" (p. 246). Overall, the field of psychology seldom integrates intersectionality as a fundamental aspect of diversity courses. As mentioned above, the intersectionality among various social categories such as race, ability, gender, nation, class, and sexuality are rarely taught in psychology, as these courses typically address only one aspect of oppression and fail to simultaneously integrate multiple oppressions or privileges. In fact, psychology diversity requirements often limit students to choosing a course focused on race or gender. While fundamental knowledge of the unique aspects of each social category and system of oppression is essential to learning, intersectional integration leads to deeper understanding of the impact of these systems on various populations that are rarely recognized when studied as distinct concepts.

As they incorporate intersectional analyses into course work, instructors begin to challenge "traditional disciplinary boundaries and the compartmentalization and fixity of ideas" (Dill & Zambrana, 2009, p. 2) that currently dominate student learning environments. The intersectional approach provides instructors and students with a sophisticated critical framework for validating subjugated knowledge, unveiling power and privilege, examining the complexity of identity, and constructing a vision for change (Collins, 1990; Dill & Zambrana, 2009). In an effort to transform the learning environment, students and I (Kim) redesigned a graduate diversity course, serving psychology and women's studies, with an explicit and persistent intersectional focus. Using a model of student-instructor collaboration, the course was transformed to explicitly emphasize intersectionality with respect to social identity and social forces that differentially impact people located at various positions within the matrix of domination and privilege (Collins, 1990).

Student-Instructor Collaborative Course Design

Student critiques of a master's level Psychology of Women course offered insight into students' curricular expectations. Students typically expressed surprise and discomfort with coverage of racism and white privilege in readings, discussions, and assignments. The first step in addressing student misconceptions involved updating the course title to Psychology of Gender, Race, and Sexuality as a more accurate reflection of content that also provides a pedagogical platform for introducing intersectionality. Next, the course design and pedagogical approaches were overhauled to meet articulated learning goals associated with conceptualizing intersectionality at the theoretical and applied levels. The strategic course redesign included careful textbook and reading selection, assignments emphasizing intersectionality, and most important, a student-instructor collaboration to reimagine the course.

Four master's students in social science disciplines, including two coauthors of this chapter, met with the professor to develop pedagogical approaches for incorporating intersectionality into a women's studies course in which they enrolled for the upcoming semester (fall 2010). The team agreed that graduate-level course work should challenge students to integrate new concepts with previous knowledge, and assignments should have a minimal amount of scaffolding, or instructional guidance, to foster creativity and diverse perspectives. Reviewing the syllabus from the previous course, the group discussed which assignments might best support student learning in the new class. The students expressed that response papers, an assignment requiring students to reflect and write about the weekly readings, benefited students by encouraging them to pinpoint new perspectives, apply the knowledge to their lives, and identify actions for social change. The group decided to keep a take-home midterm essay exam to assess student comprehension, integration, and application of concepts.

Two new assignments focusing on intersectionality included a photography presentation and a public education project. The first assignment, often referred to as "photovoice" (Chio & Fandt, 2007; Wang, 1999), asked students to take photos representing their personal social identity intersections or illustrating the overall concept of intersectionality. The redesign team felt this assignment encouraged students to apply intersectionality theory to their own lives and to integrate concepts, theories, and readings in their presentations. The final project required students to utilize their newfound knowledge of intersectionality for public education. For example, public education could be achieved by creating brochures, websites, videos, blogs, and workshops. Both assignments provided avenues for students to learn through application of intersectionality to personal social identities and lived experiences while sharing knowledge with peers and the wider community.

Student-Instructor Reflections on Learning Intersectionality

Refocusing this graduate course on intersecting identities and the benefits of intersectional analysis, I (Kim) came to realize my pedagogy has always included intersections. After all, my very first Psychology of Women undergraduate course required students to read essays by African American, lesbian, and working-class women. However, my approach illustrated a textbook case of the outdated additive model of diversity education (Andersen & Collins, 2009) rather than consideration of complex identities that grow out of marginalized and privileged aspects of the lived human experience (Dill & Zambrana, 2009). Although potentially inclusive of multiple perspectives, the additive model segregates various aspects of social identity such that courses cover gender separately from social identity based on race, ethnicity, sexuality, religion, and more. This severely limits consideration of ways that identities impact each other and exist simultaneously to affect people's lives. In contrast to previous courses, every instructional decision developed through my lens of intersectional pedagogical goals. When a student dropped by during office hours to discuss the photovoice project or the midterm exam, I repeatedly emphasized the necessity of demonstrating their use of an intersectional framework in designing their projects and writing their take-home exam papers. In class, when a student shared that the reading about the experiences of a gay Asian man (Han, 2009) introduced new perspectives in terms of complicating racism and heterosexism, I exclaimed, "That's intersectionality!" Taking advantage of these seemingly small opportunities provided immediate feedback to help students identify intersections and the benefits of intersectional analysis.

In preparation for the first day of class, I grew anxious about moving students away from categorical assumptions and ingrained expectations of higher education and toward this major focus on intersectionality. Unlike my previous syllabi, this new syllabus included more than a full page devoted to theoretical frameworks for guiding our learning and the basic tenets and assumptions of each: intersectional theory, feminist theory, queer theory, critical race theory, and critical white studies. By including these approaches directly on the syllabus, I emphasized the importance of understanding and incorporating theoretical analyses into our journey as a cohesive unit of learners. The first day of class meant setting the stage for a cultural shift from traditional classroom lectures to a community space for sharing and growing as co-intentional learners (Freire, 1970). The majority of our first class involved my purposeful and repeated explanations of the multiple ways that this course was designed to utilize nontraditional approaches to learning, challenge student assumptions, and emphasize intersecting identities and forms of oppression.

Developing a Culture of Student Engagement

Students' eyes widened as I explained that the classroom space would be transformed each week into a circle and that everyone in the room held shared responsibility for discussion and engaged learning. By transforming the room to allow us to face one another, our space directly challenged the traditional model that reinforces the power of the instructor lecturing at the front of the room. The circle setting made the classroom environment more student centered, rather than instructor centered, and incorporated everyone's knowledge while promoting shared responsibility for learning. We (Angela and Shaprie) felt this inclusive environment helped us to get to know our classmates on a more personal level. By building these relationships, we began to see that our diverse social identities contributed unique world perspectives to the class discussions. Although the majority of the class consisted of white heterosexual females (including Angela and Shaprie), the class also included gay, lesbian, bisexual, transgender, Black, Asian, and biracial students. A range of religions included Christianity, Judaism, atheism, and agnosticism. These varied perspectives enabled us to see how intersections of our social identities shape our individual perceptions enhancing our understanding of intersectionality. Each week of the class, I (Kim) intentionally created ways to remind students of our commitment to supporting one another as a community of learners working to complicate the social constructions that perpetuate oppression and privilege within the matrix of domination (Collins, 1990). Upon recognizing that previous friendships created clique-type situations in class, I used one class meeting to assign seats so that every single student was sitting beside two people they did not know prior to the course. The next week, during each activity I required students to choose partners with whom they had never teamed up previously. The group bonded as they grew together creating a culture of support, teamwork, and safety with one another that allowed uncomfortable moments to develop into powerful instances of shifting paradigms.

During our fifth class meeting and discussion, one female and one male student (pseudonym Donny) began speaking at about the same time. Donny, also African American and gay, paused and said, "Oh, ladies first," indicating that the white female student, Tiffany, should comment before him. His comment sparked a direct, yet friendly, challenge to the gendered nature of this framework from his classmates. The class erupted in laughter and verbal recognition of his gendered behavior in that moment. When he responded that he was "raised to be a gentleman," he received even more enthusiastic objections to his gendered constructions. Although this moment could have caused Donny to feel chastised, perhaps leading him to retreat or completely shut down, the class approached the challenge in a warm, friendly way. Their responses allowed him to understand they were not judging him, but merely challenging him to reflect on the relationship between his words and the perpetuation of social constructions. Due to the students' community building and sense of shared responsibility for learning, Donny processed the feedback from female classmates as positive rather than as an attack. In fact, he reminded us of this challenge almost seven weeks later as an illustration of moments that helped him reflect on his own areas for improvement. This particular situation represents a key turning point for the class as a community of learners. From that moment going forward, students advanced to a higher level of shared responsibility for the learning taking place among their peers and colleagues.

As students in the first class to experience this redesigned course, we (Angela and Shaprie) felt the new format of the class created an inclusive social environment and encouraged an open learning style, one in which we felt free to explore, debate, and critique controversial subject matter. For instance, viewing and discussing the film *Race: The Power of an Illusion (Episode 2)* (Adelman & Cheng, 2003) shed new light on racial social constructions and efforts to maintain socioeconomic class boundaries that privilege whites. In-class learning opportunities helped to spark debate and brought up ideas that instructors typically avoid in class.

Promoting Active Learning, or "Keeping Students Awake"

My (Kim's) strategy to maximize student engagement involved creating in-class activities that required a high rate of student involvement and incorporated new concepts to build a concrete foundation of intersectionality principles. I designed these customized activities to help students remember the terminology and to foster the application of theories to real-world experiences. Given that intersectionality was new to the majority of the students, essential to the foundation of the course, as well as abstract and difficult to grasp, I planned an activity to motivate students to think more deeply about defining the concept for themselves. After reading Dill and Zambrana's (2009) explanation of the tenets of the theoretical approach, I gave students 60 seconds to brainstorm as many words as they could that they associate with intersectionality. After individually brainstorming, they spent 5 minutes with a partner sharing the associated word lists and explaining connections to intersectional analysis. Finally, the class as a whole transferred all of the words to the board and identified themes and patterns emerging from the collective list. This activity allowed students to spend individual, paired, and learning community discussion time working with complex and abstract terms that was critically essential to the foundation of their learning for the entire semester.

During this same class meeting, students experienced the "grab bag" activity by reaching into a deep bag and pulling out an item. Students were instructed to grab an individual object from the bag before being given any additional information on what the activity entailed. After each student chose an object, I gave them 3 minutes to make a connection between the item and intersectionality theory or the assigned readings for that week. The student who pulled a key out of the bag used it to discuss the access granted to those with privileged social identities that unlock doors to new opportunities. The cassette tape became a metaphor for recording history from the perspective of the group in power and connecting the tape to the reading "A Different Mirror" (Takaki, 2009). The ball of rubber bands transformed into a visual representation of the matrix of oppression, with each band serving as a specific identity either centralized (center of the ball) or marginalized (outer edges of the ball) by systematic oppression. The grab bag exercise positioned each student to think critically about intersectionality, concepts, and readings in ways that would enhance learning for the broader community of learners in the course. Out of this grab bag discussion, the metaphor of intersecting roadways emerged. A single student discussed his vision of intersectionality as a major highway intersection with six roads coming together at once. Several more students chimed in with ideas for expanding this metaphor, such as green lights for the privileged while marginalized groups navigated roadblocks, police barricades, and red lights. This synergistic moment in the classroom produced a new framework for student understanding of intersectionality that students consistently returned to throughout the rest of the term.

Expanding on the success of the grab bag, I asked students to bring items to the class the next week as representations of their personal cultural heritage or social identities in some way. Later in the course, we revisited this show-and-tell exercise with a focus on food items that share some aspect of their cultural or family heritage. In both scenarios, each student shared the object (or food item) with the class, explained the cultural or identity connection, and explicitly tied the object to course concepts or readings. For example, Angela presented a pasta spoon her Italian grandmother used to serve the family traditional Italian cuisine and raised the issue of cultural expectations requiring women to cook and serve others. She related the spoon to several readings that discussed divergent familial expectations that required women to serve the family. By sharing and discussing their own backgrounds, students used personal applications to successfully link intersecting identities with course concepts and readings.

After three weeks of readings, I sensed students were struggling with the long list of new concepts developing from the extensive readings. I felt an urgent need to provide an intervention to aid their learning without defaulting to a traditional lecture about terminology. Alas, I was faced with the task of making terminology fun and engaging. The resulting activity, which I named "Terminology Rotation," promotes community-based learning in advancing phases.

- In phase 1, each student pair draws 3 cards, each with 1 concept or conceptual phrase from the course readings.
- During this phase, students add to each terminology card by providing a definition, illustrative examples, and associated readings that match the given concept. The team had exactly 5 minutes to add to the cards and then rotate cards to a new team.
- By the end of phase 1, the terminology cards rotated through half of the student teams, with each team adding more content to build a comprehensive review of the particular concept.
- Phase 2 changes the focus to team learning, and student pairs get 5 minutes to review and discuss the concepts completed by other teams.
- After several rounds of team learning, all student pairs had spent time with every single terminology card in either phase 1 or 2.

Students responded well to this activity, indicating that it helped them clear up term confusion and better grasp the distinctions among similar terms and phrases. They also expressed an increased ability to integrate the assigned readings, real-world examples, and terms as a result of the Terminology Rotation. Following up on the activity, I created games to put their progress to the test. As students completed crossword puzzles and attempted to identify the correct terms on their intersectionality BINGO cards (as I called out definitions and examples), I overheard conversations utilizing the terminology cards from the previous activity to determine correct game answers. Along with these customized exercises to promote student engagement, learning took place through the two major projects designed to focus on intersectionality.

Photovoice Project Student Outcomes

For my photovoice presentation, I (Angela) used a game theme to describe the concept of intersectionality. First, I set up a Scrabble game with the word "intersections" spelled diagonally across the board. Then I added in crossword fashion the socially constructed categories of oppression and privilege, such as race, age, gender, class, and ability. I presented this photo as an introduction and used subsequent photos to connect the concept of intersectionality to real-world social issues. As I set up various games, such as Monopoly, Life, and Risk, I consciously worked to go beyond an additive approach. In contrast, my photos highlighted intersections of socially constructed characteristics combining to impact people's lives. Using a Monopoly board, for example, to represent intersections of race and class in housing discrimination, or "redlining," I sectioned off the low-cost property spaces with a red piece of yarn between the "Go" and "Jail" corner spaces. As a result of this project, intersectionality theory helped me unravel the social and psychological complexities connecting socially constructed identities and lived experiences.

To demonstrate the concept of intersectionality, I (Shaprie) presented close-up pictures of the parts of a sunflower and invited students to identify the object. Upon revealing the whole sunflower, I explained that focusing on individual identities prevents understanding the whole person. For instance, examining gender without considering race blocks the full view of an individual's experiences. In an attempt to connect micro-level everyday activities to macro-level social forces, I also analyzed how simple daily activities served as intersectional examples. While doing laundry at home, I realized that my high-tech, high-cost machine emphasized my intersection of class and gender. Because of this realization, I chose to use a picture of my washing machine in my presentation as a symbol of gendered division of labor intersecting with my middle-class status. The definition of intersectionality I developed as I prepared my project emphasized careful consideration of multiple identities and their complex interactions.

One presentation stood out for many students in the class and resonated with them as an aspect of intersectionality they had never considered. A Jewish woman in the class explained that her religion and gender combined to shape her identity as well as outsider judgments of Jewish women as unattractive. Displaying photos of female Jewish celebrities, on the one hand, she pointed out these women rarely disclose their Jewish identities. On the other hand, male Jewish celebrities often proclaim their Jewish identity without fear of losing sex appeal. Another woman who identifies as biracial (Black and white), bisexual, and tri-cultural presented her photovoice as a unique crossword puzzle visual aid illustrating her realization that she can effectively serve as a bridge linking many social groups that tend to maintain rigid boundaries.

Intersectionality Project Student Outcomes

As described above, the final project for this course required students to create an avenue for public education with regard to intersectional theory or some particular aspect of intersectional identities. Given no more than the goal of the project, students expressed extreme discomfort and requested additional direction from me (Kim). Rather than appease this request, I explained that less direction from me allowed them to develop their own unique vision for the project, improve their planning and organizing skills, and create their own map for arriving at the final project destination. Although unsettled and uncomfortable with this news, the students rose to the challenge and exceeded my expectations. I attempted to make the major contributions to my grading of these projects clear to all students well in advance. As we traveled through the course from the first week and moving toward the project due date, I explicitly reminded students that successful integration of intersectionality would be the greatest factor in assessing their performance. I also informed them that achieving the goal of public education was a major influence on the final project grade.

For my final project, I (Angela) decided to create a handout on intersectionality theory for pedagogical use in the college classroom. As an aspiring college professor, I wanted to create something for my own future classroom. The handout included several of my photovoice game-themed pictures, plus additional pictures such as a completed Rubik's Cube to emphasize the multidimensionality of the "matrix of domination" (Collins, 1990). As I worked on the project, I realized that although I had been learning the intricate aspects of the theory through a myriad of readings and activities in the course, the people I aimed to reach would likely never get that opportunity. Recognizing the need to convey extremely complicated concepts in a small amount of space, I chose simple wording to maximize accessibility for those new to the concept of intersectionality. After completing my handout, I offered it to sociology, women's studies, and education faculty to share with their students. I provided copies, asked them to post the handout online for their classes, and requested 5 minutes of class time to speak to each class. Several instructors on our campus took the offer and used the handout in their courses. This quick guide to intersectionality theory provides an easy way for faculty to incorporate a more complex analysis into their courses.

Due to my (Shaprie's) interest in the topic, I chose to discuss the intersection of race, class, and the educational system. For my project, I created a video (PowerPoint with voiceover) explaining links between oppression, race, and access to education and resources. Upon completing the video, I distributed it via e-mail to many of the education faculty on campus with a brief note describing my class project and its potential relevance for their students (preservice K–12 teachers). In addition, I offered to visit and provide a brief presentation to their students on this subject matter. To reach a broader audience, I also raised awareness by posting the video to Facebook and writing a blog to discuss the topic, inviting others to post personal stories involving race, class, and education. Although some video viewers vocalized their opposing views, it appeared they were struggling to recognize their privilege. In fact, I encountered less resistance than I expected from those who viewed the video. I found it to be quite rewarding compared to traditional final projects that require students to simply stand in the front of the class and present material the class has talked about all semester.

Other students' projects focused on a variety of public audiences as target groups. One male student connected with a community group to provide workshops on masculinity, homophobia, and human trafficking to boys in juvenile detention. Another contacted a nonprofit immigrant advocacy group and developed brochures for distribution to migrant domestic workers to inform them of their legal rights. Projects also included a documentary on images of race and gender in popular films and a board game designed to teach players about oppression, privilege, and intersectionality. Students expressed their enthusiasm as the public audiences responded with interest and curiosity to their specific projects. By expanding their learning beyond the classroom walls, students recognized the possibilities for applying intersectionality to social problems, identifying concrete avenues for raising awareness, and effecting social change through public education.

Pedagogical Lessons and Implications

Overall, the redesigned course helped students accomplish the goals of understanding intersectionality both theoretically and in applied practice. The inclusive and open environment brought the class together to form a bond as a community of learners, which fostered lively discussion and debate. Each class meeting included customized activities structured for team learning and peer support. As the instructor, I (Kim) consistently motivated learners with engaging exercises and group work that promoted collaboration and a supportive learning environment. Students learned how to transform their knowledge for presentation to audiences outside the classroom. Giving students only limited instruction for the two major course projects provided enormous flexibility that allowed students to personalize the course to their own unique interests. With greater agency, students committed to creating change and became fully engaged in designing projects with maximum impact through public education. The course's connection to raising awareness beyond the classroom walls brought intersectionality to life for a meaningful opportunity for learning. Some students even expressed that they planned to continue their public education and outreach that developed from their projects long after the course ends. Given that this course was taught at the graduate level, an undergraduate course might benefit from some lectures mixed in with interactive activities, along with more detailed instructions for each major assignment.

Teaching this course brought with it unexpected gifts for me (Kim) as an instructor. Witnessing the sense of community as it developed and watching several students transform from slightly resistant to deeply invested in complex lived experiences and intersectionality, I experienced my own framework shift. Originally, the thought of redesigning a course with students made me quite nervous. Stepping away from traditional models of instruction toward more feminist and liberatory pedagogical practices (Enns & Forrest, 2005; Freire, 1970; Sinacore & Boatwright, 2005) became more comfortable for me as the semester progressed. My approach to class discussion became more flexible each week and began to flow with students' immediate learning needs rather than confined by preconceived, rigid plans. Instructors aiming to emphasize intersectionality may find the ideas implemented in this course useful and potentially transformative to their own pedagogical philosophy, as I did.

Although the student-faculty collaboration to redesign the course occurred well before the semester started, the cooperative learning model extended throughout the term. Promotion of student involvement in the learning process, peer support, and action for public education created a classroom space reflective of the tenets of intersectionality theory. For example, the intersectional framework calls for applying theory to practice for social action, and student projects that educated the public achieved that goal. By centering the course on intersectionality using a student-faculty collaborative learning model, students moved from margin to center and became responsible for building knowledge throughout the semester and potentially beyond the course itself.

Notes

1   Although APA style requires capitalization of all race categories, we chose not to capitalize the words "white" and "whiteness" as a challenge to white privilege and racial hierarchy.

2   Essentialism refers to the belief that groups of people are naturally different at a biological level.

3   The matrix of domination was introduced by Patricia Hill Collins (1990) and described the interlocking systems of oppression, privilege, and identity that have simultaneous impact on individual lives and experiences. These systems, based on race, sex, religion, gender identity, age, sexuality, socioeconomic class, ability, and more, are traditionally conceptualized and studied separately rather than as interdependent and complex.

References

Adelman, L. (Executive Producer), & Cheng, J. (Producer). (2003). *Race: The power of an illusion (Episode 2)* [Motion picture]. San Francisco: California Newsreel.

Andersen, M. L., & Collins, P. H. (2009). Why race, class, and gender still matter. In M. L. Andersen & P. H. Collins (Eds.), *Race, class, and gender: An anthology* (7th ed.) (pp. 1–16). Belmont, CA: Wadsworth.

Bell, L. A., Washington, S., Weinstein, G., & Love, B. (2003). Knowing ourselves as instructors. In A. Darder, M. Baltodano, & R. D. Torres (Eds.), *The critical pedagogy reader* (pp. 464–478). New York: RoutledgeFalmer.

Berger, M. T., & Guidroz, K. (Eds.). (2009). *The intersectional approach: Transforming the academy through race, class, and gender*. Chapel Hill: University of North Carolina Press.

Chio, V., & Fandt, P. (2007). Photovoice in the diversity classroom: Engagement, voice, and the "eye/I" of the camera. *Journal of Management Education, 31*, 484–504. doi: 10.1177/1052562906288124

Cole, E. (2009). Intersectionality and research in psychology. *American Psychologist, 64*, 170–180. doi:10.1037/a0014564

Collins, P. H. (1990). *Black feminist thought: Knowledge, consciousness, and the politics of empowerment*. New York: Routledge.

Crenshaw, K. (1989). Demarginalizing the intersection of race and sex: A black feminist critique of antidiscrimination doctrine, feminist theory, and antiracist politics. *University of Chicago Legal Forum, 4*, 139–167.

Dill, B. T. (2009). Intersections, identities, and inequalities in higher education. In B. T. Dill & R. E. Zambrana (Eds.), *Emerging intersections: Race, class, and gender in theory, policy, and practice* (pp. 229–252). New Brunswick: Rutgers University Press.

Dill, B. T., & Zambrana, R. E. (2009). Critical thinking about inequality: An emerging lens. In B. T. Dill & R. E. Zambrana (Eds.), *Emerging intersections: Race, class, and gender in theory, policy, and practice* (pp. 1–21). New Brunswick: Rutgers University Press.

Enns, C. Z., & Forrest, L. M. (2005). Toward defining and integrating multicultural and feminist pedagogies. In C. Z. Enns & A. L. Sinacore (Eds.), *Teaching and social justice: Integrating multicultural and feminist theories in the classroom* (pp. 3–23). Washington, DC: American Psychological Association.

Fisher, B. M. (2001). *No angel in the classroom.* Lanham, MD: Rowman & Littlefield.

Fitts, M. (2009). Institutionalizing intersectionality: Reflections on the structure of women's studies departments and programs. In M. T. Berger & K. Guidroz (Eds.), *The intersectional approach: Transforming the academy through race, class, and gender* (pp. 249–257). Chapel Hill: University of North Carolina Press.

Freire, P. (1970). *Pedagogy of the oppressed.* New York: Continuum.

Han, C. (2009). Darker shades of queer: Race and sexuality at the margins. In M. L. Andersen & P. H. Collins (Eds.), *Race, class, and gender: An anthology* (7th ed.) (pp. 255–262). Belmont, CA: Wadsworth.

hooks, b. (1984). *Feminist theory: From margin to center.* Boston: South End Press.

Huber, M. T., & Hutchings, P. (2005). *The advancement of learning: Building the teaching commons.* San Francisco: Jossey-Bass.

Lorde, A. (1984). *Sister outsider.* Freedom, CA: Crossing Press.

Neumann, S. (2009). The "why's" and "how's" of being a social justice ally. In R. A. R. Gurung & L. R. Prieto (Eds.), *Getting culture: Incorporating diversity across the curriculum* (pp. 65–75). Sterling, VA: Stylus Publishing.

Sanchez-Casal, S., & MacDonald, A. (2002). Feminist reflections on the pedagogical relevance of identity. In A. A. MacDonald & S. Sanchez-Casal (Eds.), *Twenty-first-century feminist classrooms: Pedagogies of identity and difference* (pp. 1–28). New York: Palgrave Macmillan.

Sinacore, A. L., & Boatwright, K. J. (2005). The feminist classroom: Feminist strategies and student responses. In C. Z. Enns & A. L. Sinacore (Eds.), *Teaching and social justice: Integrating multicultural and feminist theories in the classroom* (pp. 109–124). Washington, DC: American Psychological Association.

Takaki, R. T. (2009). A different mirror. In M. L. Andersen & P. H. Collins (Eds.), *Race, class, and gender: An anthology* (7th ed.) (pp. 49–60). Belmont, CA: Wadsworth.

Wang, C. (1999). Photovoice: A participatory action research strategy applied to women's health. *Journal of Women's Health, 8,* 185–192.

Conflict Resolution Education and Intersectionality

Leah Wing

The foundational concept of neutrality within the field of conflict resolution[1] makes invisible the experiences of those at the margin of the hierarchies of power, and it serves to reinforce the transparency of privilege for those in the center. Common practice in the field of conflict resolution de-contextualizes, de-historicizes, as well as individuates conflicts (Auerbach, 1983; Chene, 2008; Grillo, 1991; Gunning, 1995), thereby creating a homogenized discourse while colluding to reinforce patterns of social inequalities (Abel, 1982; Auerbach, 1983; Delgado, 1997; Delgado, Dunn, Brown, Lee, & Hubbert, 1985; Fiss, 1984; Harrington, 1985). Such centralization limits engagement with conditions and subject positions that are located in the margins through exclusion from the "knowledge regime." This dominant paradigm permeates not only conflict resolution scholarship but also the tools for conflict analysis and intervention utilized in mediation, facilitation, and arbitration practices. Conflict resolution educators function, then, as conduits of knowledge production and dissemination that serve status quo power arrangements. Despite the desire of educators and practitioners in the field to further more democratic, equitable, and empowering dispute resolution processes, the argument that it is the universal application of neutral conflict resolution processes that creates procedural fairness is a dystopia and a fiction.

How can conflicts be effectively and fairly analyzed and resolved unless the realities of those in conflict are more accurately addressed? Literature on intersectionality offers crucial conceptual tools for this endeavor. Application of the concept of intersectionality to conflict intervention requires understanding the historical and present relationship between the disputing parties, their conflict, and their context. This can create more rigorous conflict analyses depicting the complexity and multiplicity of people's lives and, importantly, illuminating arenas of conflict that are systemically reinforced and structurally determined. Contextualizing conflicts by understanding that they are imbedded in the realities of social inequalities and systems of privilege increases the likelihood that theories and practices of conflict intervention can address these dilemmas (Chang, Basey, Carey, Coleman, & Hoban, 2008; Chene, 2008; Forester, 1999).[2] But, in order for conflict resolution to serve a social justice agenda—that is, truly offering empowerment and attending to power imbalances during conflict intervention—rather than reinforcing status quo power arrangements, it must effectively interrogate the actual sources and impacts of conflict on *real people with real identities*. And, it is only through such an analysis that fuller opportunities can emerge for the most marginalized to also achieve redress and resolution.

Yet, as noted above, such an approach runs counter to several foundational tenets of the field: neutrality, universality, and a "color-blind"[3] approach to theory and practice that permeates the discipline. Claims of universality link with a faith in neutrality as the conceptual building blocks of a culture-free conflict resolution system designed to equally serve anyone anywhere (see critiques by Chang et al., 2008; Goldberg, 2009; Hairston, 1999; A. L. Wing, 2002). This is articulated in one of the central texts of the field: "Anyone can use this method. . . . Principled negotiation is an all-purpose strategy" (Fisher & Ury, 1981, p. xiii). Fisher and Ury (1981) explain further:

> Prevention works best . . . structuring the negotiating game in ways that separate the substantive problem from the relationship. . . . Like two shipwrecked sailors in a lifeboat at sea quarreling over limited rations and supplies, negotiators may begin by seeing each other as adversaries. Each may view the other as a hindrance. To survive, however, those two sailors will want to disentangle the objective problems from the people. They will want to identify the needs of each, whether for shade, medicine, water, or food. They will want to go further and treat the meeting of those needs as a shared problem, along with other shared problems like keeping watch, catching rainwater, and getting the lifeboat to shore. Seeing themselves as engaged in side-by-side efforts to solve a mutual problem, the sailors will become better able to reconcile their conflicting interests as well as to advance their shared interests. . . . Separating the people from the problem is not something you can do once and forget about; you have to keep working at it. The basic approach is to deal with the people as human beings and with the problem on its merits. (pp. 38–40)

But, what is the effect of seeing disputants simply as generic "human beings"? And, who is best served and least served by such an approach? Spelman (1988) warns us that essentializing can be a Trojan horse—appearing innocent but carrying a heavy political load by obscuring the heterogeneity that is the reality of people's identities and lives.

A brief, critical inquiry into the impact of essentializing and de-contextualizing in conflict resolution literature and methodology—highlighting patterns of exclusion, disenfranchisement, and privileging by the discipline—will illustrate the importance of including intersectionality in the scholarship and curriculum. Our inquiry begins by asking, "Who are those generic 'human beings' conflict resolution is prepared to assist?" By separating people from their problems, students of conflict resolution are being taught that the process does not require understanding or engaging with the context and specifics of the disputants' identities and lives, since these characteristics are explicitly noted as separable from them and as irrelevant to addressing disputes. A benefit of assuming that "sailors" who are lost at sea are generic "human beings" is that we can concentrate solely on intervention theory and tools that are supposed to help anyone, anywhere, at any time (Fisher & Ury, 1981). How dramatically different might our analyses and interventions be if we made our sailors real people with the complex intersecting identities that real people carry in the world? And, from these different analyses, arguably new scholarship and approaches to teaching and intervening would emerge that would respond to those realities. Consider, for example, if the two sailors were actually a young novice sea captain who had ignored the advice of his experienced elder lookout, resulting in the ship's hitting rocks, sinking, and killing the entire crew with whom the lookout had sailed for more than four decades? Would their conflicts be imbedded in their identities and circumstances in ways that were different than if the sailors weren't actually sailors but, rather, a Black female slave and a White male slavemaster shipwrecked off the southern United States in 1864? Or, what if they were two wealthy yacht owners who had never held jobs, one of whom was blind and the other of whom could see? Or, if one was a Colombian man in his early twenties whose passport and graduate student visa had gone down with the ship—and for whom being picked up by the U.S. Coast Guard might not herald "rescue" in the same way that it might for his fellow traveler, an African American male doctor whose first language was English? What if the sailors were a White Jewish female professor of conflict resolution and a Catholic Dominican female undergraduate conflict resolution student who has just finished an assigned reading that had made it clear that her race, class, culture, religion, and gender were irrelevant to solving problems but whose life experience had taught her otherwise? Might these pairings of human beings actually face different disputes from each other?[4] Would they likely approach the conflicts they face from different positionalities, ones grounded in the complexities of their actual intersectional identities and the relationships between their identities and the larger social structure? For example, how likely would it be that the Black female captive and the White male slave master have the exact same goals to have them both land safely on the nearest shores of South Carolina so that she could then be sold by her "fellow sailor" into slavery? How might *who* each of them is impact what they see as the most immediate conflicts they face, those they will face in the future, those they will face alone, and those that exist between them? Would some sailors see the relationship between them and the historical relationships between groups to which they are connected as central to their conflicts and any potential resolution? Would others hope (even desperately!) that the relationships between their identities and their contexts would be rendered invisible and irrelevant? And, most important, *who would benefit if there was only one approach to conflict resolution framed as valid—one that separates the people from the problem* (see Figure 1) *and views identities and context as irrelevant or, at best, as less than secondary?*

Figure 1: Generic Human Beings

The language of universality and neutrality in conflict resolution does not serve all "sailors" equally when it replicates essentialized "human beings" in the image of those in the center and presents them as generic. Rather than generic, they are predominantly modeled on White, middle-class, Anglophone men, for example, and are also fairly reflective of White, middle-class, Anglophone women, who are located near enough to the center to also be significantly privileged by the paradigm (Chang et al., 2008; Chene, 2008; Grillo, 1991; Hairston, 1999, 2008; L. Wing, 2008). However, for those at the center their own experiences can seem "generic" and essentially "human" (A. P. Harris, 1990; Spelman, 1988), and thus their conflict experience can be infused with the privilege of not appearing to be related to their identity (Chene, 2008; Flagg, 1997) and their identity can appear to lack an association with conflict (Delgado, 1993). In this way, Figure 1 illustrates how generic faces without gender or many other identity characteristics, and whose color comes from the backdrop—white like the field around it—are presented as the norm. The "generic" person is supposedly raceless when in fact they are white. This supposed racial "transparency" or "invisibility" is a powerful illustration of the fallacy of the concept of color blindness; for it is really only for those in the majority that their race is seemingly invisible, as it is much more likely to be highly visible to those whose race is not presented as the norm (Flagg, 1997). Such privilege renders invisible those who lack it. The group at the center also dominates knowledge creation and dissemination in the field, thus reinforcing their position in the center (Chene, 2008; Hairston, 1999); and therefore, it is not a surprise that discussions of intersectionality have had no currency in the field.

It is in this context that research has demonstrated that the effects of the homogenization of the discipline based on essentializing have rendered it a tool capable of replicating oppression (Delgado et al., 1985; Grillo, 1991; Gunning, 1995; Hairston, 1999; Trujillo, Bowland, Myers, Richards, & Roy, 2008; L. Wing, 2009). An example helps to illustrate this. Typical strategies for intervening in multiparty environmental disputes do not consider patterns of disenfranchisement most commonly experienced by populations who are targeted[5] for the siting of polluting facilities because of the intersection of their identities: being disproportionately low income and people of color of specifically African, Latino/a, Hispanic, and Indigenous descent (Bullard, 1993; Cole & Foster, 2001). Research over the past several decades has consistently found that businesses and governmental agencies have targeted these populations for hazardous facilities due to a lack of political power, racial discrimination, and the economic benefits derived from siting in poor communities with low property taxes, for example; and, significantly, it has demonstrated the pervasive pattern of disproportionate poisoning of poor communities of color (see an extensive annotated bibliography of this research in the appendix, Cole & Foster, 2001, pp. 167–183). Yet, the theory and practices for intervening in environmental and public policy disputes do not take this into account. In addition, they fail to respond to the fact that many disputants view themselves as survivors who have to negotiate with those they view as perpetrators, as "the [already] environmentally polluted face the polluters" (Forester, 1999, p. 217); this is common, as many who are disputing the siting of a new plant live in communities already housing other hazardous facilities (Bullard, 1993; Cole & Foster, 2001).

The lack of attention to the importance of intersectionality in environmental justice conflicts permeates environmental and public policy dispute resolution (EPPDR) and, thus, serves to perpetuate this oppression. For example, when the siting of a potentially polluting facility is in dispute, the dominant strategy is to facilitate a risk assessment about exposure to pollutants in which "usually the exposure and resultant 'safe dose' derives from a model that uses a healthy adult white male as criterion" (Head, 1995, pp. 53–54). It can be a lethal misnomer to present the "safe dose" as based on "generic" scientific data when it is actually based on a population with intersecting identities that are more privileged than those who would be disproportionately put at risk by where the polluting facility is most likely to be sited: in a community with low-income African Americans, Latinos, Hispanics, and/or Indigenous peoples likely already absorbing pollution from other nearby facilities (Cole & Foster, 2001). And since the ways in which the disproportionate risks are experienced are not the same for all these people, it is all the more important that actual risk factors should be assessed given the specificity of the population near the proposed site and the national data that correlate with their particular identities. An intersectional analysis of health risks would reveal that, for example, African American women have a significantly higher risk for facing health and safety hazards at work than White women and men and African American men (Lucas, cited in Cole & Foster, 2001, p. 178; Shrader-Frechette, 2002), that those who do not speak English and have few financial resources face multiple barriers to political and medical access when living near polluting facilities (Cole & Foster, 2001), and that girls and women (who are disproportionately of color) who live near a polluting facility face greater vulnerabilities to cancer than boys and men in their neighborhoods due to physiology (Tarter, 2002). The health of real people whose identities place them at exponentially higher risks due to their intersectionality should be accounted for in environmental dispute resolution processes (Cole & Foster, 2001; Shrader-Frechette, 2002). Clearly, therefore, more research is needed, in general on this topic; and when practitioners intervene in an EPPDR conflict, the cumulative effects of multiple sources of health risks must be assessed for the actual populations who would be exposed to the facility under dispute.

Just a cursory look at some of these national patterns of disproportionate health risks illustrates how basing a consensus-building intervention on data collected on healthy White adult males skews the use of science in ways that advantage those favoring the siting of a polluting facility. Therefore, despite the intention to be neutral, mediators are failing such communities that have been promised a fair dispute resolution process capable of being tailored to their circumstances. Moreover, the field fails our students when we inadequately prepare them for leadership in such endeavors.

When dispute resolution is capable of producing such biased processes and outcomes, it is worth questioning whether parties ought to even use them.

Importantly, such criticisms have been levied at the field, usually from outside of it (Abel, 1982; Auerbach, 1983; Bullard, 1990; Cole & Foster, 2001; Fiss, 1984; Harrington, 1980, 1985; Nader, 1980, 2001; Rouhana & Korper, 1996) and have included a few references to intersectionality, noting that those with multiple intersecting targeted identities would be the most vulnerable in dispute resolution processes (Delgado, 1997; Delgado et al., 1985; Grillo, 1991). These criticisms should be serving as an urgent research agenda, as many who risk disenfranchisement still choose to utilize out of court dispute resolution processes for a number of reasons (Gunning, 1995), for example: some disputes involve no legal claims, some parties simultaneously pursue court and alternative dispute resolution, others do not wish to be "poster" legal claimants attempting to make societal changes at the expense of their time and budget, and still others value and believe in the promise of a more relational process (Gunning, 1995) with more durable and healing outcomes. And it is noteworthy that such outcomes are not rare; however, they are merely disproportionately available to those already privileged in society (Cooper, 2001; Trujillo et al., 2008; L. Wing, 2009). Whereas use of the concept of intersectionality will not tackle all of the dilemmas these scholars have raised, it can provide a vital lens that will keep these dilemmas front and center, demanding the creation of more responsive and fair processes (Gunning, 1995). Without this, theory and practice will continue to essentialize parties and their relationship to conflict in ways that reify hegemony.

Intersectionality and Conflict Resolution Scholarship

Educators with a dedication to teaching conflict resolution from a critical perspective have needed to branch out from traditional literature to create reading lists from across the disciplines due to the dearth of scholarship by and about those marginalized by the field (Baker, French, Trujillo, & Wing, 2000; Goldberg, 2009; Hairston, 1999; Trujillo et al., 2008) and the way that it perpetuates privilege (A. L. Wing, 2002; L. Wing, 2009). Lawrence (1995) reminds us that "the way one is portrayed in literature and the way one's own stories are valued are symbolic of one's status in the culture and in the body politic" (p. 349). So, what does a resounding silence and absence of visibility in conflict resolution scholarship portray? The boundary-spanning nature of the study of conflict facilitates addressing this, to some extent, through the inclusion of literature from across a number of disciplines. Literature from critical race legal studies, law and society interdisciplinary studies, multicultural education, social justice education, cultural studies, communications, environmental justice studies, and postcolonial studies, for example, offers particularly useful paradigms and concepts that elucidate the relationships between power, identity, and conflict that are crucial to a more complete educational preparation. While there is little material within conflict resolution scholarship that addresses how to remedy the issues raised by the critiques of exclusion and disenfranchisement (S. Raines, personal communication, June 2010), it is heartening to increasingly see publications that challenge the field from within.[6]

Faculty can turn to critical race theory, in particular, for foundational texts on intersectionality that provide excellent contributions to conflict resolution courses (Crenshaw, 1995; Delgado, 1993, 1997; Grillo, 1991, 1995; Grillo & Wildman, 2000; Gunning, 1995; A. P. Harris, 1990; Harris & Carbado, 2006; Ikemoto, 2000; A. K. Wing, 1991), as well as to other disciplines such as philosophy (Spelman, 1988) and critical theory (Forester, 1999). Despite the benefits of using such texts, they remain merely a supplemental approach to add to the curriculum rather than fundamentally change it at its core; the field requires a more multicultural and critical scholarship (Sleeter, 1996)—one that responds to the actualities of oppression as it intersects with conflict. Collective efforts within the field are required to rigorously examine who and what are missing from our scholarship base and how that impacts the theory, processes, students we teach, and those with whom we work during conflict interventions. A critical curricular and pedagogical analysis that sees multivocality and power sharing as central to knowledge creation (McCarthy, 1993; Trujillo et al., 2008) calls to educators to formulate a robust critical research agenda. It is important that we all play a role in reconstructing the field (Trujillo et al., 2008) and that those of us[7] with intersectional identities closest to the center work collaboratively in nondominating ways with people whose intersectional identities are treated as further from the center, in order to de-center ourselves and re-center a new curriculum (McCarthy, 1993; Sleeter, 1996).

Intersectionality and Conflict Resolution Curriculum

Concerned about the social justice implications of the field's reliance on neutrality, universality, and "color blindness," a very small but growing number of people have been seeking to integrate critical theory into the scholarship, intervention processes, and pedagogy of formal and informal conflict resolution education. As a member of this cadre, I have been interrogating how these foundational tenets of the discipline continue to center in conflict resolution theory and practice those already privileged by the larger social structures of society. Part of this undertaking is the challenge to find ways to incorporate a critical lens into the discipline, which inevitably means expanding teaching materials and creating new strategies for intervention. Intersectionality contextualizes and grounds the inquiry in the realities of people's lives, thereby becoming a key foundational concept in critical conflict resolution.

As part of these efforts, I have sought to incorporate into the curriculum some of the outstanding scholarship on intersectionality for the purpose of elucidating how dominant conflict resolution theory and processes are able to replicate oppression, to assist students in understanding the major critiques of the field and encourage their development as reflective researchers and practitioners (Kressel, 1997). An understanding of intersectionality can help students not only to thoughtfully interrogate the field but also consider what their role and contributions within it could or should be. In this way, students are poised to use critical theory to move beyond solely analyzing destructive practices to help construct a positive future for the field. In other words, I see educators as having a relationship with the legacy and present-day realities of social injustice and being in partnership with other disciplines, educators, practitioners, and students to either perpetuate or eradicate such conditions. Clearly doing our own ongoing work in this regard is crucial—understanding the impact of our intersectional identities and how that impacts our work as educators. Curricular and pedagogical choices, like research agendas, are central to these endeavors and offer us multiple opportunities to both role model and collaborate as agents for positive change.

What follows is an exploration of several pedagogical strategies for introducing and utilizing intersectionality in the curriculum through reading assignments, classroom activities, discussion sections, and homework assignments. They are designed to foster student understanding of the complexity and fluidity of overlapping identities—ones that are integrated within individuals and connected to larger groups and systems of support, community, and oppression—and, importantly, to see that they are inseparable from disputants, their conflicts, and their resolutions. The examples provided can be adapted as educators consider when they might be most appropriately used in their curriculum—for example, as a way to first introduce intersectionality, or after the class has already studied it in some depth. While this discussion concentrates on conflict resolution curriculum, faculty in other disciplines will hopefully find some of the material transferable with adaptations to their area of study. Sample questions for in-class discussions and writing assignments can be altered to fit the education level of the students, the course, and the timing of their use.

Several criteria are helpful to consider in selecting a reading to introduce intersectionality; for example, I consider how the author's method for communicating aligns with my pedagogical goals. Many critical race legal theory articles utilize narratives for conveyance of concepts and analyses, and this approach matches my pedagogical style of teaching conflict resolution from a social constructionist perspective, highlighting the role of socially constructed meanings in the contestation and resolution of disputes. Additionally, narratives often capture the imagination of students, making the material more accessible to explore new theoretical concepts. Diverse authorship is another factor I consider when selecting a reading list for any course in order to expose students to a variety of perspectives and scholar role models. Since almost all articles on intersectionality are presently coming from outside the field, this has required developing in-class activities and examples for lectures that help illustrate the relevance to the study of conflict of an author's presentation of intersectionality from another disciplinary perspective. A benefit of this is the illustration to students of the trans-disciplinary nature of conflict analysis.

Introducing Intersectionality: Grillo's "The Mediation Alternative: Process Dangers for Women"

Professor Grillo's (1991) article on process dangers women face in mandatory divorce mediation offers an excellent opportunity to introduce the need for and benefit of applying an intersectional lens to conflict resolution. While Grillo does not explicitly provide an introduction to the concept of intersectionality, the article effectively integrates some discussion of social position and overlapping identities with a critique of mandatory mediation. She provides some illustration of how the intersectionality of race, gender, and experiences with domestic violence affects disputants differently and criticizes mediators for not considering the realities of the social context in which the disputing parties live. The analysis is enriched by statistics and vignettes from actual cases and provides students with concrete examples of the problematics of assuming homogeneity and universality in mediation. This is particularly apparent when she dissects actual (and unfortunately common) interventions that are based on mediator assumptions of equal access to employment and equal pay which disparately impact the parties, and mediator attempts to suppress some disputants' anger based on their race and gender. Grillo's analysis of mediators' de-legitimation of Black women's anger introduces students to the importance of understanding the relationship between narratives spoken and enacted in the mediation room and society's master narratives. Grillo reveals how mediators are gatekeepers of discourse, reinforcing dominant narratives in the process and directly impacting outcomes in ways that unequally affect all disputants. Exposure to and analysis of Grillo's article can prepare students to utilize intersectionality to understand how mediator attempts to apply concepts of neutrality through de-contextualization and color blindness can replicate privilege and disenfranchisement.

Thus, it is through the presentation of the problem of unequal treatment and empowerment opportunities for all disputants that students are exposed to the importance of intersectional identities. By offering a counternarrative demonstrating how common practices actually undermine parties' self-determination and access to procedural fairness, the article cleverly uses the master narrative's expectation of universality and neutrality to illustrate its absence in the ways that Black women survivors of domestic violence, for example, are treated in mediation. Students can begin to see that context and identities matter when studying conflict resolution practices.

Since Grillo does not go into depth explaining how intersectionality applies to all people or explicating its complex relationship with privilege, marginalization, and social location, for example, to assist students in analyzing the dilemmas presented in the article, faculty can assign additional readings that specifically address intersectionality (as outlined in the following section) which can then be utilized for a more in-depth analysis of Grillo's article. She provides a rare examination of discrimination due to intersectionality in mediation, and therefore, it is an excellent choice for faculty hoping to teach conflict resolution students the importance of using the concept as a tool of analysis. Visuals can also assist in illustrating intersectionality and Figures 1 and 2 can be used to highlight the insufficiency of ignoring the overlapping identities which make up real people. The small circle at the center of Figure 2 represents an individual who has many overlapping identities that link them to larger social groupings which can bring them solidarity, community, and targeting for oppression or privilege, for example.[8] Just like the narrative vignettes presented in Grillo's article can bring to life for some the realities of how intersectionality affects parties differently in mandatory mediation, for others who are more visual learners, images such as Figure 2 can help students see the multiplicity and complexity of intersectional identities that all people have. I have found visuals especially useful in demonstrating to students that all parties, including mediators, have intersectional identities, and this can stimulate a rich critical discussion about neutrality and universality as related to Grillo's findings.

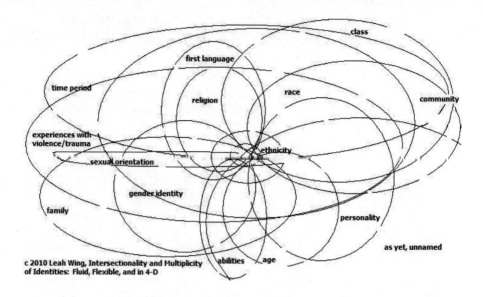

Figure 2: Intersectionality and Multiplicity of Identities: Fluid, Flexible, and in 4-Dimensions

The use of such visuals can also assist in preventing or unpacking the common practice in mainstream White feminism of framing women of color—Black women, in this case—as being "women plus" being Black (Harris, 1990; A. K. Wing, 1997), as many classroom discussions on Grillo's article are likely to move toward homogenizing the dilemmas presented as something that all women or all abuse survivors face. For example, in the midst of discussing Grillo's findings on how mediators carry the master narrative demeaning and framing as inappropriate anger expressed by Black women into the mediation room by attempting to suppress it, it can be common for a White woman to shift the focus to include White women and de-racialize the analysis by stating that any woman who experiences domestic violence faces process dangers in mandatory mediation. This reference to "generic women" decontextualizes the analysis and does not address Grillo's actual findings. In addition, by de-racializing the problematics of typical mediator practice, it undermines the critical examination of how hegemonies of racial discrimination enter mediation through the conduit of mediator behavior.

This offers an important "teachable moment" that can be both anticipated and responded to whenever it emerges. If Figures 1 and 2 are projected as an image for the class to look at or given in handouts, for example, as the discussion of Grillo's article is underway, they are readily available for analyzing the power of the master narrative of de-racialization and homogeneity which centralizes White women as "generic." It is an important opportunity to not only redirect attention to analyze Grillo's actual findings rather than follow the move to inaccurate homogenization, but it also offers a chance to discuss the importance of self-reflection for all of us in the field—students and faculty, researchers and practitioners—since we each have varying degrees of gatekeeping responsibilities and power. The images provide a powerful touchstone for exploring the dynamics of who benefits if we stop discussing intersectionality and the data on experiences of real Black women who are being disenfranchised through mediation and, instead, only focus on shared "generic" identities. These teaching tools and strategies can serve to introduce intersectionality as part of the architecture of our analytic paradigm and show students how it is directly tied to their learning and their future roles in the field.

Introducing Intersectionality: Other sample reading assignments

Readings such as Crenshaw's "Mapping the Margins: Intersectionality, Identity Politics, and Violence against Women of Color" (1995), A. P. Harris's "Race and Essentialism in Feminist Legal Theory" (1990), A. K. Wing's "Brief Reflections toward a Multiplicative Theory and Praxis of Being" (1991), Spelman's *Inessential Woman: Problems of Exclusion in Feminist Thought* (1988), and Grillo and Wildman's "Obscuring the Importance of Race: The Implication of Making Comparisons between Racism and Sexism (or Other-Isms)" (2000) are foundational texts that are relevant across the disciplines. They explore intersectionality's relationship with interconnectivity (Valdes, 2000), interrogating the links between macro-structural and institutional oppression and the micro-level implications for individuals and groups, an exceptionally useful framework for students of conflict to understand. The elucidation of how dominant narratives, and some counternarratives, such as feminism, have structurally determined the invisibility of intersectional identities provides a tool for analyzing conflict resolution as a movement and as a discipline. This can be undertaken in an introductory course, for example, when students study the development of an academic field that is also part of a social movement which has impacted the culture at large and permeated its leading institutions (legal, commercial, environmental, labor, educational, etc.) in ways that are framed as benefiting all of society. Reading key articles on intersectionality provides students with necessary concepts for analyzing how it has often structurally determined the replication of privilege and disenfranchisement, thereby actually fostering conflict.

To accomplish this, in addition to assigned readings on the field's history and major themes, faculty can assign readings on intersectionality and inter-connectivity. To assist students in applying an intersectionality critique of the conflict resolution movement, faculty can draw parallels with how the authors utilized intersesctionality to critique other disciplines (i.e., the law) and other movements (i.e., feminism). By presenting this to students at the beginning of their studies it conveys the importance of intersectionality as central to critical analysis of conflict resolution.

Applying intersectionality to students' own lives and to the field: Sample in-class discussion formats

The goals of these activities are to help students see how intersectionality affects their own identity, to see its relevance to conflict in their own lives, and then to apply this to an analysis of the field, in general.

Exploring intersectionality in dyads.
Students are asked to find a partner with whom to talk about their own intersectional identity. Figure 2 can be used to illustrate that identities intersect, are fluid, and can change over time and with geographical movement. Faculty can provide a few examples, perhaps from their own lives, to demonstrate how to frame intersectional identities. They should ask pairs to ensure that each speaker has time to (a) state some of the intersecting identities that combine to create the person they are right now; (b) describe a real or theoretical example of a conflict that has impacted/could realistically impact them because of their intersectional identity; and c) consider how interconnectivity—their identity links with macro structures—is connected to both their identities and conflicts. Faculty should let them know in advance that they will not be required to report to the class as a whole; however, if they choose to, that they are only to talk about their own story.

Exploring patterns in the relationship between intersectionality and conflict; large group discussion.
After some students briefly and voluntarily share their responses with the entire class, the students will begin to see the reality of intersectionality and how it impacts people's experiences with conflict. This can elucidate a clear pattern in the link between intersectionality and the interconnectivity to larger systems and groups and how these impact people's experiences with conflict, including some people's privilege in being able to avoid it. It is an opportune moment for role modeling by faculty who have personal stories, for example,

of how their intersectional positionality has protected them from or easily reduced conflict in their lives; or how they have risen to challenges they have faced due to conflict related to their intersectional identity (see endnote 8 for further discussion).

Intersectionality and the conflict resolution field; small group discussion.
Students should be asked to analyze the abstract value of universality in the conflict resolution literature in light of what they have learned about the impact of intersectionality on real people's experiences with conflict. Faculty should be prepared to lead an analysis if many who lack multiple consciousnesses (A. K. Wing, 1991) begin by using the master narrative of imagining that rhetoric means reality and defending the field as equally accessible to all. This may be a likely response since they can rely on the literature which repeatedly states this. Their recent discussions with their own classmates and the readings by Grillo and others that challenge this can provide this positive opportunity for students to integrate their learning about intersectionality into a critical analysis of the field.

Designing Intersectionality: A right-brain activity

Another learning methodology for engaging students in an analysis of intersectionality is through the creation of visual images and/or objects. They can provide multiple advantages: as devices that approach a difficult point for discussion and externalize it away from an individual speaker by projecting it on a wall or onto a three-dimensional object, by providing a source of conversation that can allow for a variety of interpretations, and by offering a change of pace from the routine of written and oral/aural learning activities. Faculty can assign students a right-brain group activity to create a visual design or object representing the complexity and multiplicity of intersectionality. This could spark creativity, provide an opportunity to do collaborative work across identities, and help those who are visual learners to integrate their learning more fully. And this is increasingly relevant as students are depending more than ever on visual media for learning and communicating their ideas (McCarthy, 1993). Posting completed designs on the web could increase the visual vocabularies (Machida, 2008) and tools available to others working on intersectionality in any discipline. Such public engagement can also highlight to students that they are knowledge creators who can contribute to the field.

Conclusion

The field of conflict resolution remains a fertile ground for the perpetuation of theory and practices that ignore the real lives of those who are disadvantaged and targeted in ways specific to their intersectional identities as well as perpetuating privilege for those whose intersectional identities place them close to the center. Intersectionality provides a conceptual tool that can illuminate these dynamics and help undermine their continuance. More research and new pedagogical inventions are required to challenge the paradigm of neutrality, universality, and color blindness and the architecture of the field upon which it is built. Central to this endeavor must be recognizing our own positionalities, as educators, and the privileges imbedded within them as we make choices about our pedagogy and the curriculum we use. This is important, since whether educators use the dominant paradigm of conflict resolution or critically examine it significantly impacts the scholarship, pedagogy, and curriculum to which students are exposed. The challenge is ever present for faculty to seek to ground their pedagogy in an understanding that positionality and the multiplicity and intersection of identities are crucial to the study and resolution of conflict. In fact, each gatekeeping juncture in the field offers the chance to contribute to change: curriculum selection, pedagogy, research, hiring practices, publication selection, conflict interventions, public policy advocacy, theory building, and mentoring. These are places of opportunity to support a new multicultural generation of theory builders and intervenors who will not settle for less than a field fairly and effectively serving all disputing parties by being multipartial to their needs based on—not despite—their real identities. Therefore, a critical, emancipatory, and socially just pedagogy has a place in teaching conflict resolution. If we are not using such an approach to study conflict's development and resolution, then whom are we serving?

Notes

1   The geographic focus of this chapter is the United States; however, it is worth noting that its dominant approaches to conflict resolution—theory, methodologies, and intervention techniques based in Western cultures—are acquiring global hegemony.

2   See Wildman and Davis (2000) for a more general discussion about making hierarchy and privilege visible in order to address them.

3   The centrality of the master narrative of color blindness in U.S. society is powerfully reinforced through the law (Delgado & Stefancic, 2001; Lawrence, 1995), and I argue elsewhere that dispute resolution also serves as a conduit of the master narrative (A. L.

Wing, 2002; L. Wing, 2008). Here, I refer to color blindness as both a legal concept and the common metaphor for valuing the lack of seeing differences as a salve for and strategy to prevent discrimination.

4   These questions are an intellectual exercise to challenge essentialism since one cannot merely substitute a generic human being for a generic male Colombian graduate student in an actual conflict analysis. Using an intersectional lens in conflict assessment requires interrogating the overlap of identities and their impact on disputants' lives and their disputes within a society imbued with systemic inequalities—and this demands contextualization and specificity.

5   For example, see the Cerrell Report (1984) commissioned by the State of California outlining the description of the communities to be targeted for the siting of waste treatment plants. Its research findings outline those populations least likely to resist siting of a hazardous facility. The lower levels of political power for mounting effective resistance are articulated as due to poverty, low education levels, language barriers, distance from urban centers, and willingness to follow hierarchy due to religious socialization as Catholics, among other factors. Numerous other studies have found that the overlap of targeted racial groups (people of color) and poverty are the leading characteristics that determine where polluting facilities are to be sited (Cole & Foster, 2001; Shrader-Frechette, 2002) and that race is the number one determinant (Mohai & Bunyan, cited in Cole & Foster, 2001, p. 179).

6   See the colloquy issue of *Conflict Resolution Quarterly*, "Challenging the Dominant Paradigms in Alternative Dispute Resolution" (Raines, 2009), and an entire book similarly dedicated to this topic, Trujillo et al. (2008).

7   I write as someone who has multiple overlapping identities that mutually reinforce privilege, as a White woman and faculty member whose first language is English, for example. While not all my overlapping identities privilege me, my experience these days is that my positionality is most often treated as close to the center. This affects my educator role, creating important responsibilities and challenges for naming my cumulative and compounded privileges at times as well as the reality of experiencing particularized kinds of privilege and targeting due to my intersectional identity at others. Continual work on understanding our own intersectional identities and their impact on our pedagogical choices is demanded of critical educators, and sometimes this has meant using my own life as an example, and other times, it has meant not centering myself in the discussion.

8   I created Figure 2, "Intersectionality and Multiplicity of Identities: Fluid, Flexible, and in 4-Dimensions," prior to my reading Stephanie M. Wildman's reference to an image of a Koosh ball used to describe a person at the crux of many intersections (Wildman & Davis, 2000).

References

Abel, R. (Ed.). (1982). *The politics of informal justice: The American experience* (Vol. 1). New York: Academic Press.

Auerbach, J. S. (1983). *Justice without law?* Oxford: Oxford University Press.

Baker, M., French, V., Trujillo, M., & Wing, L. (2000). Impact on diverse populations: How CRE has not addressed the needs of diverse populations. In T. S. Jones & D. Kmitta

(Eds.), *Does it work? The case for conflict resolution education in our nation's schools* (pp. 61–78). Washington, DC: CREnet.

Bullard, R. D. (1990). *Dumping in Dixie: Race, class, and environmental quality.* Boulder, CO: Westview Press.

Bullard, R. D. (Ed.). (1993). *Confronting environmental racism: Voices from the grassroots.* Boston: South End Press.

Cerrell Associates, Inc. (1984). *Political difficulties facing waste-to-energy conversion plant siting.* Los Angeles: State of California.

Chang, A., Basey, D., Carey, V., Coleman, A., & Hoban, K. (2008). Race, (in)justice, and conflict resolution: Injustice in the African American community, effects on community, and the relevance of conflict resolution. In M. A. Trujillo, S. Y. Bowland, L. J. Myers, P. M. Richards, & B. Roy (Eds.), *Re-centering culture and knowledge in conflict resolution practice* (pp. 108–127). Syracuse, NY: Syracuse University Press.

Chene, R. M. (2008). Beyond mediation? Reconciling an intercultural world: A new role for conflict resolution. In M. A. Trujillo, S. Y. Bowland, L. J. Myers, P. M. Richards, & B. Roy (Eds.), *Re-centering culture and knowledge in conflict resolution practice* (pp. 32–36). Syracuse, NY: Syracuse University Press.

Cole, L. W., & Foster, S. R. (2001). *From the ground up: Environmental racism and the rise of the environmental justice movement.* New York: New York University Press.

Cooper, C. (2001). Mediation in black and white: Unequal distribution of empowerment by police. In J. Asim (Ed.), *Not guilty: Twelve black men speak out on law, justice, and life* (pp. 125–141). New York: Amistad, HarperCollins.

Crenshaw, K. W. (1995). Mapping the margins: Intersectionality, identity politics, and violence against women of color. In K. Crenshaw, N. Gotanda, G. Peller, & K. Thomas (Eds.), *Critical race theory: The key writings that formed the movement* (pp. 357–383). New York: New York University Press.

Delgado, R. (1993). Rodrigo's sixth chronicle: Intersections, essences, and the dilemma of social reform. *New York University Law Review, 68*(3), 639–674.

Delgado, R. (1997). Alternative dispute resolution conflict as pathology: An essay for Trina Grillo. *Minnesota Law Review, 81,* 1391–1411.

Delgado, R., Dunn, C., Brown, P., Lee, H., & Hubbert, D. (1985). Fairness and formality: Minimizing the risk of prejudice in alternative dispute resolution. *Wisconsin Law Review, 6,* 1359–1404.

Delgado, R., & Stefancic, J. (2001). *Critical race theory: An introduction.* New York: New York University Press.

Fisher, R., & Ury, W. (1981). *Getting to yes: Negotiating agreement without giving in.* Boston: Houghton Mifflin.

Fiss, O. M. (1984). Against settlement. *Yale Law Journal, 93,* 1073–1090.

Flagg, B. J. (1997). The transparency phenomenon, race-neutral decision making and discriminatory intent. In R. Delgado & J. Stefancic (Eds.), *Critical white studies: Looking behind the mirror* (pp. 220–226). Philadelphia: Temple University Press.

Forester, J. (1999). *The deliberative practitioner: Encouraging participatory planning processes.* Cambridge, MA: The MIT Press.

Goldberg, R. M. (2009). How our worldviews shape our practice. *Conflict Resolution Quarterly, 26,* 405–431.

Grillo, T. (1991). The mediation alternative: Process dangers for women. *Yale Law Journal, 100*, 1545-1610.

Grillo, T. (1995). Anti-essentialism and intersectionality: Tools to dismantle the master's house. *Berkeley Women's Law Journal, 10*, 16-30.

Grillo, T., & Wildman, S. M. (2000). Obscuring the importance of race: The implication of making comparisons between racism and sexism (or other -isms). In R. Delgado & J. Stefancic (Eds.), *Critical race theory: The cutting edge* (2nd ed.). (pp. 648-656). Philadelphia: Temple University Press.

Gunning, I. R. (1995). Diversity issues in mediation: Controlling negative cultural myths. *Journal of Dispute Resolution, 1*, 55-93.

Hairston, C. D. (1999). African Americans in mediation literature: A neglected population. *Mediation Quarterly, 16*(4), 357-375.

Hairston, C. D. (2008). Reflection on African Americans in mediation literature: A neglected population. In M. A. Trujillo, S. Y. Bowland, L. J. Myers, P. M. Richards, & B. Roy (Eds.), *Re-centering culture and knowledge in conflict resolution practice* (pp. 159-164). Syracuse, NY: Syracuse University Press.

Harrington, C. (1980). Voluntariness, consent and coercion in adjudicating minor disputes: The neighborhood justice center. In J. Brigham & D. Brown (Eds.), *Policy implementation: Choosing between penalties and incentives* (pp. 131-158). Beverly Hills, CA: Sage.

Harrington, C. (1985). *Shadow justice: The ideology and institutionalization of alternatives to court.* Westport, CT: Greenwood.

Harris, A. P. (1990). Race and essentialism in feminist legal theory. *Stanford Law Review, 42*(3), 581-616.

Harris, C. I., & Carbado, D. W. (2006). Loot or find: Fact or frame? In D. D. Troutt (Ed.), *After the storm: Black intellectuals explore the meaning of Hurricane Katrina* (pp. 87-110). New York: The New Press.

Head, R. A. (1995). Health-based standards: What role in environmental justice? In B. Bryant (Ed.), *Environmental justice: Issues, policies, solutions* (pp. 45-56). Washington, DC: Island Press.

Ikemoto, L. C. (2000). Traces of the master narrative in the story of African American/Korean American conflict: How we constructed "Los Angeles." In R. Delgado & J. Stefancic (Eds.), *Critical race theory: The cutting edge* (2nd ed.) (pp. 302-312). Philadelphia: Temple University Press.

Kressel, K. (**1997**). Practice-relevant research in mediation: Toward a reflective research paradigm. *Negotiation Journal, 2*(13), 143-160.

Lawrence, C. R., III (1995). The word and the river: Pedagogy as scholarship as struggle. In K. Crenshaw, N. Gotanda, G. Peller, & K. Thomas (Eds.), *Critical race theory: The key writings that formed the movement* (pp. 336-351). New York: New York University Press.

Machida, M. (2008). *Unsettled visions: Contemporary Asian American artists and the social imaginary.* Durham, NC: Duke University Press.

McCarthy, C. (1993). After the canon: Knowledge and ideological representation in the multicultural discourse on curriculum reform. In C. McCarthy & W. Crichlow (Ed.), *Race, identity, and representation in education.* New York: Routledge.

Nader, L. (Ed.). (1980). *No access to law: Alternatives to the American judicial system.* New York: Academic Press.

Nader, L. (2001). Harmony models and the construction of law. In P. K. Chew (Ed.), *The conflict and culture reader* (pp. 38–44). New York: New York University Press.

Raines, S. (Ed.). (2009). Challenging the dominant paradigms in alternative dispute resolution. *Conflict Resolution Quarterly, 26*(4), 381–495.

Rouhana, N. R., & Korper, S. H. (1996). Case analysis: Dealing with the dilemmas posed by power asymmetry in intergroup conflict. *Negotiation Journal, 12*(4), 353–366.

Shrader-Frechette, K. (2002). *Environmental justice: Creating equality, reclaiming democracy.* Oxford: Oxford University Press.

Sleeter, C. E. (1996). *Multicultural education as social activism.* Albany: State University of New York Press.

Spelman, E. V. (1988). *Inessential woman: Problems of exclusion in feminist thought.* Boston: Beacon Press.

Tarter, J. (2002). Some live more downstream than others: Cancer, gender, and environmental justice. In J. Adamson, M. M. Evans, & R. Stein (Eds.), *The environmental justice reader* (pp. 213–228). Tucson: University of Arizona Press.

Trujillo, M. A., Bowland, S. Y., Myers, L. J., Richards, P. M., & Roy, B. (Eds.). (2008). *Re-centering culture and knowledge in conflict resolution practice.* Syracuse, NY: Syracuse University Press.

Valdes, F. (2000). Sex and race in queer legal culture: Ruminations on identities and interconnectivities. In R. Delgado & J. Stefancic (Eds.), *Critical race theory: The cutting edge* (2nd ed.) (pp. 334–339). Philadelphia: Temple University Press.

Wildman, S. M., & Davis, A. D. (2000). Language and silence: Making systems of privilege visible. In R. Delgado & J. Stefancic (Eds.), *Critical race theory: The cutting edge* (2nd ed.) (pp. 657–663). Philadelphia: Temple University Press.

Wing, A. K. (1991). Brief reflections toward a multiplicative theory and praxis of being. *Berkeley Women's Law Journal, 6*, 181–201.

Wing, A. K. (1997). *Critical race feminism: A reader.* New York: New York University Press.

Wing, A. L. (2002). Social justice and mediation. (Unpublished doctoral dissertation). University of Massachusetts at Amherst.

Wing, L. (2008). Whither neutrality? Mediation in the twenty-first century. In M. A. Trujillo, S. Y. Bowland, L. J. Myers, P. M. Richards, & B. Roy (Eds.), *Re-centering culture and knowledge in conflict resolution practice* (pp. 93–107). Syracuse, NY: Syracuse University Press.

Wing, L. (2009). Mediation and inequality reconsidered: Bringing the discussion to the table. *Conflict Resolution Quarterly, 26*, 383–404.

"Check Your Head"
Teaching and Learning
the Intersectionality of Whiteness

Anna Creadick, with Jalisa Whitley, Patrice Thomas,
Amber Jackson, Katy Wolfe, Martin Quigley, and Reina Apraez

To identify, analyze, and oppose the destructive consequences of whiteness, we need what Walter Benjamin called "presence of mind."
—George Lipsitz, "The Possessive Investment of Whiteness"

Check your head.
—Beastie Boys

Six years into my position as an English/American Studies professor at a small liberal arts college in western New York, I began to despair about the varieties of privilege, ignorance, and arrogance I saw in some students. Though we are fairly diverse for an institution our size, the campus culture seemed dominated by a predominantly white, upper-middle-class majority. Often, after they had taken a number of courses, I could see incremental shifts in awareness of privilege in my juniors or seniors. But why wait? How could I trigger a sense of consciousness in them sooner? I began to consider that *whiteness* could be a place to begin.

Patricia Williams has written of the "exnomination" of whiteness: "In our culture, whiteness is rarely marked in the indicative there! there! sense of my bracketed blackness. And the majoritarian privilege of never noticing them-selves was the beginning of an imbalance from which so much, so much else flowed" (1997, p. 7). If I could just get these privileged students to become *conscious* of their whiteness, I thought, they might begin to see "race" as every-body's problem. For my working-class white students and students of color, I thought, demystifying whiteness could reveal the shaky foundations upon which many structures of privilege and power have historically been built. If "so much else flowed" from the invisibility of whiteness, then *seeing* it might shape their academic, work, and social relationships for the next four years, and reverberate beyond them.

So, in the fall of 2007, I launched a first-year seminar entitled Seeing Whiteness. Because my graduate training in American Studies had encouraged a critical understanding of the intersectionality of difference, my pedagogy has always been politicized, highlighting issues of diversity and social justice in a complex way. Seeing Whiteness demanded an intersectional approach. By connecting race to other categories such as class, gender/sexuality, ethnicity, and region intersectionally, I worked to bring students past the personal to understand the structural underpinnings of sameness and difference.

What happens when students are asked to confront white privilege—historically, theoretically, and personally—in their first semester of their first year? Was whiteness an effective lens through which to introduce the social construction of race to undergraduates? Is intersectionality the most effective lens through which to teach about whiteness?

To address these questions, this chapter opens with an overview of my course design and a description of my research methodology, followed by a series of thematic discussions drawn from a prose "roundtable" discussion between myself and six of the most thoughtful and articulate student-graduates of my seminar. In a concluding section, I assess the risks and benefits of using intersectional pedagogy, as seen through this experience. Ultimately, I argue that if collegiate education reproduces structures of privilege, the college *classroom* can be a site for the destabilization of privilege if an intersectional approach is taken.

Course Overview

My motivation for designing and teaching Seeing Whiteness was both intellectual and ethical. A long-standing academic interest in the unmarked categories of identity, such as masculinity, heterosexuality, middle-classness—and eventually "normality" (Creadick, 2010)—made an inquiry into "whiteness" resonate with me. At a personal level, since reading Toni Morrison's landmark study *Playing in the Dark*, I had been acutely attuned to my own responsibility, as a white person, to write and teach about race and racism, and to do so in a highly self-reflexive way.

Intersectionality suited my subject. Audre Lorde's (1983) early discovery that "there is no hierarchy of oppressions" indelibly shaped my understanding of all difference, so it was important that I acknowledge whiteness as one among many sites of sameness/privilege against which difference/oppression is measured/enacted. The intersectionality of the course was explicit in my course goals: "interdisciplinary course readings, lectures, discussions, and films" would allow students to investigate "the roots and consequences of white privilege"; "the ways in which whiteness can intersect with class, sexuality, gender, region, and other identity categories"; as well as "strategies" for "an active and reflective anti-racism." Because my topic conveniently sprawled in multiple directions, we were able to investigate whiteness as identity but also as a commodity, as a colonial tactic, as performance, as privilege, as symbol, and as beauty standard.

To encourage students to think about race intersectionally, the syllabus pointed students toward considerations of how different categories of identity inflect whiteness in different contexts, mediating its privileges. For example, an early section on the history of whiteness exposed the ways in which national origin, ethnicity, and citizenship have intersected with race. Learning that Jewish or Italian or Irish immigrants did not arrive white but rather "became" white was a revelation that served to denaturalize whiteness into a quality neither biological nor obvious (Adelman, 2003; Jacobsen, 1998). If whiteness is not biologically stable, what is it? Next, a series of readings on "whiteness and class" asked students to analyze, for example, the tongue-in-cheek website/book *Stuff White People Like* and Martha Stewart's home-decorating websites to track the alignment of whiteness with expressions of middle-class taste. As Patricia Williams has argued, "Middle-classness . . . is so persistently a euphemism for whiteness, that middle-class black people are sometimes described as 'honorary whites' or as . . . deracinated in some vaguely political sense" (1997, p. 35). Other readings and examples engaged the intersections of race, class, and region, where we saw how particular labels have distanced poor whites—labeled "hillbillies," "rednecks," "white trash"—from the rest of the white population, so that they become, effectively, *nonwhite* whites. Intersections between race, class, location, and gender were further illuminated by a sociological study of African American girls raised in predominately white suburban environments. These "brown-skinned white girls," the author argues, did not understand themselves as black until college, where identitarian politics and black student activism sparked a shift (Twine, 1997, p. 215). Kathe Sandler's documentary *A Question of Color* (1993) allowed us to investigate the way whiteness, or "lightness," is privileged *within* communities of color through racialized standards of beauty, color/caste hierarchies, and the exoticization of desire. Finally, in a section on white violence, we looked at lynching—especially the 1955 Emmett Till case—to unpack the ways whiteness, masculinity, and sexuality converged when the rhetoric of Till's "crime" was steeped in deeply racialized notions of manhood, womanhood, and rights.

While intersectionality was part of the course design, it also emerged in more unpredictable and unharnessed ways via the discussions, experiences, investments, and reactions of the students and myself as the course unfolded. In order to recapture some of the layers of this intersectional teaching and learning, I invited six students, three from the 2007 iteration of the course and three from the 2009 version, to collaborate with me on this chapter.

Methodology and Research Design

The model of "dialogue" with students was appealing for this chapter because the course meant different things to different people. I adapted the polyvocal model of a published "roundtable"—which I had experienced in writing academic review essays by invitation in the past (Creadick, 2004)—to allow those various voices to analyze the course content: We would write about and evaluate this common experience, share our responses over e-mail, then respond to one another's responses in a kind of dialogue on paper. I selected these particular students (comprising roughly one-fifth of the total enrollment for each class) because they were some of the most articulate. Either in class discussions, written assignments, or both, these students engaged fully with the course content and participated fully in the "collective production of knowledge" that I strive for in the classroom (Freire, 1970/2006; Shor, 1992; Shrewsbury, 1987).

In retrospect, I now realize that these students' depth of engagement stemmed at least in part from their own fraught relationships to "whiteness": From the 2007 class, I invited **Jalisa Whitley**, a middle-class, African American student from Geneva, NY, who would go on to study sociology and public policy, specializing in race and social justice; **Reina Apraez**, a light-skinned student of Colombian descent who explored our course concepts deeply through creative work and teaching as an arts scholar and studio art/education major; and **Katy Wolfe**, a white, middle-class arts scholar whose long-standing interest in Africa led her toward study abroad in Ghana and an Africana Studies/Peace Studies curriculum. From my 2009 section, I invited **Patrice Thomas**, a Haitian American student from New York City, and a scholar, poet, and activist who quickly became a campus leader around race and rights; **Martin Quigley**, an especially perceptive white student from the Catskills of New York whose relationship to race privilege had been complicated by his experiences with regional and class bias; and **Amber Jackson**, an arts scholar in creative writing whose experience growing up with urban poverty and racial isolation in Syracuse, NY, gave her an ambivalent relationship to her own whiteness as "privilege."

Like everyone in the course, these students each had something serious at stake. But unlike everyone in the course, they were willing and able to take the risk of confronting and articulating, often powerfully, what that "something" was. Our "roundtable" discussions brought forth some central themes I have used to structure the remainder of this chapter. These themes might be said to characterize the teaching and learning of intersectionality: *vision, context, positionality,* and *consciousness.*

Teaching and Learning VISION

On the first day of class in my 2009 Seeing Whiteness seminar, 15 students and I sat around a table in a small corner classroom in Gulick Hall. To begin, I asked them to do an in-class writing in which they tried to "see" whiteness in our classroom:

ASSIGNMENT: Where is whiteness in this room? Is it visible/can you see it? What is your personal relationship to whiteness, and how might that relationship shape your work in this class? What interests you about this course subject?

By posing these questions I triggered their "vision" on the first day, in the first moments of the class. The first question was intentionally ambiguous, and some students (especially the white ones) described "white walls, white paper, shoes, the whiteboard." The African American students in the class were unequivocal, however. One wrote, "Whiteness is in the majority of this room. Ninety-eight percent of the people sitting in this room are white." The second question about "visibility" pushed everyone to consider how whiteness is not always apparent on the surface, and student responses got more complicated: "Skin color does not show the background or history of a person's descent." The subsequent questions encouraged students to begin to establish their own stakes in the course topic and to consider their own positions as relevant to their learning. Here some students even began to move from the personal toward the structural in their thinking: "I was always curious why Caucasian folks are called 'white,'" wrote one of my current coauthors, Patrice Thomas, on this first day. "Their skin color is obviously not white. Is it something symbolic?"

As we shared our responses to the questions, I read from my own answers to the questions, which I had written alongside them:

ANNA CREADICK: White walls. White socks. Pinkish-brown people who appear racially white. Are they? White noise. White liberal arts college. Maybe "Gulick" was a white person. Probably. Buildings tend to be named after the wealthy philanthropists who give the money for them. . . . I am white. I have its privileges, with some limits because of class and region (I am not *as* white as Martha Stewart). Illuminating whiteness makes me feel *raced*, and therefore *e-rased* in some ways. It makes me part of a group, less of an individual. It feels confining, uncomfortable. My whiteness means I get to teach about race and not be viewed with suspicion.

My response highlighted these more institutional elements of whiteness and tried to model the kind of critical self-reflexivity I would be nudging them toward all term.

Beginning with whiteness (rather than blackness) had helped to disorient students, shaking their sense of familiarity with racial conversations and incorporating all of them into a racial terrain in ways that were largely inescapable. As the semester continued, other assignments required students to continue to "see" whiteness inside and outside the classroom. In the 2007 course, students kept personal reading logs/journals in which they could make the course content personal in a more private way. In 2009, students were required to attend any weekend academic or social event (such as frat parties, lectures, or dances) with the charge to "see whiteness," then write about how it played out in these specific campus contexts. These kinds of reflective components of the course required students to recognize and articulate their own relationship to race privilege and to understand their own identities as complicated by race but not reducible to it.

These assignments made for some of the more highly charged moments in the course, as when, after the first weekend of the '09 term, we discovered that most of the white students had attended a "highlighter party" at a campus fraternity which required them to wear all white and draw on one another's bodies under black lights. Meanwhile most of the students of color had attended a dance sponsored by the black student organization. Metaphors of whiteness abounded in these examples, but students only partially "saw" them. "Was there crossover?" I asked. Not much. "Why did you all, in your very first weekend here, already divide yourselves up along these racial 'party' lines?" I asked. Silence. Though they were beginning to "see" whiteness, they did not necessarily understand it nor understand their own complicity in reproducing its boundaries.

By the end of the course, as a selection of coauthors' comments illustrates, the conceptual language of "vision" or "sightedness" became deeply incorporated into how students would articulate their understanding of the significance of the course and of race more generally:

JALISA WHITLEY: It seemed so provocative, yet simple to "see whiteness." Before taking the course I had thought of whiteness as something that I "saw" daily and which was easily noticeable to me and my friends and family . . . , [but] I thought it would be interesting to see what spin this course would put on "seeing whiteness," [by] making the previously invisible, visible.

AMBER JACKSON: The first step is actually seeing that there is a problem before we can fix it, and since most people don't even see whiteness, digging deeper into the subject of whiteness can help.

REINA APRAEZ: It is only by isolating and disseminating [the] structure [of whiteness] that we can first truly "see" it.

KATY WOLFE: From where I stand, I can only see benefits from learning how to "see" whiteness. It made me understand the term in a more honest and truthful light.

PATRICE THOMAS: Ultimately, seeing whiteness signifies seeing this society in its entirety.

The title Seeing Whiteness thus contained several layers of intention for the course. White students were asked to "see" their own whiteness, to step outside the privilege of being racially unmarked. All students were asked to "witness" race more honestly—to engage, to pay attention to the way they enact and support the social construction of race on a daily basis. Assignments were designed to make the invisible visible, since seeing race—something they have pointedly been taught *not* to see—was a first step toward dismantling its power. More broadly, the course encouraged a kind of cognitive *vision*: to encourage habits of critical reflexivity around all experiences of power and privilege.

Teaching and Learning CONTEXT

An emphasis on history can be critical to teaching intersectionally. My own background in cultural history shaped my sense that showing how whiteness had changed over time would be key to demystifying and denaturalizing it. Early readings such as Matthew Frye Jacobsen's *Whiteness of a Different Color* (1998) and Stephen Jay Gould's *The Mismeasure of Man* (1981) let students understand the historical invention of whiteness, and the pseudoscience at its root, while assessing the reality of its influence on the past, present, and future.

The first time I taught the course, however, I felt the students becoming bored and bogged down with the academic prose of these Ivy League intellectuals, so for the 2009 iteration, I used a smaller section of Gould, and then arranged students into small groups and asked them to prepare and "teach" specific chapters of Jacobsen to the rest of us. This tactic of turning the tables and asking the class to teach class worked: it gave them a sense of mastery over at least one significant body of evidence proving whiteness as something cultural and changeable. Listening to one another's presentations reinforced the lesson that whiteness has not always meant the same thing, that it has been invented and defended over time not by bigoted individuals but by social institutions and their laws, policies, typologies, and practices. My student coauthors regularly pointed to the significance of historical context to their understanding of race and the intersectionality of that understanding:

> PATRICE: Prior to taking this course, I equated "whiteness" to simply the color of one's skin. I was unaware of the historical mutability, the vicissitudes of "whiteness," and how the whole conception of "whiteness" is a political and economical deployment used to burden some and privilege others. . . . With this knowledge, I could juxtapose the true history of the majority in this country with that of the minority to see how they intersect and influence one another . . . (i.e., the Jews did not become white until their class status was improved; their class status did not improve until they became white).

> REINA: Class issues emerged in the class often, particularly when we began to discuss and read *Whiteness of a Different Color* and understood what qualifiers within "whiteness" exist, and how long they have [such as what] whiteness lost or gained from allowing Japanese immigrants versus other Asian immigrants potential citizenship.

> KATY: One's race does not determine that person's other identities. However, because of certain aspects of America's history, such as the legality of owning slaves, segregation between blacks and whites, etc., it would be a great challenge to avoid discussion of how various identities were forced into correlation.

We were able to enter the "vicissitudes" of whiteness that Patrice mentions (a term that Jacobsen uses repeatedly) because we opened the door of historical inquiry, to find that, for example, landmark legal cases Reina alludes to, such as *U.S. v. Ozawa* and *U.S. v. Thind*, saw the Supreme Court rewrite racial definitions repeatedly, from whiteness as visibility/skin color, to whiteness as genetic (being of "Caucasian" ancestry), to whiteness as subjectively determined (by the judgment of the "common man"). The reverberations of these legal decisions were intense: after *Thind*, formerly naturalized South Asian Americans were stripped of both citizenship and property (Adelman, 2003). Studying FHA lending practices in the post–World War II era helped students understand how class and race privilege (or oppression) have been "forced into correlation" in this country, as Katy puts it. Looking back, Jalisa concludes:

> JALISA: I don't think there is any way to discuss race without its intersecting categories because of how closely they are all intertwined in America.

[Intersectionality] starts to dismantle some of the myths that are rampant on campus and in the larger society that "all white people are rich and all black people are poor" and begins to give light to the fact that different people are privileged in different ways. We may be disadvantaged in some ways but privileged in other ways we do not consider when we look solely at race.

Beginning our discussions with context broadened and complicated the scope of our subject, nudging students past the interpersonal and individual to see the complex, shifting ways in which differences intersect as a consequence of structural forces.

Teaching and Learning POSITIONALITY

Some of the most potent learning that took place in the course involved "experiential" techniques of having students actually position their bodies on the terrain of the subject matter. The "fieldwork" assignments to go to parties or events and "see" whiteness were examples of this, but students' relative silence regarding their own positions during such experiences suggested that they were writing as observers, without holding up mirrors to themselves as participants. Instilling critical reflexivity required a higher-risk assignment.

Around midterm, I decided to do a "privilege walk" exercise with the class (Adams, Bell, & Griffin, 1997; Center for Academic Excellence, 2011; College of Communications, 2005; University of Arizona Residence Life, 2010). Though I sometimes use such experiential exercises early in a class, I purposefully waited until midterm for Seeing Whiteness, because I wanted the students to have developed a closeness, a rapport. These bonds of friendship and trust were necessary to navigate the divisions that the privilege walk would inevitably illuminate. The experience would remain a powerful memory for all the graduates of the course.

On this day, I had the students walk silently outside together, hand in hand, to the quad, where they lined up along one edge and dropped hands. I began reading aloud a list of examples of privileges and hindrances—race, class, gender, and otherwise—and the students were instructed to take a step forward or back, depending on their relationship to each example: "If you have ever experienced racial profiling, take a step back"; "If you went to a private high school, take a step forward"; "If you have ever worried about having enough money for food or heat, take a step back." Quickly, our tight-knit group of 16 students had spread across the quadrangle, those out front blissfully unaware (unless they *chose* to look back) of how far ahead they were, and those at the back painfully conscious of their position in relation to everyone else's. In the 2007 section, all the students in the rear were the students of color. Because I had inadvertently begun the walk at the base of a hill, the students of color had the added insult of having to walk backward *uphill,* and, with poignant symbolism, had instinctively reached out to help one another balance, as they looked out at their white peers moving ever forward. The 2009 section had most students of color toward the back as well, but the fractures among and between the white students were more palpable. The experiment became a powerful metaphor for "seeing" (and not seeing) privilege, and it "exposed" some students more punishingly than others, as my student graduates' comments explain:

> MARTIN QUIGLEY: For students that were comfortably middle-class, [the privilege walk] was not particularly traumatizing. However, for students who were either hyper-privileged or under-privileged, this activity "outed" them to their new classmates. Becoming suddenly aware of one's place in the world is not a particularly good feeling, and unfortunately studying "whiteness" intensely will always result in that feeling. Remaining unaware of privilege may save an individual from feeling uncomfortable, but it takes a toll on all of those who are disadvantaged.

> REINA: There are multiple identifiers which keep people from assimilating into the system or, rather, being absorbed by it. Those who cannot be absorbed are left along the border to suffer. These identifiers emerged most in the classroom when we had exercises like the privilege walk, where we confronted our own class, gender, religious, etc., differences with ourselves. We became aware of "growing up with more than 50 books in a house" as a class privilege, and where that placed us, and knowing that other people around you were also putting their feet forward or backward.

> AMBER: The questions in the [privilege] walk addressed not only race and whiteness but other intersections as well, specifically class. At the end of the privilege walk, I stood in front of only one other student in the class and equally with another. Everyone else was far ahead. I am white, but I was in the back anyway because class, like race, is exceptionally oppressive. I think most people in the seminar were shocked that I was so far behind because they didn't take class into consideration.

The privilege walk had illustrated, most potently, the ways students could simultaneously experience race privilege *and* class oppression, or class privilege *and* race oppression, or both class and race privilege *but* gender oppression—all in the same body. This experience of individual positionality—what Martin refers to as "becoming suddenly aware of one's place in the world"—was also, inevitably, an experience of establishing a sense of community position—the alignment of groups in relation to others. This discovery of both oneself and one's community was especially powerfully expressed when those students walking uphill backwards decided to reach out and help one another balance.

In the follow-up discussion of the privilege walk, I began by letting students write/vent on unsigned papers about how the experiment felt, what they learned, what they could see. Then, I asked for volunteers to share some impressions. Some of them (often the students left behind, with fewer privileges, or those far ahead) were quite upset or angry or interested and ready to talk. Others (often those in the middle) remained disproportionately silent. Students noted how the only "safe" place was in the anonymous middle, that there was "shame" both for those positioned at the front (for their unearned privilege) *and* at the rear (for their supposed failures). I asked students to contemplate the significance of holding hands, and they reflected on what they had in common before and after the walk: all first-years, all 17 or 18 years old, all in the same seminar, all in the same dorm, at the same college, receiving the privilege of a fine liberal arts education. We discussed visibility, and the fact that those in back had no choice but to observe their peers moving forward, while those in front literally did not have to "see" others' oppression unless they turned around to register it. Finally, and most importantly, I emphasized to them that nearly every item on the list I had read—whether an advantage or a disadvantage—was beyond their control: these were the "unearned" factors derived from the circumstances of their birth.

Because it so effectively and indelibly marked the structural roots of social differences onto their individual bodies, the privilege walk became a touchstone for establishing positionality in the course. Once the hierarchies of privilege had been embodied by individual students, then plotted onto the graph of the quadrangle, there might have been different rates of moving forward, but there was no turning back.

The privilege walk thus brought many of the students (including most of the students I've invited to be coauthors here) more fully into the space of the classroom. Once their positions—for many, their alterity—had been established, they had less to lose in fully interrogating the politics of whiteness. From this point on, they became significant participants not just in the learning but in the *teaching* that transpired in the course.

Teaching and Learning CONSCIOUSNESS

The 2007 version of the course was overloaded with texts we didn't get to discuss enough, and also, I fear, left students feeling helpless or hapless in the face of whiteness as an insurmountably structural social problem. As a result, in the second iteration of the course I wanted to focus on empowering students individually, encouraging them to consider how they might carry their understandings beyond the classroom through new habits of thought, or actual actions/interventions. Most pointedly, to accomplish this goal, I assigned two readings: philosopher Charles Mills's "White ignorance" (2007, an article derived from his monograph *The Racial Contract*, 1997) and activist/writer Tim Wise's autobiography *White Like Me* (2007). This pair of texts worked well together: Mills worked to raise the students' consciousness, while Wise worked to prick their conscience.

Charles Mills, a Jamaican critical race theorist, argues that "white Igno-rance" is a way of seeing the world that is distorted by the delusion of white superiority. Because race is intersubjectively constructed as a social system, "white ignorance" is not strictly an individual but a social epistemology (Mills, 1997, p. 134). Mills points out that "white ignorance" is not passive, resulting from a lack of knowledge but is active, the consequence of a deliberate refusal to know. This "collective amnesia" is "not uniform across the white popula-tion" and is not confined to white people alone (Mills, 2007, pp. 14–15). My coauthor Jalisa Whitley's analysis of a campus racial incident that occurred the year following our Seeing Whiteness seminar illustrates the way white igno-rance can operate:

> JALISA: The perfect example of [class] intersecting with race is the infamous "crew team incident" on campus, where a group of [white] students on the crew team dressed up as slaves and had the one black team member dress up as the slave master. This incited the most divisive racial incident on campus that I have ever seen and allowed all those feelings that had been boiling right below the surface to come out about how far we as a campus and as a society still have to go in dealing with everyday issues of racial tension. There was a largely black/white divide, where most black students felt that this was an assault on black people at large and that they felt unsafe on campus, while most white students felt that it wasn't that big of a deal and was just a joke, a play on an outdated historical experience that we all should be able to laugh at by now.

Jalisa's analysis points to an awareness that such an incident is not the re-sult of racist individuals but is a social epistemology, a way of thinking about race that is structural and entrenched. Yet her individualistic and black/white analysis of the events refuses to explain the black student's participation in the stunt—a perfect example of Mills's point that white ignorance can incorporate non-whites, as well (2007, p. 16).

Patrice Thomas made a series of shrewd observations about the ways in which "white ignorance" could persist, even in the face of the new knowledge the course offered:

> PATRICE: My experience in the "Seeing Whiteness" course taught me that isolating whiteness as a subject of intellectual inquiry is very difficult not only for the white students but also for the non-white students. It seems to me that there exists this sense of contempt amongst the white students, especially the privileged ones, when discussing and learning about whiteness. They appear to be uncomfortable learning about themselves. I often watched the "uncomfortableness" suffocating the room. Often they would speak, but their speech would really be forced because the professor

stared at them. Often they would speak, but their words tend to have little substance; it is as if they completely missed the point. Often they speak, yet they remain mentally silent. So it's me and my blackness seeing whiteness for everyone else, trying to break this "mystifying" silence.

Tim Wise's memoir *White Like Me* (2007) was, to some degree, an anti-dote to the hollowness Patrice perceived in the white students. Wise's book helped to lessen students' despair and diffuse white guilt and shame by offering white anti-racist activism as a potential solution. Wise first establishes a term—"collaboration"—to describe the act of perpetuating systems of power and privilege by doing nothing. Next, he offers a number of strategies for how to respond to racism and resist the unearned privileges of whiteness.

One of my favorite memories from my Seeing Whiteness course was the moment when Patrice announced in one of his assignments that if whiteness was socially constructed and was laden with connotations of goodness and light, he would simply "declare" himself white for the rest of the semester. If race is so invented, he seemed to suggest, then I'll just invent myself a different one. But he and I both knew that he could free his mind, but that the structures surrounding him would not translate that cognitive shift into a material change of conditions. Worse, as Charles Mills notes, with pain, "what people of color quickly come to see—in a sense the primary epistemic principle of the racialized social epistemology of which they are the object—is that they are not seen at all" (2007, p. 8). Patrice's brief experiment was a pointed and poignant exercise in the limits of consciousness as the end point of change.

The course concluded with Patricia Williams's essay collection *Seeing a Color-Blind Future*, in which she critiques the ideology of "color blindness" as a solution to racism. Color blindness, Williams argues, is actually a dangerous refusal to see. While ending her study with hope, that "racism is not inevitable, however entrenched," Williams notes that finding solutions requires us to "negotiate, consider, ponder" (1997, p. 64).

Conclusions

When I first decided to collaborate with students on this chapter, I decided a good first step would be to gather the students first in person for a focus group to brainstorm ideas and generate some questions together. The students all agreed to meet me at the local coffee shop on a Friday morning before final exams were to start. When that Friday came, only Jalisa and Patrice, the two African American students, showed up. Our course had trained us to "see" whiteness, and so we did. "Talk about white privilege," we chuckled gloomily, pained at the reality that some conspiracy of oversleeping, forgetting, broken alarm clocks, and the like had made *all* of the light-skinned students miss our meeting, while the only two African American students had somehow made it, on time and well prepared. After several minutes of waiting and some heavy sighs, we ordered our tea and smoothies and got to work, engaging quickly in a rich dialogue through which they helped to establish some of the central questions of this article and early insights into the meanings of our course.

For a time, I considered cutting the four other students and coauthoring this chapter with Jalisa and Patrice alone. But in the end, I decided I needed a fuller range of student voices—even if it meant reinforcing white privilege, yet again. Patrice's insights helped me contextualize "seeing whiteness" as a project that would take longer than one semester to accomplish:

> PATRICE: The privileged students not only did not want to remit their privileges but oftentimes refused to acknowledge them. . . . However, this mental silence is very understandable because it is extremely difficult to become conscious of something that has been planted in the subconscious since birth.

The very first lesson of this project thus mirrored the first, middle, and last lesson of my course: white privilege runs deep. To resist it, you must constantly, carefully, "check your head." Doing so allows us to fight what Patrice calls "mental silence," in order to observe, reflect, and connect with the ways in which the simultaneity of privilege and oppression positions us as individuals and as groups.

Taken together, these dialogues with my students suggest that the aims of the course were largely successful. By the end of this class, whiteness had ceased to be an unmarked category. By the end of the course, students understood whiteness as inextricable from other identities, such as class, region, ethnicity, or gender. Jalisa Whitley, now studying race, public policy, and social justice as a senior, rearticulated these goals beautifully:

> JALISA: [The course] starts a discussion about race that is still necessary, and it delves into the discussion in a deeper way than looking at racism as hating black people. It looks at how whiteness as a system, rather than a skin color, plays into the everyday fabric of how race operates in America. There are the costs of separating people on racial lines, each side defending their race, but I think this is only initial, [because] as the course goes on people begin to see the historic, systemic and cultural ways that whiteness plays into each of our lives. We begin to see that it's not just something that bad white people did to good black people. It is a system that we all play into and we all receive advantage from in differing ways. From here it allows students and faculty to work together to propose solutions and next steps in changing our classroom, our campus, and our world by dismantling untruths.

As Patricia Williams writes, "Creating community . . . involves this most difficult work of negotiating real divisions, of considering boundaries before we go crashing through, and of pondering our differences before we can ever agree on the terms of our sameness" (1997, p. 6). My hope in teaching Seeing Whiteness was for this class to create a stronger campus community, one that was not so fractured along class and racial lines. But for white students, especially, I found that "seeing whiteness" actually fractures community, at least at first. The "community" that the students had constructed in their first semester of college was an imagined one, built on assumptions and performances of sameness. That fantasy of sameness had to be dismantled in order for a *true* community, consisting of deeper understandings of intersecting identities, to be built.

The privilege walk was a metaphor for the teaching and learning process: At first, the students have found a ground on which to feel the same. By the end of the course, my students have drifted apart. My hope is that, over the next four years, they work to come together again, forging relationships that are more truthful and less blind.

References

Adams, M., Bell, M. A., & Griffin, P. (Eds.). (1997). *Teaching for diversity and social change: A sourcebook*. New York: Routledge.

Adelman, L. (Producer). (2003). *Race: The power of an illusion* [Documentary film]. San Francisco: California Newsreel.

Center for Academic Excellence, University of North Carolina at Pembroke. (2011). Privilege walk. Retrieved from www.uncp.edu/cae/seminar/privilegewalk.doc

College of Communications, California State University–Fullerton. (2005). Privilege walk. Retrieved from commfaculty.fullerton.edu/ . . . /Privilege%20Walk%20Activity.doc

Creadick, A. (2004) Location, location, location: A response to *Cold Mountain*. *Appalachian Journal, 31*(3-4), 327–332.

Creadick, A. (2010). *Perfectly average: The pursuit of normality in postwar America*. Amherst and Boston: University of Massachusetts Press.

Freire, P. (1970/2006). *Pedagogy of the oppressed* (M. B. Ramos, Trans.). New York: Continuum.

Gould, S. J. (1981). *The mismeasure of man*. New York: W. W. Norton.

Jacobsen, M. F. (1998) *Whiteness of a different color: European immigrants and the alchemy of race*. Cambridge, MA: Harvard University Press.

Lipsitz, G. (1998) *The possessive investment in whiteness: How white people profit from identity politics*. Philadelphia: Temple University Press.

Lorde, A. (1983). There is no hierarchy of oppressions. *Interracial Books for Children Bulletin, 14*(3-4), p. 9.

Mills, C. W. (1997). *The racial contract*. Ithaca, NY: Cornell University Press.

Mills, C. W. (2007). White ignorance. In S. Sullivan and N. Tuana (Eds.), *Race and epistemologies of ignorance*, (pp. 11–38). Albany: SUNY Press.

Morrison, T. (1993). *Playing in the dark: Whiteness and the literary imagination.* New York: Vintage.

Sandler, K. (Director). (1993). *A question of color* [Documentary film]. United States: California Newsreel.

Shor, I. (1992). *Empowering education: Critical teaching for social change.* Portsmouth, NH: Heinemann.

Shrewsbury, C. M. (1987). What is feminist pedagogy? *Women's Studies Quarterly, 15*(3–4), 6–14.

Twine, F. W. (1997). Brown-skinned white girls: Class, culture, and the construction of white identity in suburban communities. In R. Frankenberg (Ed.), *Displacing whiteness* (pp. 214–243). Durham, NC: Duke University Press.

University of Arizona Residence Life. (2010). Privilege walk. Adapted from M. Adams, L. A. Bell, & P. Griffin (Eds.). (2007), *Teaching for diversity and social justice* (2nd ed.). Retrieved from www.life.arizona.edu/residentassistants/ . . . /PRIVILEGE_WALK.pdf

Williams, P. J. (1997). *Seeing a color-blind future: The paradox of race.* New York: Farrar, Straus and Giroux.

Wise, T. (2007). *White like me: Reflections on race from a privileged son.* Berkeley: Soft Skull.

Using a Pedagogy
of Intersectionality in the
Community College Classroom

Linda McCarthy & Laura M. Larson

When I started this class, I didn't have a full understanding of the idea of privilege. I always felt resentment when anyone suggested that I was privileged because of my skin color. "Privileged" conjured up images of silver spoons and free rides, which were as foreign to me as hover cars and time machines. What I've come to understand . . . is that I was missing half of the concept (white working-class female, late twenties).

Introduction

This chapter offers a pedagogical framework for effectively teaching low-income students about privilege and oppression and provides practical tools for educators to help students understand the impact of intersectionality on society. Through the discipline of sociology, the authors suggest that a pedagogy of intersectionality can help achieve the social justice education goals of equity, activism, and social literacy. A pedagogy of intersectionality is especially valuable when teaching community college students because a majority of students view their socioeconomic identity as a master status (Goffman, 1956). Almost 50% of low-income students attend college at some point (Institute for Higher Education Policy, 2010), and many of them begin (and sometimes end) their education at a community college. At the same time, these low-income students have a range of other identities, some of which are considered dominant identities in mainstream U.S. culture. A pedagogy of intersectionality helps students loosen their grip on their individualized experiences of poverty enough to recognize the impact of intersecting identities.

According to Ayers, Quinn, and Stovall (2009), there are three principles of social justice education: equity, activism, and social literacy. Equity means providing all students with "equal access to the most challenging and nourishing educational experiences" (p. xiv). Activism is a goal rooted in the notion of democracy—that students should strive for "full participation" in society and be provided with opportunities "to develop their citizenship skills through critique . . . as well the opportunity to actively change their schools and communities" (Quijada Cerecer, Alvarez Gutierrez, & Rios, 2010, p. 156). Social literacy suggests that educators should provide students with "opportunities to critique and analyze how their role and existence in our global society are interconnected with others' lives" (p. 156). We argue that using a pedagogy of intersectionality is central to attaining these objectives.

A Pedagogy of Intersectionality

Given the emotional nature of classroom conversations about oppression, teaching low-income students about privilege requires thoughtful and intentional pedagogy. Like social justice pedagogy, the central goal of using a pedagogy of intersectionality is to promote a more equitable and just society. It gives attention to both content and process in the classroom, balancing "the emotional and cognitive components of the learning process," and paying "attention to social relations and dynamics within the classroom" (Adams, 2010, p. 75). In addition, a pedagogy of intersectionality centralizes the principle that the diversity in our society produces multiple perspectives based on our dominant and subordinated identities and the particular ways that they intersect. In order to support dialogue across a range of social identities, educators must normalize the notion that different social identities produce distinct experiences in relation to privilege and oppression and that they can exist simultaneously.

In his textbook on identities and inequalities, Newman (2007) writes about "privilege as well as disadvantage, 'otherness' as well as similarity, invisibility as well as visibility" (p. xvi). Newman's point is that teaching about inequality means teaching about privilege, not just about the "othered" groups. Too often, students focus only on the experiences of targeted groups when thinking about and discussing social identities. Teachers are often guilty of this as well, as they teach about racism by focusing on people of color, sexism by focusing on women, etc. It is critical to remind students that oppression is about more than subjugated groups; it is a dynamic process that relies on the construction of a binary wherein some groups have more social power than others.

Content

Sociology offers a number of concepts to help students understand intersectionality: social status and roles; social structures; social group membership, including dominant and subordinated identities; the difference between individual bias and prejudice; and institutionalized oppression. As students come to understand how social structures such as culture, institutions, and social statuses all give meaning to everyday social life, they learn to critically examine their experiences not as random, individualized acts but as part of larger social patterns that serve to keep some groups in power and others subordinated.

Students are often confused about the difference between prejudice, discrimination, and oppression and are unaware of how social power functions in society (Johnson, 2006). Clarifying these concepts with an analysis of individual, cultural, and institutional levels of discrimination (Newman, 2007) can help students make meaning of the difference between the individual acts of prejudice that they may have experienced (racial or class bias) and those that are embedded within the structures of our society (racism or classism). Students come to understand that their lives are defined by their embodiment of social statuses, including ascribed social group memberships such as race and gender, and how those statuses are constructed within a particular historical moment. Using student-generated examples as content helps foster connections between personal experience and concepts such as social power, marginalization, and institutionalized oppression. Concepts such as horizontal oppression and internalized oppression (Fletcher, 1999; Tappan, 2006) are critical to helping students understand how power structures are maintained by both dominant and subordinate groups. Clarifying how the dynamics of oppression and privilege work helps students to examine their role in the system. The concepts of *mitigated oppression* and *mitigated privilege*, which explain how one's privileged identities can mitigate the experience of oppression in specific contexts, contrast with the master narrative about categories of race, class, gender, and other social identities being singular points of analysis and help students understand the complex dynamics of intersectionality.

Privilege, as defined by McIntosh (1988) in her seminal work on white privilege, is a set of unearned advantages given by society to members of dominant groups. It is based on social group membership and is systematically awarded to some and denied to others (Johnson, 2006). McIntosh distinguishes between unearned entitlements, which play out on an individual level, and conferred dominance, which refers to one group having power over another. Many authors since McIntosh have expanded on her original list of privileges associated with white identity and male identity (Johnson, 2006;

Kivel, 2009). While privilege is experienced on an individual level, the ramifications are much broader. According to Goodman (2001), "domination is created and maintained through interpersonal, cultural, and institutional forces. The privileged group creates systems and structures that reflect its values, embody its characteristics, and advance its interests" (pp. 13–14).

Process

A positive learning environment that fosters lively conversation and values multiple perspectives is critical to teaching about privilege and oppression. A community-based approach to learning provides equal opportunity for students and teachers to learn from one another (hooks, 2003); creates a safe, open, and supportive learning environment (Adams, Bell, & Griffin, 2007; hooks, 1994, 2003); and helps to promote the goals of equity and social literacy by giving students equal access to rich and "nourishing educational experiences" (Ayers, Quinn, & Stovall, 2009, p. xiv). Utilizing an intersectional framework requires intentional community building and frequent attention to the classroom environment to ensure respectful dialogue across differences.

Group guidelines lay the foundation for the learning environment. Guidelines can be designed to inoculate against students continually shutting down or opting out of conversations, can foster community responsibility for learning, and can set the tone, goals, and processes for the class. While instructors may suggest some guidelines, they should be set primarily by the students and worded in a way that ensures that they take responsibility for maintaining them and for addressing their peers when they feel a guideline has been compromised. After the initial creation of these group guidelines, they can serve as a touchstone whenever necessary.

Icebreaker exercises such as common ground (Adams, Bell, & Griffin, 2007), dyad work, and small group exercises help students get to know each another through low-risk, structured interactions. Intentional pairing of students from different identity groups for active listening exercises encourages students to articulate their own experiences within the content of course concepts and offers the opportunity to understand other perspectives. Advising students that "we don't know what we don't know" reminds them that others' experiences may be different from their own and that the development of empathy and deep learning requires that one maintain an open mind (hooks, 2003). As students share information about their upbringing and life experiences, they can identify how those experiences mirror or differ from others'. Identifying these differences can help students recognize that advantages and disadvantages accompany all social identities, which leads to a better understanding of privilege and intersectionality. This kind of dialogue promotes an understanding that multiple truths coexist within the classroom and fosters a sense of shared experience across age, ethnic, and racial group identity; ability levels; sexual orientations, etc. Further, using the concepts of intersectionality, educators can help students make connections between their shared experiences and cultural and institutional manifestations of privilege and oppression.

Fostering student investment in being part of a community of learners depends heavily on persuading a student to see her- or himself as having a role in helping the group understand oppression. For example, a young, working-class white woman wrote in a reflection paper:

> After talking to [two students of color] and thinking more about [the instructor's] feedback . . . I realize that . . . when I listen to people of color I hear them, but if I don't agree with what they're saying, I just tune them out. This is what I've been doing in class. . . . How do I become more open-minded? How do I stop seeing just black and white and instead see gray? . . . I don't know how to do it, but I want to.

This kind of opening up—the beginnings of real learning for this student—comes not just from instructor prodding but from the student's own desire to be part of the classroom community. She is invested in seeing herself as part of the group and does not want to be left behind, yet she struggles to understand how to reconcile others' experiences with her own perception of how the world works. Effective dialogue and small group exercises foster an environment in which students come to recognize that their classmates' experiences are not the "exceptions," but rather are representative of larger social patterns that are determined by social group membership.

The Community College Population

Community colleges fulfill a vital and significant role in our society, providing educational opportunities for those who cannot afford other higher education institutions (Institute for Higher Education Policy, 2010). "Characterized by student diversity in all its facets—racial, gender, and socioeconomic, as well as by wide differences in ability, educational readiness, motivation, and age" (Brookfield, 2002, p. 31), community colleges are truly locales of intersecting identities and experiences. We teach at two vastly different community colleges: one is urban and extremely diverse, and one is small and rural, with a fairly homogenous population of white low- and middle-income students.

Unlike other types of colleges, community colleges provide open enroll-ment, which means that anyone with a high school diploma or GED can enroll, allowing "a second chance for students who did poorly in high school, who made mistakes in their earlier plans, or who have immigrated to this country and need to start anew" (Grubb & Lazerson, 2004, p. 72). Further, community college classrooms may include advanced high school students, adult learners returning to school after many years in the workforce, recent immigrants with incipient English language skills, veterans, and the typical first-year college student. Of undergraduate students, 47% of black students, 55% of Hispanic students, 47% of Asian/Pacific Islander, and 57% of Native American students attend community college (American Association of Community Colleges, 2007). Over 80% of community college students are employed, with about 54% working full-time. Many students are responsible for children or other dependents, and over 16% are single parents (Laden, 2004). While there is a huge range of diversity on all levels, many community college students share the experience of commuting to school, with many attending part-time, and dropping in and out of school (Grubb & Cox, 2005). This ever-changing student population impacts the larger campus community and affects classroom dynamics.

First-generation college students often grow up seeing their parents work long hours in low-paying jobs, usually involving menial or unsatisfying work. These students often enroll in college with the explicit goal of improving their earning potential so that they can sustain themselves and their families. Grubb and Cox (2005) argue that community college students are "highly vocational" (p. 95), employ an "intense utilitarianism" (p. 96) in their assessment of learn-ing and time, and enroll in school explicitly to procure a (better) job, not to attain a broad liberal arts education. Their focus on credits and grades, rather than on knowledge and understanding, Grubb and Cox argue, undermines students' learning. This is a view that is not unique to community college students but rather is reflective of a larger narrative on the purpose of higher education—to give students higher economic status and specific career oppor-tunities, not to become well-informed, critical, and actively engaged citizens. A corollary of this narrative is that a true liberal arts education, with its emphasis on the development of critical thinking skills, exposure to a broad range of ideas and ways of thinking, and the ability to express one's self in multiple forms, is reserved for the middle and upper classes. Intellectual pursuits that do not lead directly to increased wages are seen as an indulgent luxury. This idea, that the only value of attending college is increased income, is supported by the ongoing national discourse about the value of community colleges as sites of job training and workforce development. For example, recent federal educational grants include the language "to improve [students'] knowledge and skills and enable them *to obtain high quality employment to support their families* [italics added]" (United States Dept. of Labor, Employment and Training Administration, 2009). All of these factors give context to the perspectives that students bring to community college classroom learning.

Given the complexities generated by the diversity and other particularities of this population, using a pedagogy of intersectionality is critical to facilitating students' understanding of their personal experiences of both privilege and oppression and to contextualizing these experiences in relation to social justice and inequality. Further, a pedagogy of intersectionality can help students recognize the need for low-income people to work together across racial boundaries to address classism, as well as all other forms of oppression, in order to build a more just society.

The Intersection of Class and Other Identities

In a classroom context where the majority of students are low income, we find many contradictions in how students articulate their class identity. The myth of meritocracy and the accompanying corollaries about individualism and success (Marger, 2008) feed the idea that individual characteristics such as hard work and determination can overcome any obstacle, and that social identities such as race and gender need not limit anyone's achievements. Poor students may identify with individual experiences of poverty without recognizing that these experiences are shared by poor people as a whole.

Given the stigma associated with poverty in the United States, some students understandably distance themselves from a working-class or poor identity. And, like much of America, some low-income students mistakenly believe that they are middle class (Marger, 2008). Rural students may equate poverty with urban environments rather than with their small towns or otherwise associate poverty with people of color. Similarly, students of color may misidentify as middle class because they see themselves as better off than their black or Latino neighbors who have fewer resources, depend on public assistance, or who are not in college. Further, working-class or poor people of color may feel that their racial identity is more salient than their class identity, which may limit their awareness of common ground with their white low-income counterparts. These complexities of race and class impede a class consciousness that transcends racial boundaries.

Low-income students often cannot, or are reluctant to, see beyond their own struggles with economic inequality. For example, white students' ability to recognize how institutionalized racism impacts people of color in today's society is eclipsed by their own experiences with poverty. Correspondingly, low-income students of color are often reluctant to recognize that while they may experience race and class discrimination, they may also possess heterosexual privilege, Christian privilege, able-bodied privilege, or other types of agency. A representative statement, in this case made by a white 29-year-old female in an Introduction to Sociology class, is, "I've never felt privileged because I've lived in poverty my entire life." In general, students' daily struggles with poverty inhibit an understanding of the privileges associated with other aspects of their social identities. A pedagogy of intersectionality can help students understand that they can experience privilege while simultaneously experiencing poverty.

Teaching Low-Income Students
Using a Pedagogy of Intersectionality

A pedagogy of intersectionality plays an important role in interrupting the prevalent narrative that higher education is simply a means to employment for low-income students. As educators, our experience is that once low-income students begin to engage with the topics in sociology and other disciplines that challenge how they think about the world, they develop an appreciation for learning, and many want to continue their education beyond their original two-year college plan. Using inductive pedagogy and instructor modeling, a pedagogy of intersectionality helps students move from an individual perspective to one that fosters alliances across differences.

Inductive pedagogy

When discussing issues of privilege and oppression, using particular vocabulary terms, such as "oppressor," can evoke instant student resistance. While it is important to provide common terminology in order to create a shared understanding of concepts, the more important point of the learning is that students understand that those from different identity groups experience the world differently. An inductive approach, in which students are led to the ideas through dialogue and discussion, rather than a deductive approach, in which students are told what words mean, is more effective. In this way, students feel ownership of their learning and are more apt to apply the terms to their own lives because they feel they have discovered them. Adams and colleagues (2007) call this an "invitational" approach, which is preferable to a "confrontational" approach (p. xx). For example, when two teachers were co-teaching about racism, one asserted that, "All white people are racist." His own understanding of racism, based on the concept of "power plus privilege equals oppression" (Adams, Bell, & Griffin, 1997) led him to believe this. While this may be a reasonable understanding of the social dynamics of racism in the United States, students in this class had not yet been exposed to this particular characterization of racism. As previously mentioned, it is important for students to be able to maintain a positive self-image in order to remain open to learning about the role of white people in racism. For the white students in the class, being racist meant something akin to saying, "I hate all Black people." Throwing out such a provocative phrase put white students on the defensive and diminished the possibility of their acknowledgment and eventual ownership of white privilege.

One alternative to this approach is to first build an understanding of racial dynamics in modern society, discussing statistics and facts about a variety of social structures. Films like the Public Broadcasting System series *Race: The Power of an Illusion* can provide an excellent historical context for understanding institutional racism (Adelman, 2003). Discussions of how the word "racist" has been used throughout history and in modern society can draw out the images that come to mind when the students hear this word. It will be evident that no one would want to claim this identity for themselves and will likely resist any application of this term to anyone other than men in white sheets (Schmidt, 2005). With a broad understanding of how racism is embedded in virtually all U.S. institutions and culture, students can come to appreciate the concept of white privilege and the role of white people in racism.

An inductive approach can also be used to lead students to an understanding of privilege. For example, in an Introduction to Sociology course, students were asked to examine statistics about violence against women, comparable-worth salaries in the employment sector, and facts about women's lack of equal representation in government. They then juxtaposed their findings with sexualized depictions of women in popular magazines and cultural expectations of women's responsibility to perform the bulk of domestic work. Through conversations across gendered groups, male students identified clear examples of the messages they were given about their conferred dominant status in relation to women, and their privileged position as a group. By utilizing materials in class that depicted both cultural standards and institutionalized practices that disadvantage women, male students readily identified the ways in which they do not share women's disadvantage, thereby seeing themselves as privileged in the area of sexism. As mentioned in the editors' introduction to this volume, there are particular contexts in which students with dominant group identities are in the minority. For some students, this has been their prevalent experience. Differentiating between individual acts of racial bias or exclusion and broader social patterns allows students to hold their personal experiences while understanding that they are not representative of national trends. It is important to validate their individual experiences of exclusion and marginalization while also helping them to identify how these experiences are exceptional in the context of larger social patterns.

Shifting from individualism to a sociological perspective

Many students of the millennial generation are reluctant to embrace any information that goes against their personal experience (or that of their friends). Social science data and established theories do not trump what they have experienced firsthand, and some students will outright dismiss such factual evidence as merely an opinion with which they disagree (Diangelo & Sensoy, 2009). A conversation about anecdotal evidence, research methods, and empirical data collection that validates students' personal experiences but situates those experiences within a larger context can decenter the personal experience as reliable evidence. In the context of this conversation, verifiable statistics that demonstrate structural inequality can effectively interrupt resistance in all but the most defensive students. In addition to examining irrefutable data, it is important to lead students in a critical analysis of statistics. For example, an uninformed look at incarceration rates might lead one to conclude that African American men are more likely to sell drugs than white men. A critical examination helps students understand the dynamics of the prison industrial complex and the unequal sentencing processes for blacks and whites (see www.sentencingproject.org). In addition to examining empirical data, looking at the ways that fairy tales, parables, television shows, and movies support the individualistic perspective rampant within U.S. culture is an effective strategy to facilitate students' understanding that they have been socialized to believe that individual actions can always supersede larger social forces.

Without a sociological perspective, low-income students may call on a variation of epistemic privilege (Wylie, 2003) to dismiss material they are uncomfortable with. Further, they may reach for individual, personality-based reasons to explain their classmates' experiences of discrimination with comments such as, "She seems like she's always looking for something to complain about," or they may dismiss someone as a "whiner." This blame-the-victim tactic effectively dismisses the notion that structural inequality is linked to social identities. It is unlikely that the students would see themselves as whiners when they object to cuts in social services or to the cost of higher education. Blaming an individual for his or her individual circumstances is a form of resistance embraced by low-income students more than people from other identity groups, because they have internalized the myth of meritocracy as the explanation for their own oppression. Since they construct individualistic explanations for their own circumstances, they also construct individualistic explanations for the circumstances of others. It is key to help students recognize that their struggles with class-based oppression are parallel to those experienced by others from different identity groups. This connection can help students realize that systemic forces, rather than individual circumstances, are at the root of the issues.

The following example illustrates some of these issues. In a paper assigned for a Group Dynamics class, a young, working-class white woman from a small New England town justified her own racism rather than address the assigned topic (Why is it so difficult to talk about racism?). She wrote, "I've met far more ignorant African Americans than I have ignorant white people. How are you going to not believe the stereotypes if your experience tells you they're true?" This student's comment exemplifies the particular obstacles that prevent low-income white students, particularly those from rural areas, from being willing to give credence to experiences that differ from their own. They have had limited experience interacting with people of color and yet focus on these individual incidents as central evidence for their perspective. Students may fear being labeled as racist, homophobic, or sexist and therefore exempt themselves from participating in any discussion of these topics. This particular student opts out of the conversation by refusing to engage with the topic, even in her response paper. Lastly, the student blames the victim, by suggesting that African Americans are ignorant and therefore deserving of whatever comes their way. Teaching low-income white students about white privilege, then, involves addressing the social messages that reinforce individualistic explanations of social life.

Guided by the master narrative of individualism, when discussing social issues, students may focus primarily on individualized acts of oppression such as stereotyping and personal bias, rather than identifying structural inequality. Further invoking individualism, students ignore the larger social dynamics of power and tend to rely on false parallels (Johnson, 2006) to demonstrate that anyone can be a victim of oppression. The idea that everyone is oppressed at one time or another, and therefore no group can claim anything unique, is illustrated in this statement, made by a 25-year-old white man in an Introduction to Sociology course:

I feel like sociologists are saying that women are growing up with fewer advantages than men. And . . . in most places around the world, this is true. But throughout my lifetime and through my eyes, what I have seen is that we can all go through tough times.

While this statement shows resistance, it also provides a teachable moment. This young man is dismissive of the differences in how people from different identity groups experience the world, but perhaps he is also drawing common ground. The concept of intersectionality is key to helping this student recognize that he does not need to deny his own oppression as a low-income individual in order to acknowledge the distinct oppression of women. Similarly, being oppressed does not preclude one from receiving privilege based on another social identity. Using a lens of intersectionality fosters intellectual persistence and allows students to sit with this cognitive dissonance.

An individualistic perspective also prevents low-income students from recognizing the impact of social structures. For instance, one student wrote, "I don't think society is racist. I think there are some racist people but I feel it's wrong to say all white people are racist. I'm not racist; I wasn't raised that way." This student holds firmly to the belief that although individuals may be racist, society is not.

Giving up an individualistic analysis of why people experience oppression is not easy for students. However, utilizing sociological concepts, a pedagogy of intersectionality can help facilitate students' understanding of the larger social structures at work behind their individual experiences. There are a number of benefits that come when students are able to embrace a sociological perspective. Students can stop blaming themselves or their parents for circumstances related to classism, racism, religious oppression, etc., and understand that others in their social identity group share their struggles. Students from dominant groups can identify how their privilege manifests and begin to interrupt stereotypes and take other actions in their spheres of influence. As instructors, we frequently see students' enthusiasm for course material increase dramatically once they have made these connections. When they are able to connect individual experiences to larger social forces, they begin to see the ways in which these forces operate all around them, and they bring these examples to the class. In particular, the concept of internalized oppression (Fletcher, 1999) can help facilitate reflection among low-income students and highlight the role of the media and other social institutions as the mechanisms that keep an unequal system in place.

Instructor modeling/storytelling

In reflecting on our own narratives, instructors model an understanding of intersectionality and how privilege and oppression can manifest over the course of a lifetime. By using a model such as the Cycle of Socialization (Harro, 1997), instructors can show how agents of socialization lead us to construct meaning of the messages we receive about our own identities and about those of other groups. For example, in her classes, Laura introduces the model by reviewing her experiences growing up female in Southern California, giving detailed examples of the messages she received about women's bodies, how she internalized those messages, and how those negative messages impacted her sense of self as a woman. She uses her personal experiences to illustrate the concept of internalized oppression and how the objectification of women serves to limit women's self-confidence and what women believe they are capable of achieving. She then elicits examples from both female and male students to identify how gender socialization operates and the ways in which it hurts both men and women.

Because our dominant identities are typically less salient for us and because society normalizes members of dominant groups (Tatum, 2003), it is important for instructors to model how their agent identities have manifested in their lives. For example, Linda discusses her background growing up upper middle class and the process of coming to recognize that she had opportunities and experiences that others did not. By normalizing her initial lack of awareness, she models an emerging understanding of the impact of class privilege. Students can then be asked to think about the early messages they received about their dominant identities and identify how they have benefitted from the social structures that confer dominance on agent groups.

Storytelling can be a critical vehicle for establishing a tone of openness and candor, for identifying the links between theory and personal experience (Freire, 1972; hooks, 2003), and for illustrating the complexities of intersectionality. For example, Laura calls on her identity as a white lesbian to discuss some of the impacts of homophobia that are common to other forms of oppression, such as marginalization, powerlessness, and violence (Young, 1990). She then contrasts those experiences with the privileges she receives for being white, such as being seen as normal, having authority, and expecting fair treatment. Instructors who model self-disclosure via storytelling not only foster comfort with self-reflection in the classroom but also disrupt the traditional mode of education that positions the teacher as a guarded authority figure (hooks, 1994). Through storytelling, the instructor makes her- or himself fully human to the students, normalizing human fallibility as well as the potential for great personal transformation (hooks, 1994, 2003).

Activism: Creating allies in the classroom

As noted in the introduction to this chapter, activism is a key goal of social justice education (Ayers, Quinn, & Stovall, 2009). Being able to critically analyze injustices in their personal spheres and in society at large is an important skill for students to develop if they are to achieve "full participation" in society and be able to positively "change their schools and communities" (Quijada Cerecer, Alvarez Gutierrez, & Rios, 2010, p. 156). As Freire (1972), Memmi (1991), and other liberationists have pointed out, oppression hurts everyone, and it will take everyone working against it to create true liberation. If students can see themselves as distinct from, but also aligned with, students of other social identities, they can broaden their vision of where there is common ground and perhaps envisage new alliances in the struggle for social justice.

For disempowered populations, it can be a transformative process to rec-ognize privilege and explore the accompanying opportunities to become an ally to subordinate groups. Intersectionality builds empathy for others' experi-ences and creates a shared sense of social injustice that inspires students to act. Through modeling and inductive pedagogy, instructors can foster both an awareness of social injustice and opportunities for taking action against it. As students develop a sense of connection to the classroom community, they cultivate an investment in one another that enriches the learning environment and provides an opportunity for creating alliances across differences in social identities.

Conclusion

A pedagogy of intersectionality offers low-income students a lens which can help them see that every member of society encounters both struggle and fortuity. An understanding of multiple identity groups (Young, 1990), an examination of how privilege functions in one's life, and challenging the idea of a hierarchy of oppression (Lorde, 1984) can help low-income students begin to see beyond their own individual struggles and envision themselves as part of a collective group struggle across social identities. As students from dominant identity groups come to recognize that whites, males, heterosexuals, etc., receive unearned advantages, they can begin to see themselves not just as recipients of these privileges but as actors who have a role to play—either in supporting them, or in disrupting them. With a combination of support, validation, and gentle prodding, students can make radical transformations. In this process, students begin to consider the power that is afforded them based on their agent identities, and the impact that they may have on their social spheres.

Low-income students face many challenges, and it is not surprising that they would be reticent to acknowledge that they also hold some advantages in society. In contrast to other generations, class consciousness is weak among young people in this historical moment. Further, as Johnson (2006) points out, we tend to be identified by our lowest social identity. Low-income students therefore may be slow to recognize the commonalities they share across racial differences and instead may focus on the advantages they perceive the other groups to have. Building alliances and awareness of common ground can help foster a new shared sense of class consciousness. As students come to understand the concept of intersectionality, they come to realize that they do not need to minimize or deny their own class-based oppression in order to acknowledge that other groups of people also experience oppression.

References

Adams, M. (2010). Roots of social justice pedagogies in social movements. In T. K. Chapman & N. Hobbel (Eds.), *Social justice pedagogy across the curriculum: The practice of freedom* (pp. 59–85). New York: Routledge.

Adams, M., Bell, L. A., & Griffin, P. (Eds.). (1997). *Teaching for diversity and social justice*. New York: Routledge.

Adams, M., Bell, L. A., & Griffin, P. (Eds.). (2007). *Teaching for diversity and social justice* (2nd ed.). New York: Routledge.

Adelman, L. (Producer). (2003). *Race: The power of an illusion* [Television series]. San Francisco: California Newsreel. Retrieved from http://www.pbs.org/race/000_General/000_00-Home.htm

American Association of Community Colleges. (2007). *Facts 2007*. Retrieved from http://www2.aacc.nche.edu/pdf/factsheet2007_updated.pdf

Ayers, D., Quinn, T., & Stovall, D. (2009). *Handbook of social justice in education*. New York: Routledge.

Brookfield, S. D. (2002). Using the lenses of critically reflective teaching in the community college classroom. *New Directions for Community Colleges, 118*, 31–38.

Diangelo, R., & Sensoy, O. (2009). "We don't want your opinion": Knowledge construction and the discourse of opinion in the equity classroom. *Equity & Excellence in Education, 42*(4), 443–455.

Fletcher, B. R. (1999). Internalized oppression: The enemy within. In A. L. Cooke, M. Brazzel, A. Saunders Craig, & B. Greig (Eds.), *Reading book for human relations training* (8th ed.) (pp. 97–102). Alexandria, VA: NTL Institute for Applied Behavioral Science.

Freire, P. (1972). *Pedagogy of the oppressed*. New York: Herder and Herder.

Goffman, E. (1956). *Presentation of self in everyday life*. Garden City, NY: Anchor Books.

Goodman, D. J. (2001). *Promoting diversity and social justice: Educating people from privileged groups*.

Thousand Oaks, CA: Sage.

Grubb, N. W., & Cox, R. D. (2005). Pedagogical alignment and curricular consistency: The challenges for developmental education. *New Directions for Community Colleges, 129,* 93–103.

Grubb, N. W., & Lazerson, M. (2004). *The education gospel: The economic power of schooling.* Cambridge, MA: Harvard University Press.

Harro, B. (1997). The cycle of socialization. In M. Adams, L. A. Bell, & P. Griffin (Eds.), *Teaching for diversity and social justice* (p. 81). New York: Routledge.

hooks, b. (1994). *Teaching to transgress: Education as the practice of freedom.* New York: Routledge.

hooks, b. (2003). *Teaching community: A pedagogy of hope.* New York: Routledge.

Institute for Higher Education Policy. (2010). A portrait of low-income young adults in education. Retrieved from http://www.ihep.org/publications/publications-detail.cfm?id=138

Johnson, A. G. (2006). *Privilege, power, and difference* (2nd ed.). Boston: McGraw-Hill.

Kivel, P. (2009). The Christian holiday cycle. Retrieved from http://www.christianhegemony.org/wp-content/uploads/2009/12/Christian_Holidays1.pdf

Laden, B. V. (2004). Serving emerging majority students. *New Directions for Community Colleges, 127,* 5–19.

Lorde, A. (1984). *Sister outsider.* Trumansburg, NY: Crossing Press.

Marger, M.N. (2008). *Social Inequality: Patterns and Processes.* 4th Ed. Boston: McGraw-Hill.

McIntosh, P. (1988). *White privilege and male privilege: A personal account of coming to see correspondences through work in women studies.* Wellesley, MA: Wellesley College Center for Research on Women.

Memmi, A. (1991). *The colonizer and the colonized.* Boston: Beacon Press.

Newman, D. (2007). *Identities and inequalities: Exploring the intersections of race, class, gender, and sexuality.* New York: McGraw-Hill.

Quijada Cerecer, P. D., Alvarez Gutierrez, L., & Rios, F. (2010). Critical multiculturalism: Transformative educational principles and practices. In T. K. Chapman, & N. Hobbel (Eds.), *Social justice pedagogy across the curriculum: The practice of freedom* (pp. 144–163). New York: Routledge.

Schmidt, S. L. (2005). More than men in white sheets: Seven concepts critical to the teaching of racism as systemic inequality. *Equity & Excellence in Education, 38*(2), 110–122.

Tappan, M. (2006). Reframing internalized oppression and internalized domination: From the psychological to the sociocultural. *Teachers College Record, 108*(10), 2115–2144.

Tatum, B. D. (2003). *Why are all the black kids sitting together in the cafeteria? And other conversations about race.* New York: Basic Books.

United States Dept. of Labor, Employment and Training Administration.(2009). Introduction to the trade adjustment assistance community college and career training program (TAACCCT). Retrieved from http://www.doleta.gov/pdf/Factsheet_FAQs_FINAL_100610.pdf?target=http://frwebgate.access.gpo.gov/cgi-bin/getdoc.cgi?dbname=111_cong_public_laws&docid=f:publ005.111.pdf

Wylie, A. (2003). Why standpoint matters. In R. Figueroa & S. Harding (Eds.), *Science and other cultures: Issues in philosophies of science and technology* (pp. 26–45). New York: Routledge.

Young, I. M. (1990). *Justice and politics of difference.* Princeton, NJ: Princeton University Press.

The Rhetorical Nature
of Intersecting Identities

Actualizing Intersectionality in the Classroom

Neeta Bhasin

Recently, a colleague, who is one of the few international faculty members at a small liberal arts institution, confided to me her difficulties and challenges as a headscarf-wearing Muslim woman teaching not only about Islam but particularly about gender in Islam. It seems, she bitterly complained, as if her faith and her head-covering somehow disqualified her from talking about feminism and excluded her from being accepted as modern, liberal, or progressive. She is constantly struck by how "unfair" and misplaced the criticism is from her students on her course evaluations, which more often than not imply that she lacks teaching credentials and knowledge, that she has a "biased" and "narrow" view of the West, and that she holds a "one-sided and overly critical" perspective of the current debates in the United States and the West about women in Islam.

My colleague's remonstrations should not be a surprise to anyone who has seen how increasingly the veil, or the *hijab*, has become a powerful visual marker of Muslim women's oppression in the past two decades. This response to the veil has often served to fuel the absurd claims of the "dangerous" rise of Islamic fanaticism and militancy. In fact, the veil has, erroneously, come to represent Islam itself and is taken, falsely, as a sign of inability and/or refusal to adopt progressive "Western values" by Muslims. Besides being not taken seriously by her students, what was perhaps more disturbing was her suspicion that even her colleagues in the department and the college might (silently) share some of the same views of her as her students. Her dilemma captures the shifting, multiple, and intersecting positionings that many teachers, particularly those who are marked in some way as the "Other," come to occupy in meeting the demands and challenges of teaching in American academia.

An interesting paradox here is that this grappling with varied and inter-meshed identities (in her case of a woman, a Muslim, a feminist, a professor, an Asian, to name a few) has to occur alongside the constant confrontations with the narrow, one-dimensional, and culturally essentializing[1] understand-ings of identity rampant all around. Kimberle Crenshaw (2000) views these essentializing attitudes as a sign of the "invisibility" of the intersections of Identities.

Recently, the need to integrate teaching and learning as interactive prac-tices informed by intersecting identities has begun to be addressed in higher education (Akom, 2008; Edelstein, 2005). As the experience of my colleague illustrates, this integrative development is crucial for educators aiming to guide students to engage responsibly in critical conversations within academia and beyond. It is also a critical foundation from which educators must examine their own pedagogical practice.

Where I Enter This Discussion

The salience of intersectionality and the rhetorical nature of identities are not merely of academic concern to me, and grasping their significance was not just a theoretical impulse. Rather, the impetus to actively create a new pedagogical framework that highlights intersectionality emerged from my own life as an immigrant from South Asia in American academia. The visa stamp in my passport now clearly indicates that my immigrant status lasts only for the duration of my employment in this country. So technically, I am not an immigrant to this country. Even though I think of myself as a sojourner, a mere career migrant, and not a permanent resident, I'm sure that my experience of displacement, "culture shock," and "fitting in" has something in common with those who have uprooted themselves to make their home in another country in search of a better life. I should emphasize, there are always differences of class, age, ethnicity, religion, and occupation, to name just a few. These differences and the power relations that constitute them are significant enough to indicate to me that the linguistic, ideological, rhetorical, and cultural resources that these immigrants used to hone their ways of being in America can differ from the ones that I would have chosen. It is also not surprising to find that most people have a rather limited exposure to the lives of marginalized and disenfranchised immigrants.

Scholars have tended to focus on the most conspicuously noticeable constructions of national, racial, gendered, and ethnic identities and have often neglected the equally creative activities and motivations of "rank-and-file" people in their everyday practices. Rarely do we listen to immigrants explain themselves in their own words, and therefore, we often fail to understand why, when, and how they interpret their social experiences in national, racial, gendered, or any other terms. The question, then, is partly of methodology. Can we understand and, indeed, teach about discursive practices only by studying them textually? The answer for me clearly was that only analyses that illustrate and elucidate rhetoricity, fluidity, and intersectionality of (constructed) identities can dislodge shallow and essentialist understandings of identities and thus promote a more robust dialogue around power structures in which these are embedded.

Framing the Discussion

In keeping with Kimberle Crenshaw's (1991) call for the need to account for the multifarious axes of identities to understand the social world, this chapter explores the ways my pedagogy emphasizes the rhetorical dimensions of identities and explores the way different identities of race, class, gender, ethnicity, and nationality intersect in immigrant concerns. I argue that to understand the intersectionality theory of identity, one has to understand intersecting, overlapping, and sometimes competing identities that are largely rhetorical in nature. This approach to identity not only illuminates the robustness of intersectionality but also underscores the importance of agent-centered analyses that allow for the identification of agency, understanding of the way human initiative interacts with social structures, and the power dynamics entailed in such interactions.

For this chapter, I will use my course Immigrant Experiences: Voices and Discourses as an example to illustrate how the concept of intersectionality can be operationalized to bring alive and make visible the dynamic nature of identity construction, particularly the multiple axes of oppression, and also of empowerment. If classroom practices are to assist students in developing an ethical perspective toward not only their own education but also toward the nonacademic communities they are members of, then we need to understand and utilize the very permeable boundary between academe and the outside world. My intent is to consider pedagogical strategies that can instill in students a sense of themselves as agents and interlocutors in a larger, ongoing historical and political dialogue in which they and we, particularly as teachers, have much to contribute.

Intersectionality and the Rhetorical Approach

The inspiration to attempt an alternative theoretical framework of this particular chapter comes from scholars Kimberle Crenshaw and Rita Dhamoon, among a plethora of other scholars, teachers, and students who have contributed greatly to this undertaking of revisiting and revising the concept of identity and its real-life impact on college campuses. Crenshaw is one of the major and early proponents of intersectionality and its usefulness in understanding the multifarious axes of identities needed to explain the social world. An intersectional approach holds that the classical models of oppression within a society, such as those based on race/ethnicity, gender, religion, sexuality, class, disability, and other markers of difference, are not hermetically sealed from one another nor do they act independently of one another (Crenshaw, 1991). Instead, these forms of oppression interrelate, thus giving the approach its name. This insight is now readily applied in various fields like sociology and cultural studies, and in this chapter it will be applied to the field of Writing and Rhetoric. It is also often applied to social work, advocacy, and activism.

Rita Kaur Dhamoon's (2006, 2011) work on the politics of intersectional identity borrows from Crenshaw and the other theorists of intersectionality but takes it further to provide a much-needed critique of liberal multiculturalism. According to Dhamoon (2006), liberal multiculturalism essentializes cultures and identities and contributes to the depoliticization of these concepts, thereby crystallizing the everyday production and legitimization of racism and discrimination. Dhamoon has also researched and written extensively on multiculturalism, teaching and learning about race and racism and feminist theories and practices of intersectionality. The critical examinations of Crenshaw and Dhamoon can help us to dislodge the single-axis analysis preferred by those who increasingly avoid the talk of power and privilege and uphold multiculturalism through discourses of diversity and inclusion in which the Other is merely tolerated and accommodated (Dhamoon, 2006).

The rhetorical approach to identity eliminates the presuppositions regarding the preconstituted categories such as gender, race, ethnicity, or class that are often used as a bag of tricks, which when opened can miraculously explain people's identities and sometimes their whole lives. While many of the theories of race, class, and gender used in Identity Studies, and particularly regarding diasporic and postcolonial settings, are conceptually rich and sophisticated (Gilroy, 1993; Hall, 1989, 1990; Minh-ha, 1989), they explain little about the complex and endless boundary negotiations that are entailed in people's daily lives. There is no detailed account of the ways in which people cultivate affiliations and solidarities and disavow them in the arena of micro-politics of interethnic interaction. Many of the teaching materials used in classrooms do not and arguably cannot capture the contingent, process-oriented, and intersectional nature of identities. By rhetorical nature of identities, I mean that they are constructed to communicate, persuade, and accomplish the goal the rhetors/speakers set for themselves in a communicative situation or interaction. I subscribe to the view that there is rhetorical purpose in the construction of reality, and social identities of people are created and deployed as part of that purpose. To understand the rhetorical character of identities, one must go beyond the presumed, the innate, the supposedly biological or the primordial nature of identities and look for how, why, when, and where they are constructed and the purposes they serve in everyday lives of people. A rhetorical approach to identity can allow for balancing both structural analysis and individual agency and illustrating how both structure and agency interact and intersect with each other.

Therefore, the starting point of my rhetorical approach consists of assuming an agentive stance of viewing human beings as agents who are engaged in exercising their ability to reconstitute and change the world to suit their purposes. Identity, then, is a rhetorical resource in this endeavor, and nation, race, ethnicity, etc., are inventional materials, or practical categories that people utilize to position themselves socially in their daily interactions. Furthermore, everyday social interactions are the primary arena where the will and creativity of people are displayed and honed, and to understand agency, one has to situate it in the context of social, cultural, and political dynamics of a specific place and time out of which it arises and by which it is constrained, rather than regard it as ontologically prior to context. Clearly, if agency becomes the key component in the investigation of identity, the focus on the local and the small scale necessarily and organically flows from it, and that makes it more favorable to understand social relations and contexts of marginality and privilege. So, if I appear to "fetishize" individual and local agency at the expense of institutions and structures, it is to the extent that the individual and the local often are the specific sites of agency and because this stance compels us not to be dismissive of the self-representations and narratives by the so-called subjects of our study.

I also want to make it clear that I do not equate agency with free will or naively assume that it operates without any structural or systemic impediments. I do not disdain macro-social laws or the study of large-scale patterns in society and cultures, nor ignore the structure of power relations while assuming the relativistic legitimacy of the practices of individuals and groups. In fact, I believe that the micro- and macro-levels, the local and the global, are connected to, and indeed, shape each other, and therefore, the idea of social construction of identity should not be trapped within the familiar terms of either free will or determinism. Rather, we can have better access to macro-politics only through micro-political mediation. Thus, carefully analyzing the multiple constraints on the participants in interactions or situations, and the micro-narratives they use to represent themselves and others, allows us profound insights into the interlacing of the micro- and macro-levels of discursive orders, the purposes for which the identity is being constructed (consciously or unconsciously), and a much better understanding of how power and privilege are deployed and resisted.

Taking a rhetorical approach to identity construction seems particularly propitious to call attention to the intersectionality of identities. However, most importantly, in classrooms, a rhetorical paradigm that emphasizes the overlapping and intersecting nature of identities, oppressions, and empowerments can be used to study and to teach about different social groups, social relations, and the contexts within which they are embedded. This approach can yield a richer and a fuller picture than others that facilely corral and enclose people into one conventional category at a time. While other social science methods can make social positions seem fixed and self-contained, the rhetorical-intersectional paradigm can evince the relationality and the multiple positionings that constitute daily life for people, and the power relations that are part and parcel of it. Such an approach can also be easily fused with other ways of conducting inquiries and building knowledge about complex social issues that necessitate a more humane and social justice perspective. The difficult part of this undertaking, however, is to be able to demonstrate that identities are intersecting and have shifting axes through our pedagogical practices.

Pedagogy, Rhetoric, and Intersectionality

To address the aforementioned concern about intersectionality and pedagogical practice and materials that incorporate people's daily lives and to illustrate how intersectionality can be operationalized in our pedagogical practices, I want to discuss an experimental and explorative course that I designed and offered called Immigrant Experiences: Voices and Discourses.

There were resources available at my institution through a grant from the Center for Teaching and Learning for educators interested in incorporating innovative teaching practices like service learning in their courses.

After receiving this grant, I struggled to incorporate a civic engagement or service-learning component in this course when I first offered it in 2008. Despite my initial reservation, I decided to integrate service learning largely because of the undeniable salience of immigration issues and a considerable (and controversial) presence of migrant farmworkers in the local geographical area. Fifteen students enrolled in this course and almost all of them were first years or sophomores. The comprehensive and long-term goal of Immigrant Experiences was to enhance and enrich students' understanding of the sociocultural and political contexts of immigrant discourses, to encourage them to appreciate discursive practices in other languages/cultures, and to develop and employ a variety of strategies to unpack the complexity of cultural exchanges and power relations embedded in them.

Immigration is a central component of American history and the search for identity and justice among transplanted individuals was to be a recurrent theme in this course. The course was to examine the historical, political, and economic aspects of immigration as well as issues concerning gender, ethnicity, culture, and cross-cultural divides through written discourse, discussions, films, field trips and community placements, and talks by guest speakers for additional insights. At the end of the course, I expected students to have an understanding of the centrality and complexity of immigration to the history of the United States and understand immigrant experiences in terms of an intersectional paradigm of identities; sufficiently engage in the intellectual debates surrounding immigrant issues in American culture and deepen their awareness of the varied origins of immigrants and of the diverse linguistic and cultural experiences immigrants encounter in the United States; develop a perspective on their own cultures, allowing them to denaturalize or defamiliarize it and see it as specific to time and space rather than assuming it as the norm; and finally, to build positive attitudes of curiosity, openness, and independence toward exploring immigrant discourses. It was important to have my students develop a sense of the life experiences of immigrants to this country.

Providing knowledge and understanding of different immigrant populations and issues that affect their daily lives in the United States was a major component of this course. It was impossible to delve into all the different domains of experiences of every group of immigrants in this 200-level course, so I addressed the immigrant experience as a series of topics framed as questions. Some questions for our class were: What are the factors underlying immigration? What are the processes of integration into American society and how do linguistic and cultural factors affect individual and collective social integration? How do race, ethnicity, class, gender, language, educational background, migration goals, religion, timing, area of settlement, and other factors shape the experiences of immigrants to the United States? What kind of strains and conflicts do individuals and families, and the larger immigrant community, experience? What are the work, business, and income experiences of immigrants and what is the impact of immigrants on society? Another closely related theme was the historical development of nativist movements and efforts to restrict immigration. To lend substance to our discussions we drew upon experiential accounts of immigrant individuals and groups through letters, documentaries, and oral testimonies. Through these accounts, students were introduced to the sociocultural characteristics of new immigrant groups and to the interaction between immigrant cultures and American society.

This course was divided into three sections dealing with global, national, and local immigration issues, respectively. We began by exploring immigration and migration issues in the global context and then focused our attention on immigration issues, debates, and policies in the United States. The third and largest section of the course consisted of gaining hands-on understanding by placing students "in the field" to understand local issues around immigrants and immigration in the city and surrounding areas. I designed course projects in partnership with members of community organizations and planned activities for students to meet needs in the community and advance the students' understanding of course content. From time to time immigration activists, and members of various community and local organizations closely working on immigrant issues, and indeed immigrants, both men and women, visited our class as guest speakers. I accompanied students to various sites, so I too could hear their accounts directly. The organizations that students worked with included the Rape and Abuse Crises Center, Catholic Charities, Rural and Migrant Ministries, Farmworker Legal Services, Agri-business and Child Development, and Migrant Health Services, a shelter for migrants that allowed students to meet and interact with immigrants and migrant workers in various domains of their life. As part of their civic engagement responsibilities and service-learning projects, students performed volunteer work at local organizations affiliated with immigrant issues including children and youth programs, an immigrant health clinic, legal services, farmworkers associations, and crisis centers for immigrant women, among others. In addition, the grant allowed me to take the class to New York City to visit the Tenement Museum and the Lower East Side.

Students wrote weekly reflection journals and worked on their term projects in conjunction and in interaction with the people at the site where they were working. This helped them develop an awareness of community issues and their underlying socioeconomic and political causes. Students also linked their everyday experiences in the field with intellectual inquiry, thus practicing engaged citizenship. Students were asked to focus on one or more aspects of the immigrant experience of a person or a group. For example, their projects addressed topics of immigrant lives such as language use, cultural practices, the role of women and children, the problems of cultural translation, the availability of social supports or services, intergenerational conflict, or discrimination, to name just a few. It is important to note that the course became an inquiry into the character of service learning—an evolving pedagogy in which students could both perform meaningful service to local community organizations and reflect critically upon that service, particularly its politics and ethics.

Engaging Students: Pedagogical Choices

Classes in which students are required to examine and engage in discussions about such controversial matters as immigrant experiences can be challenging for students and teachers alike. Talking about discrimination and power structures can be a daunting task as students are often reluctant to talk about these sensitive matters. My own experience has been that even when it is hard for them to articulate, students are quite aware of the enormous tensions between studying issues of race, ethnicity, class, and gender within the classroom and experiencing these forms of power relations outside its confines. Therefore, to make them understand and experience how people, and especially immigrants, establish and negotiate individual and group identities in complex rhetorical situations, I focus on examining the processes that establish meanings; the way identities come to appear to be fixed and unidimensional; the challenges posed for normative social definitions of community, ethnicity, and nation, and the way these challenges are handled by ordinary people in everyday situations—the way ordinary people make sense of their experiences, select, construct, and narrate their different identities and how these processes are both rooted in their varied material conditions that not only bestow power and privilege in relation to one another but are also necessitated by the rhetorical exigencies of their interactions. Thus, in order to help students view their learning as a means to deal with these real-life issues, so that their education can become more meaningful to them and to their communities, we must as teachers lay bare within the institutions where we teach and in our teaching practices, the multiple and complex identities that overlap, complement, and also compete with one another.

In keeping with the above observations, the issue of teaching practices, particularly in classrooms, and more generally on college campuses, comes down to emphasizing the fluidity of identities and the multiple positionings, thus drawing attention away from their purported singularity and fixity. It is also important to highlight and underscore the rhetorical nature of identities, particularly as seen in the everyday interactions of people by which they create, maintain, challenge, avow and disavow, defy and reinforce identity labels and the normative understandings of identities. Rather than adhering to overly mechanistic and rationalistic approaches that hinder us from making any meaningful change in our understanding and actions as social beings, we ought to explore how the enactments of identities in the everyday lives of people reiterate or modify our understanding of the master narratives, large patterns, and grand theories.

To operationalize these concepts in the classroom, I prompted students to compare the insights offered in theoretical and academic course texts to their experiences in the field while visiting or volunteering at specific sites, and to their interactions with immigrants and migrants. In these discussions and the required reflection papers, I try to elicit from students their thoughts on the self-representation by immigrants, the attributes they assign to themselves and to others, and the particular situations and interactions in which these narratives are embedded. The point is to go beyond the prescriptive (what immigrants should do), the normative (what immigrants normally do), and the speculative (what immigrants can and might do) to what they actually do and did. Although it is true that "immigrants" and "migrants" are *a priori* framed as subjects of study in this course, such a juxtaposition of theory with practice not only serves to triangulate the findings but also helps in immeasurable ways to unpack and make more visible the complexity of human behavior, the different modalities of social relationships, and the processes of identity construction.

Let me also add another cautionary note here. The danger of falling into the trap of a glib multiculturalism is ever present in these discussions. Often students, in their well-meaning efforts to relate and empathize, tended to overwhelmingly highlight the cultural and other similarities while minimizing differences between themselves and immigrants or migrant farmworkers. There were also occasions when the differences were so exoticized that the discussions would begin to deteriorate into jejune celebrations of diversity. It took considerable vigilance and skill honed over time to interrupt students who (admittedly, often in their desire to walk a mile in someone else's shoes) would do away with 'difference' so completely as to blur or ignore the vicious hierarchies and brutal power differentials. At these opportune junctures, I found it personally and politically imperative and useful to interject myself in the unfolding meaning-making process not as a teacher but as an immigrant. Using myself as an example, I asked my students to contemplate the differences in the immigrant experiences of an Indian (female) professor in a private liberal arts institution in upstate New York and, say, an Indian (male) cab driver in New York City. The discussion around this sometimes unflattering and thorny comparison was revealing and thought provoking. Many students in this course actively maintained their interest in immigration issues long after the term was over, and some even continued to cultivate meaningful relationships with groups and individuals they worked with during the term. I found that teaching this course allowed me to overcome the schism that often exists between students and professors by establishing bonds of empathy and good rapport. It was very rewarding to be treated not simply as a one-dimensional outsider (of color and with an accent) who stood between them and a good grade.

In sum, if teachers do not help students fully comprehend why, how, and in what situations people deploy their constructed identities to achieve certain purposes that emerge out of their routine interactions, then we are more liable to produce misunderstandings and faulty knowledge of their motivations and intentions. The aforementioned practices afford better ways, I contend, to ensure that our students' understanding of multiculturalism does not dissolve into cursory, inconsiderate, and self-serving acting out of identity politics.

Lessons Learned

The aims and objectives of the course at first were not clearly focused on intersectionality, but over the duration of the semester, it came to be incorporated more perspicuously. The civic engagement component of the course was the most fruitful one in terms of highlighting intersectionality. It provided students with the valuable opportunity to apply classroom discussions and theoretical analyses of immigrant experiences to the real community of immigrants in the area, thus integrating community-based learning with academic study.

Student responses to the course were very positive as their journals and reflection papers testified. The course evaluations at the end of the semester also corroborated their enthusiasm for the way the course was organized as they wrote expressively about the eye-opening nature of their experiences. "The class challenges and expands your notions of immigration as a cultural and political phenomenon. The guest speakers we have bring the assigned readings to life," a student observed. Another echoed the sentiment that hearing from the immigrants and interacting with them in their place of work "helped us to put faces and real-life stories to the readings we had done." Students in this class, according to him, became "emotionally invested" after these interactions with immigrants and activists for a sustained period of time. The profound impact of such an exposure to the different aspects of immigrant experiences compelled another student to note that the "treatment of migrants in this country is unfair and goes against everything that this nation is supposed to believe. The conditions that some of these migrants are forced to live under are disturbing." A student, as part of her final project, wanted to anthologize the stories of legal and illegal immigrants who took shelter at a halfway house for migrant farmworkers where she volunteered. Other term projects involved looking at the work conditions and sexual abuse of migrant women; the education of immigrant children; and the general health of migrants working on farms and orchards in upstate New York, all through sustained contact with individuals and groups in their field placements.

The trip to New York City proved very successful, both in terms of the bonding of the students with one another and with me. One student wrote eloquently in his course evaluation that "the trip to New York city made me start looking at immigration from a much different perspective. Going to Little Italy and Chinatown, rather than simply enjoying the atmosphere, I started thinking about whether immigrants in these areas saw themselves as blending in with American culture or still more attached to their respective cultures." Another student thanked me profusely in an e-mail after the trip, writing, "I was fascinated by our trip to Chinatown. Stepping off Canal Street, I felt like all of a sudden I had walked into China. And then, only a few blocks away, Little Italy could not have looked more different. I have been to New York City many times, but I have never experienced this, and was absolutely floored by what I discovered."

These responses are one, albeit an important, way to measure the effectiveness of the course and the teaching practices. It is clear that the impact of working with and learning from the immigrants in their various roles and in different domains of everyday life provided more opportunity for them to explore and understand the multiple roles and positioning of the immigrants, their representations and self-representations, and the multifarious axes of oppression and empowerment. It also drove home with clarity the point for me that it was possible to combine *both* theoretical and empirical approaches in a course. Sharing these experiences, particularly the trip to New York City, with each other in class created bonds of solidarity and camaraderie that also helped me immensely in my interactions with students. In the course of teaching this class, I did reconsider and amend my teaching philosophy to emphasize both the personal and the political in the classroom. The intersectional approach allowed me to raise personal viewpoints in class and then to discuss those perspectives and positions that differ. It is a mistake, I realized, in this class that deals with difficult and sensitive matters such as cultural differences or discrimination of marginalized social groups based on race, class, and gender, to name just a few, to present oneself as a completely "objective" observer or presenter of "facts." As Dhamoon (2011) claimed, "an intersectional-type research paradigm" can serve to not merely explain power dynamics in specific contexts but also to

> critique or deconstruct and therefore *disrupt* the forces of power so as to offer alternative worldviews. This disruption entails a self-reflexive critique of the analyst and her or his own implication in the matrix of meaning-making, specifically her or his relationship to knowledge production and research subjects. This can make intersectional-type research challenging, for it demands a willingness to address sometimes uncomfortable relations of implication in the production and organization of unequal power relations. (p. 240)

These insights reinforced my conviction that as teachers we need to locate ourselves within the debates we teach and admit and acknowledge our own influences, positions, and interpretations. No one is or can be completely objective, but it can be detrimental to the teachable moment to assume a neutral position that lets us off the hook. In the teaching of this course, I also realized it is important to demonstrate to students why one is compelled to take on the burden of representation (of one's religion, race, class, gender, ethnicity, nation, tribe, so on and so forth), and also why that burden of representation is never exhaustively representative or reflective of all of the strands, stratifications, and axes of identity formations.

This insight helped me to make sense of my colleague's frustration at the failure of her students and her colleagues to see the multiplicity and the interlocking of their teacher's identities, and to understand her choice and her need to foreground one over the other in a given situation or context. This critical awareness is necessary for all, but perhaps it is much more consequential for teachers who embody underrepresented identities on college campuses. It is vital for us to carve out not only a speaking position, for ourselves, but also to open up our classrooms for other opinions and perspectives that will help students develop a more informed comprehension of the workings of power relations in American educational settings. This will help to counter the often superficial and facile discussions that take place in classrooms and on college campuses and empower students, who possess such tremendous potential, interest, and passion, to work actively for social change.

Conclusion

Crenshaw's (1991) formulation of intersectionality reflects, according to Dhamoon (2011), the view that identifications and power are not separate and do not exist apart from each other. The intersectional-rhetorical paradigm is useful for studying identities, categories, the process of identity construction, and also the systems of domination, facets that can allow for a better, deeper, and more nuanced understanding of difficult issues, particularly related to marginalized groups. This is a more useful way of teaching than the superficial, "politically correct" but ineffectual discourses of diversity and multiculturalism that might raise the issue of inclusion yet further disenfranchise those who are underserved and underrepresented. Educators must strive to link the problems of the real world and the way they play out in classrooms and on college campuses and then tie that to what we teach. Only then can we move forward and create actual and lasting change. That there is an urgent need to change is obvious to anyone who cares to look at the state of diversity, multiculturalism, and inclusion on college campuses. As Dhamoon (2011) points out, it is only when we frame intersectionality as a form of social critique that we can bring to the fore its tremendous potential to lay bare and to impede oppressive workings of power. Hopefully, this modest contribution to the discussion on intersectionality will help in pushing out the debate from its academic confines to become more like "political praxis" (Dhamoon, 2011). This will allow students, faculty, staff, administrators, and anyone who has some stake in making educational institutions and society more fair and just to uphold the values of inquiry and social change.

Note

[1]   Essentialism, in its most basic sense, refers to the reductionist belief that people and/or phenomena have an underlying and unchanging essence. Cultural Essentialism is the tendency to believe that those who belong to a specific culture exhibit morals, ideas, or traits universally or a person born into a culture is born with its designated characteristics. Further, a person is judged to have certain characteristics based on which "culture" (often a term used for race, ethnicity, religion, and nation) he/she appears to belong to. This notion has been largely discredited both in academia and outside, but subtle forms still exist.

References

Akom, A. A. (2008). Black metropolis and mental life: Beyond the "burden of 'acting White'" toward a third wave of critical racial studies. *Anthropology & Education Quarterly, 39*(3), 247–265.

Crenshaw, K. W. (1991). Mapping the margins: Intersectionality, identity politics, and violence against women of color. *Stanford Law Review, 43*(6), 1241–1299.

Crenshaw. K. W. (2000). The intersectionality of race and gender discrimination. Position paper based on a presentation given at the UN Expert Group Meeting on Gender and Discrimination. Retrieved from http://www.scribd.com

Dhamoon, R. (2006). Shifting from "Culture" to "the Cultural": Critical theorizing of identity/difference politics. *Constellations, 13*(3), 354–373.

Dhamoon, R. K. (2011). Considerations on mainstreaming intersectionality. *Political Research Quarterly, 64*(1), 230–243.

Edelstein, M. (2005). Multiculturalisms past, present, and future. College English, 68(1), 14–41.

Gilroy, P. (1993). *The black Atlantic: Modernity and double consciousness.* London: Verso.

Hall, S. (1989). Ethnicity: Identity and difference. *Radical America, 23*(4), 9–20.

Hall, S. (1990). Cultural identity and diaspora. In J. Rutherford (Ed.), *Identity: community, culture, difference.* London: Lawrence & Wishart Limited.

Minh-ha, T. T. (1989). *Woman, native, other.* Indianapolis: Indiana University Press.

A.L.L.I.E.D. Across Our Differences

Blogging and the (Un)Reconciled Politics of Intersectionality

Lesley Bogad, Ibilolia Holder, Juanita Montes de Oca,
Andres Ramirez, and Chris Susi

> The truth is that it's the hard that makes it good. It's the struggle that takes us to deeper places. . . . We are at a tipping point. We know how to stand up when others are pressing down on us, but now those pressures are coming from within.
> —Liam, current A.L.L.I.E.D. member

In 2005, the Diversity Committee for the school of education at Shoreline State College (SSC) started exploring the issue of recruiting students of color into our education programs. In light of research that suggests that children from racial minority groups need teachers who reflect their cultures and identities (Delpit, 1994; Howard, 1999; Marx, 2009), we realized that we had a problem of numbers: in 2007, just 2% of undergraduates in our school of education self-identified as students of color, while over 70% of the public schools surrounding our college met that criterion (InfoWorks, 2007). We soon discovered in focus groups and survey research that the discrepant statistics around our so-called black and brown students were merely a symptom of larger problems of isolation, marginalization, and disconnection. One black student told us he ate lunch in his car because he did not know anyone on campus well enough to sit with in the cafeteria. A Dominican student recounted her weekly anxiety about going to class in a space where she could not visibly identify any allies. A Puerto Rican student told us that he had dropped a class required for his major because he felt that the professor attributed his struggles in math to his ethnicity. A Cambodian student shared that she was thinking about changing her major because she just could not figure out how to complete the admission requirements to the school of education and did not know who to ask (Fieldnotes, 2007–2009).

These stories made us sad. These stories made us angry. These stories made us wonder about how *other* students from historically underrepresented groups on campus—LGBTQ students, students with disabilities, parenting students, first generation college students—were negotiating their undergraduate experience at Shoreline State College. It was not just students of color who needed our affirmative efforts. The Diversity Committee began the process of recruiting *any* SSC student who self-identified as a member of a historically underrepresented group who also had an interest in becoming a teacher to join us for lunch on occasional Wednesdays to talk about his or her educational life. We started with just nine students. These lunches evolved into a one-credit course designed to formalize this mentoring and support initiative. This initiative, which has grown almost 500% in the four years of its existence, is now a joyful, messy, intersectional space where future teachers come together as A.L.L.I.E.D., the Advanced Learning and Leadership Initiative for Educational Diversity.

In this chapter, we use the lens of intersectionality to explore a moment of crisis in our A.L.L.I.E.D. community. Through the analysis of critical moments on the A.L.L.I.E.D. blog, we show how intersectionality work requires both hope and struggle (Freire, 1993): *hope* for the possibilities of community and coherence but also *struggle* as we make sense of the ways our oppressions are, to borrow from Ladson-Billings and Tate (2008), "analogous" but not "equivalent" (p. 461). We will show how our hopeful visions of shared identity in A.L.L.I.E.D. were challenged and strengthened by an intersectional intervention forged from within. Ultimately, we argue that when it comes to the complicated work of intersectional coalition building, moments of crisis are not moments of failure. Rather, we suggest that it is in struggle, in the "ebb and flow" (Allan, 2007), that the co-construction of true hopeful alliances is possible.

Methodology and Context

This project is a participant-observation study rooted in the basic tenets of qualitative research, in that it is inductive, naturalistic, and interested in how people make meaning of their lives (Bogdan & Biklen, 2003; Emerson, Fretz, & Shaw, 1995). All of the authors are members of the A.L.L.I.E.D. community—one as a current undergraduate student, two as alums of the program, and two as faculty facilitators. Our multiple identities reflect many of those represented in the group at large across lines of race, class, disability, religion, parenting status, gender identity, and sexual orientation. This intersectional dynamic offers us unique insights into how power and privilege are manifested between and among us, as a writing group and as a part of the larger A.L.L.I.E.D. community. I, Lesley, am a 38-year-old, single, straight, white woman from a privileged background who has been teaching and researching issues of social justice and schooling for almost 15 years. I am the founder and primary facilitator of the A.L.L.I.E.D. group, but my role here is one of both teacher and student. While my position as instructor grants me authority, responsibility, and privilege in this space, I also face a steep learning curve in a community where I must constantly reflect on how to name and negotiate my privilege in public ways. In a predominantly Christian community, I am underrepresented as a Jew; but my class privilege often dissipates any marginalization I might otherwise experience around religious status.

I, Ibilolia, am a straight, Liberian woman from a strong, conservative Christian background. I am a recent graduate of SSC and an alumna of A.L.L.I.E.D., currently teaching in a local public school. I was raised in all-white schools and all-white churches, and came to A.L.L.I.E.D. with the perspective that race was a nonissue for me. My experience in A.L.L.I.E.D. and in this writing group has shifted my perspectives on religion and homosexuality, and my relationship to racial identity.

I, Juanita, am a Latina, the parent of a 5-year-old, and a straight, married woman. I joined A.L.L.I.E.D. in Spring 2007 as a returning student looking for a place on campus to call "home." I've brought to the table my academic strengths, the knowledge of my experience (as a student and as a 30-something person in the world), and have served as a leader in the A.L.L.I.E.D. classroom space and on the blog as the primary administrator.

I, Andres, am a straight Colombian man from a modest Catholic background; I am the oldest of seven children, first in my family to go to college, and now the parent of two young girls. I joined A.L.L.I.E.D. in Fall 2008, as a new faculty member at SSC to assist in co-facilitating the group, but I found that it proved to be essential for my own development as well, both as an "underrepresented" teacher (as one of few faculty on campus from a culturally and linguistically diverse background) and also as a novice in the SSC community, learning the culture of this new place.

I, Chris, am a white, 23-year-old queer intersex trans-man (who identified as female for most of my years in A.L.L.I.E.D.) from a privileged background with a degree in Women's Studies and a broad history in LGBTQ activism. Throughout my years as an undergraduate member of A.L.L.I.E.D., I served as an informal peer mentor and leader to the group; currently, I am graduate assistant to the A.L.L.I.E.D. program of which I am also a founding member.

Blog as (Con)Text

In this chapter, we draw from narrative data that consist of blog entries[1] that were posted on the A.L.L.I.E.D. blog from September 2008 through April 2010. Our blog is a private, invitation-only space to which all student members of A.L.L.I.E.D. and the two faculty facilitators have access (total members = 58). All members of the community collaboratively author the blog, with two administrators (Lesley and Juanita) who control the layout, design, and permissions. Because only members of the A.L.L.I.E.D. community can read and post, we consider the space to be "private" and also informal in language, convention, and style. Spelling and grammar are not a concern; abbreviations, emoticons, and nonstandard English are commonplace, and we all post things that are both personal and academic. We have 568 unique entries over 20 months of use. For this project, we worked with the blog data in an inductive manner; we analyzed the data collaboratively, first open coding, then developing themes, and ultimately formulating arguments about how A.L.L.I.E.D. students use the blog and to what ends.

When I (Lesley) first started using blogs in my academic courses, I imagined that blogging would enhance teaching and learning in many ways. As a feminist pedagogue and a de facto teacher of writing, I liked the idea that students would be posting their written assignments to a public forum where they could read and comment on one another's work. While I understood that this made them vulnerable, I also knew that it created a safety net—on weeks that the readings for the course were dense and difficult, the class blog posts offered an immediate place for students to go to check for understanding. I also hoped that doing this would create a stronger sense of community in our classroom as we engaged one another beyond the scope of the three-hour face-to-face time each week. Finally, I wanted to capitalize on my students' digital literacies and encourage them to use those 21st-century skills to connect our course content to the world and to their own lives via YouTube, hyperlinks, photos, personal stories, and visually enhanced reflections.

While A.L.L.I.E.D. is not an academic course, it is with all these things in mind that the A.L.L.I.E.D. blog was born in 2008. As a public/private alternative space where we could create shared meaning and build community, the blog offered our group an open forum with the possibility of more—more support, more time, more feedback, more advice, more mentoring. It also offered a peer-to-peer space, less structured by the (metaphorical and embodied) voice of the white, middle-class norms that filter into the culture of higher education even when uninvited. The personal nature of the posts, informal tone, grammatical abandon, and informal "txtspk" suggest to us that students related to this online space as fundamentally different than a teacher-driven classroom.

However, as the faculty facilitators, Lesley and Andres do tend to post more formally, making announcements, posting assignments, following up on class discussions, and commenting on student posts in an affirmative (even official) way. Still, this is not to say that there are not students in the group who also take on this role. In an unsolicited post (3/5/09), Chris helps his fellow classmates by posting useful links and tips on taking the Pre-Professional Skills Test, a requirement for all students at Shoreline College who want to advance in the education program. Similarly on 10/4/09, Juanita simply posts "Math Learning Center at 555-555-5555." Still, "teacher voice" is an important part of maintaining structure and institutional validity in A.L.L.I.E.D. In this idealistic vision of support and mentorship, we did not anticipate that the blog would also provide a forum for internal conflict; yet, we knew then and still see now that the A.L.L.I.E.D. blog is a space for all the community and connection we had hoped for.

Community of Hope: Becoming A.L.L.I.E.D.

In ways beyond the scope of a traditional college classroom, A.L.L.I.E.D. members use the blog to come together in support and alliance. Casey (2005) talks about how first generation college students often lack the "common-sense" of the college experience and thus are unaware of and unpracticed in availing themselves of the multitude of resources available on college campuses. The A.L.L.I.E.D. blog is a place to model, record, and facilitate *academic* success. Whether it is around completing a course, doing well on an exam, or making it into the school of education, the blog reveals not only the academic validation that A.L.L.I.E.D. students seek and receive from one another but also how students use it to develop a culture of academic excellence. They cheer each other on, honor one another's hard work, and encourage one another to develop habits of mind that will lead to success.

This kind of academic positivity is a primary function of the blog—in our analysis we found that students used the blog for academic celebration and support more than for any other purpose. We also know that academic crisis work gets outsourced to alternative college support services. Therefore, what makes our blog unique is how the academic struggles and successes on the blog (markers of our sameness) coexist with issues of underrepresented status (markers of our difference). A.L.L.I.E.D. students use the blog to connect with other students from underrepresented groups and as an intersectional tool to define the differences among and between us.

A space with multiple identities in itself is not necessarily an intersectional space. As Collins (1998) reminds us: "The significance of seeing race, class and gender as interlocking systems of oppression is that such an approach fosters a paradigmatic shift of thinking inclusively about other oppressions such as sexual orientation, religion and ethnicity" (p. 231). What makes something *intersectional*, then, is the acknowledgment of how those differences work, how they overlap, enhance, interrupt, challenge, and change one another. Sometimes the A.L.L.I.E.D. blog is merely a place where multiple identities coexist— and other times we strive to do the difficult work of weighing the relationships of power and privilege that come to bear here.

In order to do that difficult work, we have to make enough room for each member to demand recognition and be seen while also seeing others. While she is referring specifically to schools and curriculum development, Emily Style (1996) offers an apt metaphor here. She argues that young people need windows and mirrors—windows in which they can look out and see the world outside of themselves and mirrors in which they can see their reflection shining back at them. In a blog post, entitled "Tired," Chris states: "I'm tired of not seeing anyone who looks like me, not having anyone who walks like me, talks like me, thinks and acts like me. . . . I need LGBTQ people around—but not ones who are beaten down by the system, or navigating closets, or at the end of their rope. . . . Surely there must be some who are stable, secure, unapologetic and searching for change" (10/7/09). Tiffany—also an out member of the LGBTQ community—responded to Chris's call for affirmation. "If there was a "like" button like on Facebook I would click it. I completely agree." Tiffany offered the reflection, but Chris's post is also a window for the rest of us who get to see the world through his eyes.

It does not take a mirror to feel affirmed and validated. The windows are also important because sometimes one can catch a reflection through that glass as well. On 10/21/09, Mayra posted, "Hey guys, I just wanted to say hi and tell you all that i had my baby boy last Th." Here Mayra celebrated her identity as a new parent—importantly, all of the comments that follow Mayra's post are from nonparenting students, and all are celebratory. Ana also posted about the birth of her son just two days after she had a C-section, and was met with similar enthusiasm from nonparenting students (4/5/10). These posts are two of many in which an A.L.L.I.E.D. student proudly owns her identity as a person with children.

How do these windows and mirrors—all positive interactions that celebrate our shared experiences as A.L.L.I.E.D. members—generate the possibilities for intersectional praxis? These blog entries give us a space to create coalitions across identities so that when conflicts emerge, we have enough courage to stay at the table, both literally and metaphorically. Our ability to build a community of hope is the foundation on which our intersectional potential rests. We know how to support one another academically, and how to affirm our *collective* status as underrepresented. However, our 20 months of data show one extended period of tension around issues related to LGBTQ themes that called into question our ability to see one another as partners for liberation.

Community of Struggle: When Silence Speaks

During the fall of 2009, a group of 11 A.L.L.I.E.D. members met face-to-face to prepare for a presentation they were doing at a local conference on teaching for social justice. In reviewing the PowerPoint slides the day before the conference, the group had a discussion about the term "underrepresented" as it relates to membership within an identity category. Based on the research around the recruitment and retention of minorities in higher education (Dilworth, 1992; Farley, 2002; Guarino, Santibañez, & Daley, 2006; Post & Woessner, 1987; Szelenyi, 2001), we had previously developed four criteria to define what it means to be underrepresented as it relates to our group membership: unequal treatment, distinct physical or cultural traits, involuntary membership, and awareness of subordination.

Daniel, one member in the presentation group—a long-standing member of A.L.L.I.E.D., self-identified as straight, nonwhite, and an active member of his religious community—suggested that if "involuntary membership" was a criterion for underrepresented status, then LGBTQ students did not appropriately qualify as underrepresented. Consistent with historical tensions between gay and traditional religious communities, his comment suggested that gayness is a chosen identity, not an innate one, and thus invalidated the life stories and complexities of the LGBTQ students both in the room and in the A.L.L.I.E.D. group as a whole.[2] Across the room, Chris and KT seethed. Juanita and Destin looked at them with a stare of allied recognition. Daniel did not respond, verbally or otherwise. Other members of the group, including Ibilolia, did not notice the shift in dynamic and continued to participate in the conference preparation.

In this way, the immediate response to Daniel's comment was uneventful. In a move not entirely consistent with the ethos of A.L.L.I.E.D. but evidence of the frustration he was feeling, Chris came across the hall to seek faculty intervention. He found me (Lesley) in my office to alert me of Daniel's comment and its aftermath, and I joined the meeting for a few minutes to observe and take the temperature of the room. This kind of tension was not new for me, as a teacher whose curricula are anchored by the terms "ideology," "oppression," "privilege," and "power." I have come to see discomfort as a sign of success, a sign that the things we take most for granted are becoming visible. As Allan Johnson (2006) reminds me, we are not going to get anywhere if we are not willing to say the words. Therefore, my pedagogical stance in such moments is often to sit back and offer only gentle guidance unless tone and tenor become irretrievably disrespectful. But I usually let intellectual and personal arguments ride in hopes that students can learn to articulate their positions, academic claims, and ideological frameworks. And yet, I also know that with ideological tensions come histories of power and powerlessness; as such, these conversations feel dangerous, especially if you do not know if anyone in the room will have your back.

After listening for a few minutes, I decided to clarify—unambivalently—the previously implied assumption that LGBTQ students *are* a part of the A.L.L.I.E.D. group per our history, mission, and collective understanding. I did not ask for questions or solicit any response. I just used my position as The Teacher to authorize the validity of our LGBTQ peers so that the group could move on with their work preparing for the conference. There was some comfort in this assertion. Naively, it seemed on the surface that this swift action of public support reclaimed the cohesiveness of the A.L.L.I.E.D. space. However, while at the moment this addressed the issue in a way that allowed the presentation group to continue its work for the following day, the underlying tensions it revealed would reemerge.

On the day of the conference, the presentation—titled (ironically) "Becoming A.L.L.I.E.D."—was a big success. The audience responded very positively to the stories of success and struggle that the A.L.L.I.E.D. members shared, and ultimately the group had a rich discussion about what it means to be an ally to one another based on some work we had done in a prior A.L.L.I.E.D. meeting. At one moment in the Q&A, I spoke from the audience to acknowledge that A.L.L.I.E.D. is not always a seamless collaborative, that we often entertain tensions around our multiple and intersecting identity categories even as we support one another. Daniel responded publicly and directly to this point to say that, for example, while he might not agree with or understand someone's "lifestyle," he was an ally to anyone in the group and would hold their hand to support them. This framework did not sit well with many of the A.L.L.I.E.D. members present, but again, Daniel's comment went largely unaddressed for the sake of efficiency and professionalism. Yet in the days to follow, the issue was revisited on the blog, which proved to be an important space where all of our notions of being an ally were called into question, and we were forced to confront whether or not we could practice what we preach.

Four days after the conference presentation, KT posted on the blog:

> [M]y gayness is not a "life style." It is not a "choice." And it is not something you can dismiss from my self, as in "I like you, except for that" or "I mean the gay people, but not you." You cannot separate my gayness from me any more than my race, my gender, my ability, etc. My gayness does not make me "against straight people," "against religion," "a pedophile," or "attracted to every person of a like gender to mine."

> I think it's awesome that you can "feel comfortable to hold my hand and support me even though you don't agree with my gayness." My question is, when it comes to my rights, and you have the power to vote on them, are you going to see me as a person worthy of the same freedoms you currently hold, or someone less than you who is undeserving? That shouldn't be something you have to think about.

> You say you are my Ally, but will you stand beside me even if it means marching with me for my rights?

KT's post sat silent for 24 hours. We do not know why. We do not know who, if anyone, was on the blog during that time, or whether anyone had seen it. The blog does sometimes sit silent for a day or two without post or comment. However, when I (Chris)—self-identified as an out queer member of A.L.L.I.E.D.—did comment 28 hours after KT's initial post, I was frustrated, angry, and disappointed in the silence of my peers.

> I tried not to be the first to comment on this—to challenge others to respond first, or to see if others had the conviction of an "ally" to speak first. All I can say is let the silence be a testament to the tenuous relationship between us, our identities, A.L.L.I.E.D., and the society at large as you pointed out. (11/13/09)

With this first explicit response to KT, the blog provided a forum for us to begin the difficult work of intersectionality. KT calls for the A.L.L.I.E.D. community as a whole to come out to see her, to hear her, to value her identity. But the allies she seeks remain bystanders. All four comments under KT's post—Chris's being the first—come from out members of the LGBTQ community.

In the next several days, five more unique posts follow KT's, two of which are directly related to LGBTQ issues posted by LGBTQ-identified students. Given the posts that are up on the blog, that they are visible in full text on the screen when one signs on, and the time stamps that are indicated on them, we can say definitively that at this point other non-LGBTQ-identified students have been on the blog and seen the accumulaing discourse. But no one except LGBTQ peers responds to the posts.

Notably, just one month prior, we had worked together in class to name and document what it means to be an ally to one another. Lesley facilitated a brainstorming session, in front of a full house, where we talked about "safety," "support," and "protection." We talked about "having someone's back," "putting yourself out there," and "making an effort." Our definitions of an ally included the encouraging prompt to "speak up, speak out, speak with" one another. Our collective brainstorm demonstrated the essence of intersectionality: "assuming that each system needs the others in order to function" (Collins, 1990). And yet, when theory came to practice, we were unable to "bear witness" to one another in any visible way.

I (Chris) watched the mounting silence with a deep sense of disappointment. As an established peer leader in the group, I felt torn by my responsibility to the A.L.L.I.E.D. community on the one hand and my loyalty to my LGBTQ peers on the other. Our LGBTQ network was pulsing with uncertainty and rapidly considering complete withdrawal from the A.L.L.I.E.D. space that now felt unsafe, unsupportive, and dangerously quiet. It was not that we were simply giving up. KT had tried to reach out to seek support on the blog. I had tried to solicit a response from our non-LGBTQ peers. Liam even wrote a long post calling for allies: "We are at a tipping point. We know how to stand up when others are pressing down on us, but now those pressures are coming from within. I leave you with one question. Are you ready to be ONE?" But this burden was becoming too great to bear alone. We knew that without direct action and intervention, the LGBTQ part of this A.L.L.I.E.D. community would pack up their toys and go home.

I called Lesley. "You better get on the blog and try to deal with this . . . it isn't good." She did. But her response, consistent with the pedagogical strategies around "letting it ride" that she names above, was not enough. Lesley commented, "Amazingly powerful, Liam. You are a beautiful writer and I think you capture so much here . . . now the only question is who is listening? Where are the voices of our allies here? Anyone?" (11/17/09). In utter frustration, Liam finally wrote a personal letter to Lesley, an ultimatum of sorts. While KT and I trusted Lesley to be an effective ally, Liam was not so sure. At the end of three single-spaced pages, Liam wrote, "Now more than ever, I need you—Chris, KT, Destin, Emmitt, and all other LGBTQ students in A.L.L.I.E.D. and the larger college community need you—to put aside your straight privilege to advocate for us: to stop relying on the LGBTQ kids to educate the group, to bring up the 'gay issue'" (e-mail, 11/17/09).

And with that letter in hand, I (Lesley), behind the closed door of my office, broke every rule in the book about how a person with privilege can be a good ally. I disappeared into what I can only humbly call a textbook specimen of guilt, defensiveness, and self-pity. I cried. I made it all about me. I felt sorry for myself. I felt betrayed—not by the A.L.L.I.E.D. students who chose not to stand up for their peers but by the A.L.L.I.E.D. students who were doing everything we had ever taught about self-advocacy and talking back. With just enough self-awareness to keep me from a world of regret, I found Chris in the hallway coming out of a class and asked for his help. Graciously, and without any of the indignation I deserved, Chris reminded me that I was The Teacher in charge of this whole mess; it was my job to step up and join this fight. He was not asking me to do it alone, but the LGBTQ contingent was not willing to do it without me. He knew that the fate of the group rested on this, and he had enough faith in me and in A.L.L.I.E.D. to demand my immediate attention. We could not let A.L.L.I.E.D. fall apart over this issue—not on our watch. So right there in the hallway, we brainstormed an action plan to move the conversation forward.

In a move uncharacteristic of the A.L.L.I.E.D. culture, I issued a directive in the form of an assignment. On 11/17/09, I sent out an e-mail to all registered members of the course, posted it on the blog, and brought a hard copy of the assignment to class.

> We come to this group from very different places . . . so what are we going to do with these differences?
>
> - Can a white person be an ally to a person of color if she believes that "all Blacks are lazy—except for that cool woman in my A.L.L.I.E.D. class"?
> - Can a straight person be an ally to a member of the LGBTQ community if he believes that "gay people should really just try to choose a *normal* life"?
> - Can a Christian be an ally to a Jewish person if she believes that the Jewish person is flawed and sinful?
>
> Your assignment is to respond to this and/or the posts below relating to these issues—post a comment below. Every one of us needs to find a voice here. Even if you don't have all the right words, just try to articulate your confusion, your questions, your feelings, your attitudes as best you can. Our peers need us. They need to hear us speak so that they do not feel silenced. They deserve our voices so they don't have to feel invisible on our blog.

Three students commented almost immediately, within 24 hours. Vanna's comment represents the kind of "showing up" that we had hoped for: "Ohh wow, this is starting to get really deep. I am speechless. I don't know exactly what to say at this moment but will be here if anyone needs a hand." Fourteen other posts followed that including a range of support, acknowledgment, apology, reflection, recognition, and even opposition. But every single one of them broke the silence. Speaking out—no matter what you say as long as you say something—allows for the disagreement, acknowledgment, and presence that permit people across lines of difference to occupy the same space in coalition with one another. Mouffe (2005) argues that moving away from the discourse of consensus and into "antagonistic" engagement is an important political tool that empowers the disenfranchised to represent their interests with "passion" (p. 2). This is what intersectionality looks like. As Bellita put it perfectly, "Isn't this why we meet every week? To help one another with anything even if its just the simple fact of letting others know we care and that we are listening? I am happy to say that I am here listening and willing to take action if anyone needs it. :)" (11/18/09).

All of the posts in response to Lesley's assignment reflected an ethic of care. At one end of the spectrum was unapologetic support from Juanita—"I will vote, march, and not be silent. I trust you will do the same for me" (12/3/09). And at the other end, a genuine attempt from Efraim, albeit conflicted, at "tolerance"—"I am Christian and my faith is deeply rooted. I am anti gay and anti abortion. However, I embrace all creeds, all cultures and all beliefs. Everyone has the right to make their own choice" (11/18/09). We see all of these posts—while disappointing in that they required a faculty invitation—as a return to the accountability we expect from one another. Even in his direct rejection of gayness outright, Efraim shows up to speak and be accountable. KT responds in kind: "i appreciate your honesty. i do not choose to be oppressed . . . you don't have to agree with me, but you were kind enough to share your opinion so here is mine. Have a nice day."

The work of intersectional coalition building is not a process devoid of tension. It requires accountability, voice, and agency but also struggle, uncertainty, and sacrifice. Even through the time of waiting, silence, and heightened emotional tension, three of the out members of the queer contingent of A.L.L.I.E.D. put aside the divisive issues that were on the table in order to meet their obligation to the group. On 11/19/09—right in the middle of the brewing silence—KT posted advice about taking the Praxis exam. A few days before, Chris offered a celebratory post to acknowledge that we (collective we) hit 400 posts on the blog, a group success (11/13/09). Liam, Emmitt, and KT all responded in support of Marie's personal loss on 11/13/09. In this way, intersectionality is about sacrifice. Just as Collins (1998) suggests that Black women had to sacrifice their interests as women and as individuals in order to support the principles of Black political struggle, the LGBTQ folks put their interests on hold to show up for the group. Even in a time of discomfort, disappointment, and even despair—"It's why we need each other more now then we ever have before. I know it gets hard—Someday we'll have a place at the table" (Chris, 11/12/09)—these students were able (required? expected? obliged?) to put the needs of the whole above their own.

The conversation did not end—rather, these events became a part of our history, our memory, our culture to be called upon again when needed. We know enough now to be wary of still waters. From this period of upheaval, we grew into new ways of addressing the needs of the group. In our commitment to intersectionality, we altered the A.L.L.I.E.D. class content to include a more explicit introduction to issues of language and naming, particularly around LGBTQ issues. We moved meeting rooms to accommodate a larger table where we could all literally and metaphorically fit around without leaving anyone out in the margins. That table is a place where LGBTQ members have come to trust the group enough to share their lives in intimate ways, and the culture of the group is enriched by the understanding that we all belong here.

These lessons continue to impact our relationships to one another and to the world. But they also alter our perspectives as future teachers by offering a model of socially just praxis through which we struggle to find voice and challenge silence. As reflective practitioners, we are learning and living our educational endeavors as spaces of emotional investment and personal stake. Our struggles on the A.L.L.I.E.D. blog teach us to be humble in the face of uncertainty, to be ready and willing to take risks and even fail in order to re-imagine equity and justice. To borrow from Lisa Delpit (1995),

> it means turning yourself inside out, giving up your own sense of who you are, and being willing to see yourself in the unflattering light of another's angry gaze. It is not easy, but it is the only way to learn what it might feel like to be someone else and the only way to start the dialogue. (pp. 46–47)

Significantly, our analysis has shown us that the A.L.L.I.E.D. blog provides a space for students to work out and work through our multiple oppressions that are "analogous" but not "equivalent." This work is difficult and sometimes painful. As Ladson-Billings and Tate (2008) note, "Our understanding of the commonalities of oppression cannot wash out the particularities and specifics of each experience" (p. 461). While we come together as A.L.L.I.E.D. with a shared identity as members of underrepresented groups, we cannot be perfect mirrors for one another. But we can offer windows in which we find imperfect reflections of who we are and who we might become. Accepting that genuine intersectional work must include—and will not resolve—the "particularities and specifics of each experience" is the final contribution of our analysis. With a willingness to sit with discomfort and sacrifice comes movement—inward, outward, forward, and back—that takes us beyond the status quo to a place where hope and struggle can coexist.

Notes

[1] Weblogs, or simply blogs, are a recent but widespread phenomenon. They can be defined as frequently modified web pages in which dated entries are listed in reverse chronological sequence. Initially conceived as an individual and unstructured format of delivering information via the Internet, blogs are now firmly established as online communication tools not only offering both privacy and community building but collaborative activity, knowledge sharing, reflection, and debate (Williams & Jacobs, 2004).

[2] We align ourselves with the scholarly and political camp that holds gayness as a biological reality, not a personal choice.

References

Allan, K. (2007). *The social lens: An invitation to social and sociological theory*. London: Pine Forge Press.

Bogdan, R., & Biklen, S. (2003). *Qualitative research for education: An introduction to theories and methods* (4th ed.). New York: Pearson Education Group.

Bourdieu, P. (1973/2000). Social reproduction and cultural reproduction. In R. Arum & I. Beattie (Eds.), *The structure of schooling* (pp. 35–42). London: Mayfield Publishing Company.

Casey, J.C. (2005). Diversity, discourse, and the working-class student. *Academe Online* 91(4).

Collins, P. H. (1998). *Fighting words: Black women and the search for justice*. Minneapolis: University of Minnesota Press.

Collins, P.H. (1990). Black feminist thought in the matrix of domination. ReviewedDecember, 29, 2011, [from] http://www.culturalstudies.net/collins.html.

Delpit, L. (1995). *Other people's children*. New York: The New Press.

Dilworth, M. (1992). *Diversity in teacher education: New expectations*. San Francisco: Jossey-Bass, Inc.

Emerson, R. M., Fretz, R. I., & Shaw, L. L. (1995). *Writing ethnographic fieldnotes*. Chicago: University of Chicago Press.

Farley, J. E. (2002). Contesting our everyday work lives: The retention of minority and working-class sociology undergraduates. *The Sociological Quarterly*, 43(1), 1–25

Freire, P. (1993). *Pedagogy of the oppressed*. New York: Continuum.

Guarino, C., Santibañez, L., & Daley, G. (2006). Teacher recruitment and retention: A review of the recent empirical literature. *Review of Educational Research*, 76(2), 173–208.

Howard, G. R. (1999). *We can't teach what we don't know: White teachers, multiracial schools*. New York: Teachers College Press.

InfoWorks: Rhode Island Public Schools. (2007). District report cards [Data file]. Retrieved from http://www.infoworks.ride.uri.edu/2009/queries/FindDist.asp?District=28

Johnson, A. G. (2006). *Privilege, power, and difference* (2nd ed.). Boston: McGraw-Hill.

Ladson-Billings, G., & Tate, W. (2008). Toward a critical race theory of education. In A. Darder, M. P. Baitodano, & R. D. Torres (Eds.), *Critical pedagogy reader* (pp. 460–468). New York: Routledge.

Marx, D. M. (2009). The "Obama effect": How a salient role model reduces race-based performance differences. *Journal of Experimental Social Psychology*, 45, (4) 953–956.

Mouffe, C. (2005). *On the political.* New York: Routledge.

Post, L., & Woessner, H. (1987). Developing a recruitment and retention support system for minority students in teacher education. *The Journal of Negro Education*, 56(2), 203–211.

Style, E. (1996). "Curriculum as Window and Mirror," Listening for All Voices, Oak Knoll School monograph, Summit, NJ, 1988. (pp. 1–8).

Szelenyi, Katalin. (2001). Minority student retention and academic achievement in community colleges. Retrieved from ERIC Digest # ED451859

Williams, J. B., & Jacobs, J. (2004). Exploring the use of blogs as learning spaces in the higher education sector. *Australasian Journal of Educational Technology*, 20(2), 232–247.

Oprah and Obama Made It, Why Can't Everyone Else?

Utilizing Intersectional Pedagogy to Challenge Post-racial Ideologies within the Higher Education Classroom

Jennifer Esposito and Alison Happel

Introduction

The election of President Barack Obama has heralded a supposed new era in the United States in which discourses of post-racial society are now more prominent than ever. Proponents of post-racial ideologies have used President Obama's political success as proof that the United States is a meritocracy, and as such, individual and collective racial positionalities no longer need to be considered when assessing a person's or group's opportunities or accomplishments. In the United States, post-racial discourses are used as a way of obfuscating the complexities of life in a society in which racial hierarchies are still alive and present on individual and structural levels. The recent race-based, anti-immigrant law passed in Arizona is a blatant example of the ways in which race still informs public policies and individual attitudes. Proponents of post-racial discourses assert that race does not have an effect on individual choices and opportunities and does not come into play when creating laws and policies (Bonilla-Silva & Ray, 2009). Post-racial discourses perpetuate the simplistic notion that color blindness is akin to non-racist attitudes and practices. The ideology of color blindness functions in our society to mask the ways in which racial power and privilege matter (Bonilla-Silva, 2003). In political discourse, casual conversations, and classroom discussions, the notion of color blindness is often used as a tool to silence critical inquiries into the social and political dynamics of race and racism (Applebaum, 2005).

In this chapter we will argue that, given the current political climate as previously discussed, it is imperative to utilize intersectionality theories. Intersectionality allows us to interrogate the myriad of ways identities, including but not limited to race, complicate individual and structural choices, opportunities, and relationships. We utilize the site of the higher education classroom as a space to trouble simplistic understandings of identity and positionality.

Although most scholars use intersectionality as a theory to frame various analyses of individual and structural power and privilege, many feminist educators also utilize it as a pedagogy, and as an organizing principle for curriculum and course design. One important aspect of intersectionality is its emphasis on praxis (which is, as defined by Freire [1970], the intersection of theory and practice); consequently, scholars and educators utilizing this framework use it to inform classroom curriculum and pedagogy. This chapter will outline the necessity of using intersectionality pedagogically within the higher education classroom. We will begin by discussing our own positionalities. Next, we will outline the essential components of intersectionality. We will follow this by a theoretical discussion of color blindness and meritocracy. We will then discuss student attitudes within the higher education classroom regarding color blindness, meritocracy, and post-racial society. Specifically, we will use our own experiences of teaching undergraduate and graduate courses in order to apply intersectionality theories to our practices of higher education teaching. Both authors have noticed and documented an increase in students using post-race discourse and ideology during classroom discussions, and this chapter is our attempt to struggle theoretically and practically with the classroom dynamics that these discourses create and facilitate. We will show how intersectional pedagogy is necessary to transform student learning to help them better interrogate privilege and positionality. We argue that educators who are committed to utilizing education as a practice of freedom (Freire, 1970; hooks, 1994) should attend to intersectional approaches to curriculum and pedagogy.

Author Subjectivity

Because of our commitment to feminism and our recognition that individual subjectivities directly and indirectly influence how we see, exist, and act in the world, we believe it is important to outline our own unique positionalities.

We will do so in separate vignettes and then come back together to discuss how this works in the personal and professional spaces we both inhabit.

Happel

I am a White feminist originally from the Midwest. Although my family is of mostly German descent, I am often asked my ethnicity; this is especially true in academic settings in which I have made my political and professional allegiances known. I have a complicated class history; my parents both grew up on farms, and they worked hard together to achieve the meritocratic American Dream. I was raised middle class because of this, but I feel as though my working-class roots are ever present in many ways. Since I have been in graduate school for a while, I have learned how to subsist on very little income, but I recognize the very real and important differences between choosing to live below the poverty line and living below the poverty line despite attempts to live otherwise. I understand the fluidity of gender and sexuality, yet I identify as female and heterosexual. Because of my commitments to social justice, I make my alliances to GLBTQI communities well known in both my professional and personal life. I identify strongly as a feminist in all arenas of my life. This has had multiple effects; at times I have felt empowered, alienated, dismissed, righteous, and vulnerable because of this commitment. As is visible in this description of my positionality, I believe that we all have very complicated and messy identities that do not fit into easy categories, and these multiple identities all intersect in different ways and contexts to produce various meanings and experiences.

Esposito

I am a White Latina. I am racially ambiguous and often field questions such as, "What are you?" Depending upon geographical location, how my hair is styled, and whether my skin has browned from the sun, I am often misrecognized as people search their memories of what a White woman looks like versus a Latina. I have skin privilege. Yet, when I open my mouth and make claims to my multiple heritages, to oppression, to how I never quite fit in with any one group, people become confused. They want to "know," to have some irrefutable "proof" that I either belong or I do not. I am always asked to choose, racially and ethnically, whose side I am on. I grew up firmly entrenched with the poor/working-class population. We ate provisions from the U.S. government—pinto beans, peanut butter, and what became fondly known to me and my friends as "welfare cheese," a huge orange block of cheese "product" that when melted turned to orange oil. Mine is a "feel good" story. I was identified in school early on as "gifted." I was smart but quiet. The teachers liked me and wanted to save me from my circumstances. I was the first one in my family to attend college. Once in school, I learned the theoretical words to name what I felt all my life: "oppression, racism, sexism, subjectivities." I learned that people worked to problematize the daily assaults that I was told to deal with. I felt theory resonate with my soul. All of a sudden writers like Gloria Anzaldúa and Audre Lorde were speaking to me in ways that Shakespeare never could. I felt at home and knew I did not want to give up the comfort and privilege of the ivory tower. I knew then that I would stay in school for as long as I could and become a source of the type of knowledge and confidence I saw before me in my undergraduate courses. Thus, I became a professor—one whose prior class status and racial identity marginalized her. But, one who fled for cover under the title "Dr." I began living theory. For example, my belief in the fluidity of sexual identity was enacted in multiple ways in my life—sometimes I had heterosexual privilege and sometimes I did not. However, I have always been cognizant that privilege exists—that some are part of the "center," what is considered "normal," while others are marginalized.

We discuss these identities not to essentialize or fix meanings (hooks, 1999). For example, what exactly does it mean to live as a White feminist academic versus a Latina? Our identities are not stable nor do they denote consistently particular ways of viewing the world. We divulge this information, however, to assert that our experiences in the world have been shaped by our multiple subjectivities (Blair, 1998). Although it is difficult to know exactly how being a particular age, race, gender, or sexual orientation structured our meaning making, we know that these identities have informed how we see and experience the world.

Even though our histories are so different, our classroom pedagogies are very similar. We identify as feminist pedagogues, which means that we complicate power and identities directly through the ways in which we structure our classrooms, the readings we assign, and our interactions with faculty and students. We both are also "young" looking and assume a traditionally feminine appearance. We recognize that our appearances shape the ways in which students respond to us. For example, we have each been overtly challenged by male students who tried to assert dominance in discussions, and we assume this is an enactment of male privilege that may or may not be directly related to assumptions about our experience and right to authority within a higher education space.

Although our pedagogy and classroom practices are similar, we recognize that we are differently positioned in the university hierarchy. Therefore, the ways in which our multiple positionalities intersect have different consequences in relation to power and privilege. One of us is now a tenured professor while the other is a graduate student. These subject positions within the university structure directly and indirectly influence the kinds of risks we can take within the classroom. For example, because Esposito is a tenured faculty member, she has a relatively high degree of autonomy within her classrooms. That is not to say that the previous years of working towards tenure and being surveilled and monitored were not without struggle. Since she is a graduate student, Happel has significantly less autonomy in the classes that she teaches and less authority because she does not yet have her doctorate; she has, though, been recognized by her department as a highly competent instructor, and so she enjoys relative pedagogical independence because of this. We articulate this to illustrate how complicated privilege and power are. We are never solely privileged nor are we solely oppressed. We know this personally and we communicate this professionally.

Intersectionality

Intersectionality differentiates between understandings of oppression as interlocking and understandings of oppression as additive (Berger & Guidroz, 2009). In the additive analysis of oppression, one oppression is seen as primary, and other oppressions are theorized to be derivatives of the primary oppression (Spelman, 1988). Seeing either racism or sexism as primary and central disallows for nuanced and contextual ways of understanding positionality and interlocking forms of individual and structural oppression. "The additive analysis also suggests that a woman's racial identity can be 'subtracted' from her combined sexual and racial identity" (Spelman, 1988, p. 125). This hierarchization of oppression does not account for how "these systems mutually construct one another . . . how they 'articulate' with one another" (Collins, 1998, p. 63).

According to Dill and Zambrana (2009), there are four main tenets of intersectionality theory. First, scholarship must incorporate the complicated and layered lived experiences of people, especially those at the margins of privilege. Historically, people of color, and especially women of color, have been excluded from the production and circulation of knowledge. Intersectionality insists on bringing people of color's experiences to the forefront, through both theoretical and empirical research. Intersectionality builds on critical race theory, and both theoretical orientations attempt to prioritize and center experiences of people of color in order to respond to the ways in which they have been individually and institutionally silenced and ignored within the United States.

Second, knowledge must be utilized to advance social justice aims in higher education institutions. Traditionally, the production of knowledge was seen as neutral, and many scholars did not engage with ideas of the political and social ramifications of their knowledge production. Consequently, much knowledge production within the United States has led to the perpetuation of sexism, racism, and classism. Intersectionality claims that all knowledge production is political and is inevitably enmeshed in various power structures. Intersectionality theorists insist that the political nature and effects of knowledge be acknowledged, and they believe that scholars should use their institutional power and privilege to produce knowledge that benefits those at the margins of society.

Third, knowledge must make space for multiple voices, both within higher education institutions and society. This means that scholars who utilize intersectionality must prioritize listening to and representing those who have been traditionally under- or unrepresented within scholarship. It is important to work towards creating a society in which all voices are heard and validated. This points to the importance of the final tenet of intersectionality, which asserts that scholarship must participate in advancing fair and inclusive public policies. These last two tenets point to the importance of praxis within intersectionality. Praxis is important to intersectionality because it illustrates the importance of social justice to this theoretical framework. Intersectionality is not just a theory, it also seeks to inform the actions and policies of those outside of the academy. Essentially, intersectionality calls for an engaged activism from scholars. It is not enough for intersectionality scholars to theorize about multiple forms of oppression; they must actively work to change public and institutional policies in order to work for social justice for those whom intersectionality theorizes. Intersectionality theorists are expected to be political actors who make space for different voices and ways of knowing. This is important both inside and outside of the academy. This linking of theory and practice is a necessary component within intersectionality because of its essential commitment to social justice for those on the margins of society.

Color Blindness and the Myth of Meritocracy

As discussed in the introduction, the ideology of color blindness has become prominent in our society. Building upon this discussion, we want to examine the ways color blindness at an individual level denies the institutionally mandated practices of privilege as well as practices of discrimination. It allows people to avoid examining racism at a systemic level. Claiming to not see race provides a way for individuals to absolve themselves of racism (Bell, 2003). What follows then is the stance that because we do not see race, racism cannot possibly exist. The belief that racism no longer exists stems from the individualistic perspective on racism (Scheurich & Young, 2002). Defined in this manner, racism involves acts of blatant discrimination against a person based on race. Thus, people who are not actively engaged in overtly racist acts are not considered racist and do not contribute to racism. King (1991) calls the ideology of color blindness "dysconscious racism" because it sustains the culture of power. It allows institutionalized inequality to remain and strips people of color of the right to talk about the ways these inequalities have structured our lives. Bonilla-Silva (1997) refers to color blindness as "the new racism."

We argue that in addition to "color blindness" being the new racism, post-racial discourse is also a component of a new form of racism. Post-racial discourse asserts that race no longer matters, that we, as a society, have moved beyond race and achieved racial equality. This discourse became more prominent during the campaign and 2008 election of President Barack Obama. In popular and political conversations, many heralded the fact that a "Black" man was able to achieve such a prominent status in this country's political arena by being elected as the Democratic candidate. Interestingly, discussions about President Obama's race often neglected the complicated nature of his biracial heritage. He has come to be known as this nation's first Black president. The discourse about his "achievements" has centered around ideas that his race was not an impediment to his success. In other words, because a Black man was able to become the president, many, especially those on the political Right, espoused a belief that racism does not exist anymore. This is a complicated claim and for that reason we include this discourse as relevant to discussions about intersectionality. For example, President Obama most certainly experiences life as a Black man, but he was simultaneously privileged in terms of the educational level of his parents (both held doctorates) and had traveled extensively (and lived internationally) as a child. This afforded him a type of privilege and worldliness not available to impoverished Black children growing up in economically depressed areas.

So, if the claim is made that, as in the case of the election of President Obama, race no longer matters, then it becomes impossible to recognize the ways in which race structures institutional policies and practices such as those within the legal and educational domains. According to Brayboy, Castagno, and Maughan (2007), "Ignoring race erases the social and economic implications of a system where the boundaries between success and failure, poverty and privilege are drawn largely across racial lines" (p. 174). Those who recognize racism are immediately silenced because there is no way to enter into a discussion about racism if race does not exist. The status quo is reinforced while entire histories of racial discrimination are overshadowed by a renewed focus on the gains of the civil rights movement.

Using Intersectionality Pedagogically

Intersectionality directly informs our pedagogical goals and intended outcomes within the classes that we teach. Our first goal is seemingly simplistic; we aspire to challenge individualistic ideas and assumptions by shifting the analysis from the individual to the structural. Structural analyses are actively discouraged by many master narratives within the United States, and we both seek to challenge our students to make connections between their individual experiences and the larger structures and systems that shape those experiences. Second, we attempt to encourage students to become cognizant of how they are implicated in different systems of oppression. We reject binary analyses of oppression and privilege. For example, we talk about various privileges based on skin color, gender, sexual orientation, nationality, and language. We encourage students, while examining structural inequality, to critically assess how they are directly and indirectly complicit within different oppressive structures. Students are expected to examine their own subjectivities in order to better assess their complicated and multiple subject positions within the structures that we have been critically analyzing. When critical self-reflection is accompanied with our structural critiques of oppression, analyzing individual and collective complicities becomes less about individual finger pointing and more about a complicated and messy analysis of the relationships between individual choices, positionality, and systemic inequalities. Our last pedagogical goal centers on Freire's conceptualization of praxis. We encourage our students to become agents of change. Throughout the semester, we illustrate the importance of continually combining theory and practice in order to enact thoughtful, deliberate change on both an individual and institutional level. When we discuss particular problems within education in the United States, we encourage our students to theorize where and why the problem exists, possible ways in which we could address the problem, and then concrete actions that can be taken to enact change on various levels of the education hierarchy. We insist that action must be accompanied by reflection, and that reflection should be a reiterative process in order to make our actions relevant and ethical.

Before we begin our discussion about master narratives and our own uses of intersectionality to challenge these narratives within the classroom, we want to make clear that we are sharing our experiences in hopes that they can be useful when considering similar challenges within the higher education class-room. We by no means want our experiences to be read as a how-to manual, or what is known within Education as "best practices." We believe that con-text and positionality are key components to classroom dynamics; therefore, what is useful in one classroom may or may not be useful in another. As feminists, we believe that it is necessary that we share and theorize our indi-vidual experiences, but we caution against simplistic, formulaic interpretations of what has and has not worked for us.

Master narratives of meritocracy

As mentioned in the introduction to this book, there are a number of master narratives within the United States that make teaching within a social justice framework challenging; we argue, as do the editors, that intersectionality can play a key role in challenging predominant master narratives that simplify and/or obfuscate social inequalities. The first master narrative that appears within our classrooms is the myth of meritocracy. We frequently hear from White students who have crossed or straddled class lines about how hard their families have worked to succeed. In these instances they rely on the myth of meritocracy to remind us that their families put forth the effort required in this country to get ahead. They often passionately defend meritocratic ideals because they feel like their family story fits so perfectly into the narrative. These students use their beliefs in individualism and hard work to prove that it is possible to succeed within the United States, regardless of circumstances.

It is not only working-class White students who uphold ideologies of meri-tocracy. We also have students of color who sometimes support these ideolo-gies as well. They tell their stories of having "made it" and of being frustrated with people of color whom they deem "lazy." These students of color take a similar stance to White working-class students in arguing that hard work pays off. This position is often a harder one for us to interrupt because, for many White students, these narratives confirm previously held assumptions and stereotypes about ability, hard work, and "cultural differences." It is most likely due to the notion of authenticity. Whose story is it to frame—a black student who grew up in an impoverished area and now sits in a college class-room and argues that s/he got here as a result of hard work or a White or Latina instructor arguing that institutionalized power and privilege signifi-cantly shape a person's life chances? Many of the White students will gravitate towards their peer's story because it confirms the stereotypes and beliefs they already hold.

Both groups' simplistic beliefs in hard work and personal responsibility (read: meritocracy) put blame on the individual and ignore the larger, struc-tural webs of social, political, and institutional power that play a role in one's chance of success. As feminist pedagogues, we try to allow all students the chance to be heard. When they share their own personal struggles, we do try to affirm them. However, while we recognize their family's hard work, we gently ask the working-class White students to consider how skin privilege influences how much one's hard work pays off. We try to move students from placing so much weight on personal agency and responsibility (as if everyone has an equal chance) to seeing the world as an unfair place that is not a level playing field. We use the metaphor of starting a race and show how privilege plays an advantage in each student's starting position. If an individual gets to begin the race with a head start (for example: a well-funded education), that individual's hard work pays off quicker. For students of color who uncritically champion ideals of meritocracy and hard work, we inquire about all the struggles and hardships they have been through, and then we ask questions which point to the structural nature of these problems. We attempt to illus-trate how, even though it is very commendable and inspiring that they were able to succeed against the odds, the fact that it was so challenging points to the salience of structural racism and classism that still exist within the United States. We use intersectionality to point to the various ways that institutional power and privilege influence individual and familial chances of success, all the while reminding students of the importance of keeping social justice central to our analyses.

Master narratives of difference

The next master narratives that we encounter relate to how students conceptualize and consequently verbalize difference. The first way in which students interact with difference is that they deny difference or minimize differences between various positionalities. The discourse that appears most frequently in these discussions appears to be the color-blind perspective, and as mentioned earlier, we have noticed an increase in the prevalence of this discourse after the election of President Obama. Many of our students, while seeming to mean well, take the stance, "We are all human." They often follow up that statement with something along the lines of, "It doesn't matter if a student is purple, yellow, or blue. All I see is a student. I don't see color." One of the things that frustrates us about this statement is that it denies the saliency of color. Of course we know that people cannot be purple or blue or yellow. But we also know they *can* be Black, Brown, or White among many other shades of color. And, in this society we have attached particular stereotypes and connotations to particular colors. For example, in this historical moment, it does matter what shade of brown you are. In many states you can be stopped for "looking" like you are undocumented or not a "legal" (by Eurocentric definition) citizen. Thus, while it may not matter if one is purple, blue, or yellow, it *certainly* matters whether one is brown versus white.

This seemingly humanistic claim to color blindness can be challenged using ideas taken from intersectionality. As outlined earlier, intersectionality emphasizes the lived experiences of people of color, and it also points to the importance of creating space for multiple voices within higher education. We attempt to counter the "we're all human" discourse by providing examples of the lived, everyday experiences of people of color through guided classroom discussions in which personal anecdotes are encouraged and theorized and also through our usage of supplemental readings written from marginalized perspectives that point to the ways in which different positionalities influence the types of experiences people have within our society. We attempt to create space within our classroom to acknowledge and validate the experiences of people of color in order to work towards better understanding the different ways in which race, class, and gender intersect personally and institutionally in people's lives. For example, we facilitate small group discussions for which we provide detailed questions that encourage students to give personal examples of the theories and concepts that we are discussing. This provides a space for students to share their own stories, which are then supplemented with a theoretical analysis so that we all have a better understanding of the structures and institutions that have shaped particular life experiences. After providing time for small group discussions, we then have a large group discussion in which students can share their personal examples. We offer alternative ways to see and analyze current educational policies, and we use supplemental readings to encourage students to question and critique mainstream assumptions and analyses. We also bring in mainstream current event articles and ask students to critique the representation of the issue from perspectives that are often marginalized and/or silenced. For example, we encourage students to critically analyze the school choice narrative that has recently enjoyed bipartisan support. We challenge students to critique notions of choice and the invasion of market principles into educational discourse by asking them to consider which students and communities are being marginalized by the choice of rhetoric. We ask them to think about the short- and long-term effects of school choice from different positionalities: parents who rely on public transportation, rural communities, schools which are chronically underfunded and overdisciplined or communities in which the local school is the center of the community. Students are encouraged to disrupt the linear, simplistic narrative provided by the mainstream media through a critical analysis of the ways in which different individuals and communities may be affected by the school choice rhetoric and policies. These discussions often allow students to theorize their own experiences, and this is especially true for the younger students who were in high school during No Child Left Behind.

Another way that students minimize difference is by attempting to equate oppression. We have heard from many White students who choose to wear piercings or tattoos or dress in what some might term a "menacing" manner. They often recount instances in stores where they have been followed for fear they might shoplift. They feel discriminated against and targeted (as they should in this instance), and they often equate this oppression with racism or classism. Their stories often lack recognition that the signifier (fashion) which caused them to be labeled as a shoplifter is a choice. In addition, the cause of their discrimination was someone making a personal choice to be discriminatory based upon stereotypes. Some students appear not to understand that personal acts of discrimination, while wounding, are not as socially, economically, and politically damaging as institutional acts of discrimination. We attempt to use these personal examples to then discuss the difference between individual discrimination and institutional discrimination. For this, we often utilize media reports of Arizona's new immigration enforcement policy along with narratives from those affected. Currently uploaded on YouTube is a clip of Latina/o children playing a game that involves one person masquerading as a Federal Immigration Enforcement Agent while the other children play the role of "Illegal aliens" and scramble to get away. Initially, there are often chuckles in the room as our students watch these children play a seemingly fun cat and mouse chase. Yet, when we break into small groups to process the meaning of this game in the lives of the children on YouTube as well as some of the children our students know, there is less lighthearted laughter and more students recognize how lives have been shattered because of institutionalized immigration policies. They become horrified at the realization that it is not personal acts of discrimination but, instead, the institutionalized policies that enable Brown men, women, and children to be harassed. Utilizing intersectionality, we discuss the ways in which racism, sexism, and classism are institutionalized, and then we ask the class to think about how these oppressions are similar to and different from the oppression White students face when being followed as potential shoplifters. These discussions lead to students better understanding how personal choice, individual identity, and categories of positionality influence their day-to-day interactions, experiences, and opportunities.

A final way in which students negotiate difference is by attempting to hierarchize oppression. Being a Black man or Black boy in this world affords one a certain amount of suspicion as a drug dealer, criminal, or thug (West, 2000) in a different way than being a Black woman. Of course, Black women must deal with their own sets of stereotypes which are no less threatening or damaging but they are different due to gender (Jezebel, bitch, etc.) (Collins, 1990). Oftentimes, in classroom discussions about privilege and oppression, students begin to rank or hierarchize their oppressions, oftentimes either making gender or race the central identity category, with the other being tangential and not as important. As outlined by intersectionality, ranking oppression is counterproductive and obfuscates the ways in which different subject positions intersect and interact. We use intersectionality in our pedagogy by guiding classroom discussions in order to point to the problems with this additive analysis of oppression and privilege. We discourage binary thinking in which oppressors and victims are easily identified and categorized; instead, we encourage students to critically examine different situations in order to better understand the myriad and complex ways that race, class, and gender exist and how there are multiple categories within categories that make up unique subject positions that must be acknowledged. For example, we sometimes use President Obama as a way to highlight the various ways race, class, gender, education, and nationality can interact to create differing kinds of power, privilege, and oppression. As mentioned earlier, discourses that simplistically portray President Obama as a Black man obfuscate the ways in which his class, education, and gender intersect with his race to shape his positionality. There have been many media discussions of the fact that President Obama checked "Black" on his 2010 Census form. For the media, it appears President Obama is utilized as a way of having conversations about race. We think this is important. However, we use him as an example in class to also illustrate how inappropriate unidimensional analyses are; in focusing only on his race in order to "prove" that racism is no longer a hindrance, the educational, class, and gender privileges that he benefited from are neglected and even erased. President Obama does not fit easily into binary categories of perpetrator or victim because it is impossible to separate his multiple identity categories; his background allows us to illustrate the complexities of privilege and oppression and the futility of oppression hierarchies. We all inhabit both sides of the perpetrator/victim binary, albeit in different ways, and by using intersectionality within our classrooms, we are able to challenge these deleterious binaries and hierarchies.

Using Intersectionality in the Construction of Our Classes

In addition to using intersectionality to guide our in-class pedagogy, we also use it to guide the creation of our syllabi and the overall content of our classes. We both seek to highlight the lived experiences of those traditionally marginalized by institutionalized racism, sexism, and classism, and we do this by being deliberate about the readings that we assign and the videos that we watch. Both authors purposefully use main texts within their classes that are written from a critical perspective; these texts are often written by men and women who have been traditionally silenced with the academy. We also orient our readings, assignments, and classroom discussions around social justice issues within education, paying particular attention to which voices are being heard by our students and which theoretical and academic voices are being read by our students. For example, when teaching graduate-level qualitative research methods, we specifically use examples of qualitative research that investigate critical issues in education which relate to race, class, gender, and sexual orientation. This allows for these issues to be infused in class discussions of research methods; rather than having generic conversations about methods and empirical research, the types of research read by the students allow for critical conversations about the methods *and* content of the research. Students are consequently shown the political nature of research method choices, and they are expected to engage in critical conversations about methods and structural inequalities in education.

Within undergraduate Social Foundations courses, it is imperative for students to relate what they are learning from their main texts to what is happening politically within current education issues and debates. In order to make this connection, we frequently bring in articles that are read in class that investigate a current event within Education. In order to facilitate critical conversations about structural oppression, we do one of two things. First, we may bring in an article by an author who writes about the issue from the margins, utilizing a perspective not circulated in mainstream media. This allows students to consider an alternative analysis; it also makes obvious the need for students to critique mainstream media representations of educational issues. Our second approach involves bringing in mainstream media representations of an issue and then asking students to complicate the given representation with a race, class, and gender analysis. This facilitates critical thinking and hopefully models for students how to engage critically with mainstream media representations.

Finally, both authors stress the importance of praxis. After investigating, discussing, and theorizing the various issues within Education, we both ask the important question: What can we do? It is important for students to think through the ways in which they can act both individually and collectively to address the social injustices within the institution of education. Besides encouraging students to come up with their own actions and solutions to act upon, we also provide them with examples of individuals and groups who are fighting for social justice within public education. For example, in an undergraduate Social Foundations class that one of us teaches, students watch the documentary *Granito de Arena*, which delineates the fight of teachers' unions in southern Mexico. This documentary shows the adverse effects of globalization and neoliberalism on public education in Mexico. It provides a rich and provocative narrative that is easily connected to what teachers and students are facing within the current neoliberal climate in the United States. This movie shows students how teachers in other spaces are combating oppressive policy changes through direct action, and it also facilitates a deeper understanding of structural inequality. The movie makes the teachers' engagement with praxis very clear; teachers are shown theorizing their protests, and their continual processes of self-reflection are highlighted. This documentary is one way in which we can facilitate critical conversations with our students about the importance of both theory and practice and the role of the teacher in fights for social justice.

Conclusion

We have tried to illustrate our own challenges in the classroom and how we help our students understand institutionalized oppression. We know that feminist social justice principles do not speak to everyone. Some students meet these principles with much fear and disdain. In order to confront the fear, we propose discussing instances where the instructors have struggled with confronting their own practices so that students do not feel judged or blamed. While we want to hold students accountable for their personal beliefs and help challenge them to think more equitably, we know that we also have to support them along the way so they do not reject intersectionality as a theory or practice. In order for them to see us as advocates and not adversaries, we have to be vulnerable—sometimes even exposing personal aspects about our lives that are relevant to the topic at hand. If we are to challenge master narratives professionally, we have to illustrate to our students how we have interrupted them personally. For example, one of the authors shares stories regarding "passing"—the experience of crossing racial or sexual orientation borders without being detected as not belonging. It is not a conscious choice; however, people often mistake her for being of a race or sexual orientation that she does not claim. She then shares what it feels like to have access to privilege that should not be hers given the racist and homophobic practices of this society. However, the author shares openly with her students the ways privilege is seductive and that it often has to be a conscious choice to walk away from it or to openly challenge practices that might benefit her personally but that are not available to everyone else. Making oneself vulnerable to students is sometimes difficult but necessary to encourage them to engage in an honest examination of themselves.

As stated previously, we have not contributed a "how-to" chapter on teaching with intersectionality pedagogy. Instead, we have offered our experiences in helping students unpack master narratives as they begin to understand the difference between personal acts of discrimination and institutionalized oppression. Also, it is not without consequence that we engage in these tasks. Both of us are no strangers to accusations of "reverse discrimination" by irate students, and we have also had some student evaluations that evaluated our beliefs instead of our pedagogy. Of course, those are small prices to pay in the struggle for social justice.

In conclusion, intersectionality theories give feminist pedagogues a framework from which to teach, a framework that emphasizes the structural as well as the individual, and one that also points to the importance of positionality. It is urgent that intersectionality theories be used to engage with a wide range of educational issues, for example the continued implementation of No Child Left Behind, Zero Tolerance policies, and the move towards the privatization of public education. Intersectionality challenges current popular notions of color blindness and post-racism, and it can be used to begin and facilitate much-needed conversations about race, class, gender, and sexuality in relation to education. It is important for feminists to consider how to utilize these theories in both their classroom discussions as well as in their construction of syllabi and reading lists.

References

Applebaum, B. (2005). In the name of morality: Moral responsibility, whiteness and social justice education. *Journal of Moral Education, 34*(3), 277–290.

Bell, L. A. (2003). Telling tales: What stories can teach us about racism. *Race, Ethnicity, and Education, 6*(1), 3–28.

Berger, M. T., & Guidroz, K. (2009). Introduction. In M. T. Berger & K. Guidroz (Eds.), *The intersectional approach: Transforming the academy through race, class, and gender* (pp. 1–22). Chapel Hill: University of North Carolina Press.

Blair, M. (1998). The myth of neutrality in educational research. In P. Connolly & B. Troyna (Eds.), *Researching racism in education* (pp. 12–20). Philadelphia: Open University Press.

Bonilla-Silva, E. (1997). Rethinking racism: Towards a structural interpretation. *American Sociological Review, 62*(3), 465–480.

Bonilla-Silva, E. (2003). *Racism without being racist: Color-blind racism and the persistence of racial inequality in the United States.* Lanham, MD: Rowman & Littlefield.

Bonilla-Silva, E., & Ray, V. (2009). When whites love a black leader: Race matters in Obamerica. *Journal of African American Studies, 13*, 176–183.

Brayboy, B. M. J., Castagno, A. E., & Maughan, E. (2007). Equality and justice for all? Examining race in education scholarship. *Review of Research in Education, 31*, 159–194.

Collins, P. H. (1990). *Black feminist thought: Knowledge, consciousness, and the politics of empowerment.* New York: Routledge.

Collins, P. H. (1998). It's all in the family: Intersections of gender, race, and nation. *Hypatia, 13*(3), 62–82.

Dill, B. T., & Zambrana, R. E. (2009). Critical thinking about inequality: An emerging lens. In B. T. Dill & R. E. Zambrana (Eds.), *Emerging intersections: Race, class, and gender in theory, policy, and practice* (pp. 1–21). New Brunswick, NJ: Rutgers University Press.

Freire, P. (1970). *Pedagogy of the oppressed.* New York: Continuum.

hooks, b. (1994). *Teaching to transgress: Education as the practice of freedom.* New York: Routledge.

hooks, b. (1999). Eating the other: Desire and resistance. In S. Hesse-Biber, C. Gilmartin, & R. Lydenberg (Ed.), *Feminist approaches to theory and methodology: An interdisciplinary reader* (pp. 179–194). New York: Oxford University Press.

King, J. (1991). Dysconscious racism: Ideology, identity, and the miseducation of teachers. *The Journal of Negro Education, 60*(2), 133–146.

Scheurich, J., & Young, M. (2002). Coloring epistemology: Are our research epistemologies racially biased? In J. Scheurich (Ed.), *Anti-racist scholarship: An advocacy* (pp. 51–73). Albany: State University of New York Press.

Spelman, E. V. (1988). *Inessential woman.* Boston: Beacon Press.

West, C. (2000). Race and modernity. In C. West (Ed.), *The Cornel West reader* (pp. 55–86). New York: Basic Civitas Books.

Intersectional Pedagogy and Transformative Learning

Susan M. Pliner, Cerri A. Banks, & Ashley M. Tapscott

In the United States, access to quality education (both K-12 and higher education) for women, for people of color, for the poor, and for people with disabilities has been central in social, political, and economic movements aimed at equity, inclusion, and social justice (Books, 2007; Cole, 2006; Rury, 2002; Spring, 2010). Education, as a discipline, has been a leader in identifying obstacles to educational equity and highlighting the need for systemic changes to the institution of schooling in order to remove inherent barriers. Common discourses in education include: the need for culturally relevant teaching, the ways identity and systems of power inform classroom practice and interactions, and institutional obstacles to access, inclusion, and success (Fox, 2001; Gay, 2000; Johnson, 2009; McPherson & Schapiro, 2006). Many education programs at colleges and universities have theory courses in their curricula that focus on issues of equity. While not every college or university *requires* these courses, we have seen the importance of using theory to guide our teaching practices and to expand student learning.

By discipline, our collective training is in foundations of education, women's studies, special education, social justice education, and English. We represent a range of identity markers including, white, heterosexual, Jewish, bisexual, working class, African American, Catholic, middle class, and disabled. Our teaching and our scholarship reflect a dedication to a humanist approach to education, specifically to "conscientization" and transformative learning (Freire, 1970; Mezirow, 1990). We have found that an intersectional framework for thinking and practice facilitates our efforts to be educators with a social justice mission (Kumashiro, 2004).

Educators in schools, colleges, and universities have taken on a profession that carries with it great accountability. We can each identify teaching and learning interactions that pushed us to reflect on our pedagogy and the impact our choices have on students. This chapter is a manifestation of that reflective process as we describe how the concept of intersectionality informs our teaching pedagogy and practice. Susan and Cerri will discuss the choice to use intersectional theory and pedagogy in two college courses, Social Foundations of Multiculturalism and History of Disability. We both acknowledge that these courses can be taught without an intersectional lens. In this chapter, we will show that an intersectional approach provides opportunities to expand methods, content, and analysis in ways that facilitate deeper learning. Ashley, who took both courses and is now a high school English teacher, will describe how the concept of intersectionality informed her own learning in college and her current classroom teaching. This chapter demonstrates the ways teaching and learning are always in flux; are always informed by lived, historical, cultural, and social contexts; and are impacted by the relationship between student and teacher and its inherent potential for reciprocity.

Intersectionality and Pedagogy

Pedagogy that is situated in an intersectional framework addresses equity in the classroom at all levels. It encourages teachers and students to grapple with identity and power and to acknowledge the complex ways this process informs teaching and learning. Intersectional pedagogy requires that classroom content and interactions be critically analyzed to expose structural and systemic inequalities that exist within the cultural, political, social, and economic structures in everyday life.

Intersectional pedagogy expands the reach of almost any academic discussion and the benefits of this approach are both individual and collective. For example, intersectional pedagogy necessitates creating an atmosphere of mutual respect or what Dill and Zambrana (2009) refer to as "interpersonal power" in the classroom. "Interpersonal power refers to 'routinized, day-to-day practices of how people treat one another. Such practices are systematic, recurrent and so familiar that they often go unnoticed'" (Dill & Zambrana, 2009, p. 11). Intersectional pedagogy extends a discussion of interpersonal relationships far beyond how individuals treat one another. It demands that students and teachers pay attention to the "familiar and unnoticed" in the curriculum and content, lived schooling experiences, and the inherent connections to power, privilege, and oppression in schools and beyond. Intersectional pedagogy also provides strategies that interrupt inequality. It also builds a collective classroom culture with multiple opportunities and methods for engagement. This approach can dismantle resistance in the classroom and move students beyond the master narratives of guilt, shame, and blame. It can empower students to move towards complex and meaningful understanding of course content and help them develop the capacity for action.

Social Foundations of Multiculturalism

As described on the syllabus, Social Foundations of Multiculturalism is a course "that examines the institution of schooling, broadly conceived, as it is positioned in a multicultural and diverse society." The course looks at historical and contemporary debates surrounding the concept of multiculturalism and explores how the ideas are played out in education systems in the United States and in everyday public and private social experiences. When I (Cerri) designed the course my goal was to help students explore the complexities of the world we live in and the impact they have on schooling institutions. I wanted them to move past emotions, dialogue, and engagement with diversity that were based in individual experiences, to more analytical and complex interactions about what it means to live in a diverse and multicultural world. I decided early to focus on the United States and its "history, biographies, and societies" as it relates to ideals, attitudes, policy, and practice about identity and difference (Mills, 1959). Students often find it easier to focus on global issues of injustice in stereotyped, generalized, and disconnected ways where the "difference" or "other" is located across an ocean or on a continent in places many students have never visited or accessed except through media. In this course I wanted students to sit in the dynamic murkiness that is multiculturalism in the United States and explore their everyday, constant connections to it.

The theory of intersectionality is introduced early as a foundation and framework in the course. This theoretical space is examined in interaction with other theories like privilege paradigms, social and cultural capital, and representation. It is also used to discuss histories, political and economic policies, and contemporary events that engage identity and equity. Discussing the "simultaneity of privilege and oppression"—a feature of intersectionality outlined by Rose Brewer (1999)—foregrounds the stance that everyone in the class, "within and across" all identity markers, has a relationship to issues of equity. We explore the complications of those relationships (e.g., the ways the dominance of heterosexuality informs white privilege and male privilege for a gay white man in the U.S.) and the negotiations those complications require in schools and in everyday life. Grounding our discussions in intersectional theory right from the beginning builds connections. It establishes early in the

course that each of us must work daily to challenge both our own bia
those of the systems of which we are a part. By sharing my own stories of
struggle, success, and negotiation with students, they come to recognize that it
is safe in my classroom to talk about their own.

Pedagogy and practice

In this course students are required to keep a list of key concepts. This is not a
list of definitions but rather a form of note taking that helps students organize
the theoretical content. Students are required to use the key concept list and
an intersectional approach in class discussions. For example, during the
aftermath of Hurricane Katrina, when the government's response to the crisis
was slow, many residents of New Orleans were left without food, lodging, and
water. A popular question asked in the media and among politicians was
whether the slow response was an issue of racism or an issue of class
discrimination. I asked students to apply an intersectional approach to this
debate. Specifically, I asked them to examine how the discussion and proposed
solutions to this social challenge would change if an intersectional lens that
requires both race *and* class (along with other markers of identity) instead of
race *or* class was considered as part of the discussion (Brewer, 1999).

As part of class discussions, students are also expected to identify course
concepts and intersectional analysis in course materials, even when they are
not specifically named. For example, the video *People Like Us: Social Class in
America* (Alvarez & Kolker, 2001) is a tool I have used to show students that
conversations about the intersections of identity are evident in popular culture
texts like film, magazines, and television even though the term "intersectionality" is rarely used. *People Like Us* shows just how complex the conversation
about class in the United States really is—starting with the idea that no one
wants to discuss it! Each vignette in the film portrays both individual and
group experiences with social class and students are required to find examples
that articulate and illustrate the intersections of social class with other markers
of identity, like race, gender, age, and ability. For example, they discuss the
video's portrayal of the Black middle class and its variances from typical discussions of the middle class. Students are also asked to identify where the text
fails to make these connections and how doing so can strengthen the analysis.

This video has been useful in helping students clarify the difference between an intersectional and systemic analysis and an individual analysis, which
is one of the key course concepts. For example, they are asked to identify and
engage a systemic discourse about poverty (e.g., high unemployment or lack of
a living wage) and explain how it differs from an individual discourse about

poverty (e.g., poor people are lazy). They must then take this analysis further and apply and discuss what it means for political and economic debates about poverty, the middle class, and wealth as they intersect with other markers of identity like ability and race. The depth of this intersectional analysis helps students move from simply having an emotional response to the lives and stories depicted in the videotext to engagement with systemic models that critically analyze social class in the United States.

Students must also use the concept list and an intersectional approach in their writing assignments. I ask students to write a series of critical reflection papers during the semester. Students choose a theme for the paper, take an intersectional approach to the topic, and use a range of course readings to complete the assignment. Since many students are used to writing reflection papers from their own individual experiences and perspectives, they are unnerved that I am not supplying them with a topic. Once they struggle through determining a topic, students actually enjoy applying what they know to settings that have meaning for them. They learn that theory is applicable in everyday life. Over the course of the semester students see their skills of interpreting, analyzing, and applying theory grow and develop as they make clear connections between what they are learning in the classroom and what is happening in the world. Many explain that they find it empowering to recognize that they have a language, and a theoretical framework, to challenge and contribute to important social, political, and economic discourses.

As their final assignment, students are required to choose one institution, practice, area of study or curiosity, or social phenomenon and thoroughly apply the concepts we examined in class. Each paper or project must take an intersectional approach to analysis, critique, development, and problem solving. To complete this work, students have created lesson plans, blogs, videos, expanded community engagement projects, and started student organizations. They have written substantial research papers and policy briefs that engage public and social policy, and legal and medical practices. This final assessment allows students to demonstrate a depth and breadth of understanding that moves well beyond a regurgitation of content as they begin to see themselves as theorists, practitioners, and change agents.

I do not attempt to ground my goals for the course in an academically or politically neutral space. I am clear with students that my pedagogical work has a larger mission of facilitating equity and social justice in education systems and beyond. Students understand from my words and deeds (grading) that they do not have to subscribe to or take part in that mission to pass the course. They do understand that to pass the course they must engage in thinking and dialogue that are critical, systemic, intersectional, and analytical. They must defend any stance with course concepts and with experiences that extend beyond their own personal lives. If students do not feel that they have knowledge or understanding of lived experiences other than their own, the flexibility of course assignments creates room for them to seek it out. This pedagogical approach and practice facilitate the statement on the syllabus that "this course has a larger goal of learning across differences and advocacy for social change and for broadening our knowledge about being responsible citizens of the world." Students like Ashley represent the accomplishment of that goal. They decide to use theory, like intersectionality, to actualize a lifelong commitment to social justice activism in ways that make sense for their lives.

Ashley

I am a white, Catholic, young woman from a historically working-class family. I initially understood identity to be a collection of separate and unrelated pieces, but learning about the concept of intersectionality in the Multiculturalism course made me aware of how one aspect informs and affects the others. It helped me frame my own experiences as the youngest of five children in a large family. I also learned how to contextualize the larger structures of power and privilege that exist and to examine my own experiences with privilege and oppression. For example, how did the dominance of Christianity make it possible for me to attend a Catholic private grade school even though my family was working class? How am I affected and defined by gender roles and how is that informed by my race and sexuality? What inherent power is granted, based on the fact that I am able-bodied? Utilizing the concept of intersectionality helped me to understand the complexities of these questions, situate them in a larger societal context, and use this reflective work as a foundation for my teaching. The concept of intersectionality, as a framework for teaching and learning, initiates a need to recognize student identity as a dynamic concept and to understand the complexities of student narratives. Students come from a range of family histories, racial backgrounds, social class statuses, gender constructions, and states of ability, each of which brings privilege, power, and oppression simultaneously (Harry & Klingner, 2006; Irvine, 2003; Korgen, 2010). At the high school level, students are colossally aware of these differences but are often unable to contextualize them in a social framework. I make a conscious effort to help students understand the forces of power, privilege, and dominance at play not only in the literature that I choose but also in their perceptions of themselves and their classmates.

Pedagogy and practice

The documentary we watched in the Social Foundations of Multiculturalism class, *People Like Us: Social Class in America*, traced the social class experiences of several American people and groups. Even eight years later, there is one woman from the text who stands out in my mind. She was white, very poor, lived in a run-down trailer, and walked 10 miles to work at Burger King because she could not afford a car. She discussed her decision to refuse welfare benefits and her son's feelings of embarrassment toward her worn-out clothing and lack of expendable income. This woman was shown in contrast to a teenage girl who was also white, who attended a suburban high school and drove a forty-thousand-dollar car that her parents had purchased for her. This depiction forced me to question the role of power and privilege in our society as well as how they are impacted by the intersections of race and class. Which one of these women really worked "hard"? Which one was more "deserving" of their social situation? How does an analysis of poverty as laziness make invisible a person's 10-mile walk to a job that pays minimum wage? What and who do we value in our society? Who has access to the American Dream? "Hard" work, access, and family legacy took on a new meaning for me. Watching the film and engaging in this analysis sparked an understanding of the powerful ways the consequences of the intersections of social class, race, gender, and ability inform people's lives.

Furthermore, the documentary showed that our clothing, cars, homes, vacations, and even the food we eat are inevitably connected to and determined by social class, race, and gender. For me, this has translated into a socially conscious approach to teaching F. Scott Fitzgerald's novel *The Great Gatsby* to my eleventh grade students. Gatsby is a straight, able-bodied, white male who purportedly belongs to the careless upper-class culture of America in the 1920s. At the heart of the novel lies the question: What is social class and how is it informed by the fallacy of the American Dream? Students are able to compare the historical context of the prosperous Roaring Twenties to the devastation of the Great Depression. What changed? Was it solely money, or did the views of society as a whole change as a result? What power structures contribute to the carelessness of the upper class in the novel? An intersectional approach offers students a way to extend their discussion of the content beyond typical character analysis and historical perspective. For example, typically students are able to question their own understanding of the American Dream in 2011. Does it exist? What opportunities make it possible to achieve such success? Who has access? What visible tokens of success make us think that the American Dream is attainable by everybody? Can one person's version of the American Dream be different from another person's? An intersectional approach helps students expand the discussion to include questions about the unequal distribution of power among characters from the novel to discuss its modern ramifications. The Roaring Twenties gave birth to the Jazz Age, which allows for discussions of race and social class. Daisy, a woman in the novel, who was not able to determine her own fate, sparks a dialogue about power and gender identity. Extending the lessons I learned as a student, namely, critical intersectional analysis, helps me build my own students' understanding of power and privilege as I use literature to help them to make connections between history, society, and their own lives.

History of Disability

Designing the History of Disability course with an intersectional framework is a pedagogical choice. My (Susan's) goal is to help students gain accurate and comprehensive theoretical knowledge, while also exposing them to the real-life complexities of categories of identity. While a vibrant body of literature about disability has emerged since the passage of the Americans with Disabilities Act (1990), current educational practices continue to rely on oppressive beliefs and ideals of normalcy, maintaining disability is located within the individual or body rather than an analysis of systems, theory, and practice. The result of this entrenchment is an unequal and inherently discriminatory educational system that reinforces and perpetuates ableist ideals, beliefs, and actions.

In education departments at colleges and universities, special education courses most often cover strategies to address the types of disabilities teachers will come across in their classroom. Rarely do these courses examine the meaning of disability as a socially constructed identity in historical and current contexts, nor is there an analysis of the connection and intersections with other socially constructed identities, such as race, gender, social class, and sexual orientation. While understanding variations in learning is essential for teachers, this approach places the focus on the individual student with a disability rather than on an intersectional analysis of how concepts of normalcy, ability, and disability are reified in educational systems. Davis (2006) articulates this concept:

> To understand the disabled body, one must return to the concept of the norm, the normal body. So much writing about disability has focused on the disabled person as the object of study, just as the study of race has focused on the person of color. But as with recent scholarship on race, which has turned its attention to whiteness, I would like to focus not so much on the construction of disability as the construction of normalcy. I do this because the "problem" is not the person with disabilities; the

problem is the way normalcy is constructed to create the "problem" of the disabled person. (p. 3)

The theory of intersectionality abandons ideological divisions by acknowledging that there are "simultaneous and overlapping" areas of oppression and privilege inherent in our identities (Collins, 2000). It is an effective lens to frame the complexities of social locations and evaluate historical and contemporary implications of social experience. Embedding analysis of disability historically, politically, economically, medically, and educationally as well as drawing direct connections to other socially constructed identities provides an entry point for students who feel they have no connection to disability. For instance, an intersectional approach exposes how course concepts of normalcy, immigration, and eugenics are tied directly to racist ideology and the impact that ideology has had on historical and contemporary attitudes and practices regarding education and institutionalization.

Exposing students to personal narratives about disability legitimizes the impact of this marker of identity on real lives. It is important to examine narrative with a systemic approach, that is, in conjunction with systems, institutions, policies, and practices. This helps students understand disability beyond individual experience and emotion (sympathy, pity, guilt). It also prepares teachers to use this knowledge to develop the tools necessary to avoid replicating oppressive practices as they work to develop inclusive classrooms.

Pedagogy and practice

In order to engage students in critically analyzing their beliefs, knowledge, and experiences in relationship to the core course concepts of normalcy, deviance, stigma, and empowerment, at the end of the first day of the course students are given an assignment that requires them to interview themselves with a protocol. The "Taping Project," adapted from an exercise developed by Beverly Daniel Tatum (Wellman, 1977), requires students to record themselves asking and answering questions related to major course concepts. The recordings and a short reflection paper on the process of completing the assignment are collected during the following class period. Students understand that I will not listen to their recordings since the purpose of this assignment is for them to think deeply about the subject matter of the course prior to our study and to voice their beliefs and values aloud. After a semester with full engagement with course content, I return the tapes and require students to listen to their interviews and complete a new writing reflection reacting to the self-interview.

The final taping assignment produces significant responses from students about having gained new knowledge and about their learning process. When they hear themselves on tape, initially, answering questions with authority and conviction in ways that they now know are often erroneous or heavily laden with cultural and social misperceptions and stereotypes, it makes visible how ideas about normalcy, for example, are enacted in unconscious or superficial ways in their own lives. Using an intersectional framework to analyze their initial responses challenges students to make connections between their previously held beliefs of disability as well as other socially constructed identities. This assignment is designed for students to track their own learning and take ownership of their beliefs in critical and transformative ways.

In this course, I include personal narrative and lived experiences in multiple ways including guest lectures, memoirs, videos, and class outings. The semester Ashley was enrolled in this course, there was a local exhibit of Willard State Mental Hospital patients called *The Lives They Left Behind: Suitcases from a State Hospital Attic*. The exhibit was a perfect example of deeply and historically entrenched views of disability in the United States. The suitcases told the stories of individual patients committed to the hospital prior to the deinstitutionalization movement and hospital closures. Students were able to see intersections of identity in the exhibit by seeing that patients were committed against their will because of reasons such as: language barriers (race and ethnicity), unemployment and poverty (class), and postpartum depression and hysteria (gender). The exhibit was a tangible example of eugenics, immigration, the significance of the intersections of identity, and the impact of notions of normalcy in each of these areas.

Using personal narratives of people with disabilities is an effective method for connecting students to the theoretical course concepts. I do offer a caution here. Introducing personal narrative without an examination of systems can lead to students reducing the impact of systemic oppressions related to disability to a story about one person's "misfortune." That said, having students use narrative after we have established and practiced the examination of systemic discrimination, prejudice, and oppression assists them in shifting from compassion and empathy to awareness for the need for action.

Ashley

As a MAT student, I enrolled in a class entitled History of Disability to gain background knowledge in special education as I prepared to become a high school English teacher. I took away a deeper understanding of disability through an intersectional lens: as a coinciding piece of identity, not the sole indicator, which affects normalcy, deviance, and power in our society.

The taping project in the disability class asked us to reflect on how characterizations of disabilities have changed over time. We verbally recorded our answers to a set of questions at the beginning of the semester and then listened to our responses at the end of the course. My initial answer revolved around historical exclusion and pity. I discussed how people with disabilities have been marginalized and treated poorly throughout history and used the Americans with Disabilities Act to address the surprisingly recent legislation that advocates for equity. However, I said nothing about eugenics, institutionalization, and immigration—showing that most of my learning in the course revolved around the relationship of these three concepts. Eugenics, institutionalization, and immigration are not always associated with disability, but have ultimately determined the value historically assigned to identity. For example, eugenics deemed people with disabilities unfit to have children while institutionalization regulated their access to freedom and often resulted in a life of subjection. Immigration shed light on the powerlessness historically tied to people who are different—whether they have a disability or not. This project forced me to consider the historical implications of social construction, normalcy, and deviance, thus taking ownership of my own learning.

The concepts of eugenics, immigration, and institutionalization were brought to life by a class trip to the Willard suitcase exhibit in Auburn, New York. The visit to this exhibit breathed life into the names, faces, hobbies, and story lines that would otherwise be textbook theory. This exhibit showed that eugenics and institutionalization are historically tied to normalcy and deviance. It showed disability as an evolving concept that is constantly affected by the intersections of gender, cultural barriers, and poverty. For example, a man who was an immigrant was put in the Willard State Mental Hospital because he had yelled from the top of his home as it burned. In his native country, this is a warning to inform neighbors of the danger. Using an intersectional approach crosses borders and expels the rigidity that can consume traditional analyses. The immigrant man was not "crazy." His fate, a label of disability and lifelong institutionalization, was determined by the intersections of social and cultural ideas of normalcy, a language barrier, and the inability to change his situation. Willard showed me that without an intersectional approach, identity runs the risk of being oversimplified.

Pedagogy and practice.

The taping project has impacted the way I structure learning in my classroom. Interdependence among students is encouraged through differentiated instruction and student choice, thus forcing students to take ownership of their own learning experience. They research, discuss, and defend their own viewpoints while also listening to others. From such an approach, varying social backgrounds can become a source of rich dialogue. Structures of productive group work are modeled, and guidelines are generated by the students and posted as an anchor chart; all of which are targeted at meeting the needs of all students. If I had not heard my own voice on the taping project in the History of Disability class, I would not have realized the importance of self-examination and reflective dialogue.

The Lives They Left Behind exhibit encouraged me to use personal narratives and intersectional analysis as a way for students to connect with literature. For example, my students study John Steinbeck's novella *Of Mice and Men* in ninth grade. The plotline follows the story of a man with a developmental disability in 1930s America. Through a web quest and a poster project, students re-search how identity was determined in 1930s America: the poverty of the Great Depression, the circumstances of the Dust Bowl, the effects of racial segregation, the rigidity of gender roles, and the treatment of people with disabilities. This historical context sets the stage for a discussion of identity and the unequal distribution of power among the characters in the novella. This intersectional approach helps students readily see the intersections of social class: Lennie was poor, and disability determined his eventual death in the novella. Through this historical time line project focused on the 1930s, students learn that disability was, and still is, informed by intersections of class, gender, race, age, and sexuality.

Susan Pliner and Cerri Banks made conscious decisions to allow for stu-dent ownership in their curriculum. Opportunities such as the Willard suit-case exhibit, the taping project, and the documentary *People Like Us* allowed me to take advantage of reflective practices, own my own knowledge, and learn from the lived experiences of others. *The Lives They Left Behind: Suitcases from a State Hospital Attic* used historical narratives to show the impact of personal stories and the complexities therein. The taping project forced me to expand my own thinking and instill reflective teaching practices. *People Like Us: Social Class in America* advanced my concept of what social class is and the ways it intersects with other markers of identity. For an English teacher, literature is an effective way to examine how identity intersects and is informed by the social locations of race, class, gender, religion, ability, and sexuality, while also crossing the boundaries of history, perspective, and time. Being able to learn about intersectionality and practice intersectional analysis in my education courses has directly translated into a skill set and an enthusiasm for instilling what I have learned into my own teaching practices.

Conclusion

Teaching is political and personal, and it should be, at its essence, transformative and liberatory. Teaching is not a neutral or generic endeavor, and this chapter represents our deliberate commitment to teach using the theory of intersectionality with an ultimate goal of creating an equitable and socially just world. As educators, we desire to ignite a passion for social justice and critical inquiry in our students. Constructing a course with the specific intentions of teaching students to challenge course content, as well as their own values and beliefs and those of others, is a difficult endeavor that requires specific attention to classroom environment. This includes attending to issues of power and privilege within the classroom, within the institutions in which we teach, and in the world.

Intersectional pedagogy pays close attention to building and maintaining authentic relationships in the classroom and showing respect for personal narratives and lived experiences. It calls for the selection of course content that is engaging, that provides multiple perspectives, and that highlights and disrupts destructive master narratives, all of which require developing the skills for critical analysis.

Also, intersectional pedagogy requires educators to think deeply and reflectively about their pedagogical choices, desired learning outcomes, and the multiple opportunities necessary to engage students where they are. We never know whether the factual content, narratives, personal storytelling, or experiential lessons will be the catalyst for passion and lead students to take responsibility for creating social change. We do know from experience that providing students with the knowledge to apply intersectional theory to whatever work they choose allows them to envision ways to create social change that is personally meaningful.

While we highlighted the benefits of using an intersectional approach and provided practical examples, we realize we did not represent the challenges that arise with students who hold firmly to their knowledge, beliefs, and values while resisting contradictory information and the opportunity to critically examine their ideology in deep and meaningful ways. Ashley represents the student who fully engages and internalizes the necessity for employing an intersectional framework in her work and life. We are all deeply grateful for the opportunity to have learned from and worked with one another in a traditional classroom and as coauthors of this chapter.

References

Alvarez, L., & Kolker, A. (Producers, Directors). (2001). *People like us: Social class in America* [Documentary]. United States: Center for New American Media.

Books, S. (2007). *Invisible children in the society and its schools* (3rd ed.). Mahwah, NJ: Lawrence Erlbaum Associates.

Brewer, R. M. (1999). Theorizing race, class, and gender: The new scholarship of black feminist intellectuals and black women's labor. *Race, Class, and Gender, 6*(2), 29–47.

Cole, M. (2006). *Education, equality and human rights: Issues of gender, "race," sexuality, disability and social class* (2nd ed.). New York: Routledge.

Collins, P. H. (2000). *Black feminist thought: Knowledge, consciousness, and the politics of empowerment* (Rev. ed.). New York: Routledge.

Davis, L. J. (2006). Constructing normalcy: The bell curve, the novel, and the invention of the disabled body in the nineteenth century. In L. J. Davis (Ed.), *The disability studies reader* (pp. 3–15). New York: Routledge.

Dill, B. T., & Zambrana, R. E. (2009). Critical thinking about inequality: An emerging lens. In B. T. Dill & R. E. Zambrana (Eds.), *Emerging intersections: Race, class, and gender in theory, policy, and practice* (pp. 1–21). New Brunswick, NJ: Rutgers University Press.

Fox, H. (2001). *"When race breaks out": Conversations about race and racism in college classrooms.* New York: Peter Lang.

Freire, P. (1970). *Pedagogy of the oppressed.* New York: Continuum.

Gay, C. (2000). *Culturally responsive teaching: Theory, research, and practice.* New York: Teachers College.

Harry, B., & Klingner, J. (2006). *Why are so many minority students in special education? Understanding race & disability in schools.* New York: Teachers College Press.

Irvine, J. J. (2003). *Educating teachers for diversity: Seeing with a cultural eye.* New York: Teachers College Press.

Johnson, R. G. (2009). *A twenty-first century approach to teaching social justice: Educating for both advocacy and action.* New York: Peter Lang.

Korgen, K. O. (2010). *Multiracial Americans and social class: The influence of social class on racial identity.* New York: Routledge.

Kumashiro, K. (2004). *Against common sense: Teaching and learning toward social justice* (2nd ed.). New York: Routledge.

McPherson, M. S., & Schapiro, M. O. (2006). *College access: Opportunity or privilege?* New York: College Board.

Mezirow, J. (1990). *Fostering critical reflection in adulthood.* San Francisco: Jossey-Bass.

Mills, C. W. (1959). *The sociological imagination.* New York: Oxford University Press.

Rury, J. L. (2002). *Education and social change: Contours in the history of American schooling* (3rd ed.). New York: Routledge.

Spring, J. (2010). *Political agendas for education: From change we can believe in to putting America first* (4th ed.). New York: Routledge.

Wellman, D. (1977). *Portraits of white racism.* Cambridge: University of Cambridge Press.

Intersectionality and My Practice of Teaching Mathematics

Jennifer Bowen

Introduction

In the sixth week of the fall semester of my junior year of college, I looked around the room and discovered that I was the lone female in my Combinatorics math class. Almost simultaneously, I also recognized that everyone in this upper-level math class was white, including me and my male professor. I had an immediate sense of isolation and unease, even though I could not name it. I remember feeling surprised both by my position and the amount of time it took me to become aware of this location. As a successful undergraduate mathematics student, I continued my education at the graduate level with the intention, and ultimate end, of becoming a college professor. It was during this time that my own learning grew about identity markers and the impact of their intersections, specifically, the ways that the interplay of race, class, gender, and ability provides privilege and oppression while simultaneously depending on the social location held. This realization gave me a language and foundation with which to understand what I had experienced related to gender and race as an undergraduate mathematics major.

Finding myself now teaching at a small liberal arts college of about 2,000 students, I champion equity and access in the undergraduate mathematics classroom and community. Motivated by my own rocky but triumphant experiences as a female mathematician, I argue that the stance that identity work is not relevant in the Science, Technology, Engineering, and Mathematics (STEM) disciplines is erroneous and shortsighted. While in recent years there has been an increase in scholarship related to diversity in the STEM fields, there is still a historic deficit of diversity in the STEM disciplines and disparities in student participation and achievement still exist (Gutstein, 2006; Hill, Corbett, & St. Rose, 2010). Colleges and universities must focus on not only on getting diverse students in our classroom seats but also on retaining and seeing them thrive mathematically. I argue that whether it is intentional or not, the results of the intersections of student and faculty identities influence teaching and learning in the mathematics classroom. Henrion (1997) writes, "More work needs to be done to understand the complexity of how ethnic and racial backgrounds intersect with gender in the context of mathematics" (p. 190). In my work, it is my goal to take up this intersectional approach provided by Henrion, and expand it to include social class and other identity markers. This has not been a typical approach in mathematics pedagogy but I believe it is an important one.

As a mathematics professor, I have sought out opportunities to engage in dialogue and discussion that focus on the impact of intersectionality on teaching and learning as a way to hone my classroom practice. Born out of research and scholarship in sociological and feminist theory, intersectionality examines social location and cultural identity, how each interacts and "intersects," specifically in cases of oppression and privilege on multiple levels. For example, Dill and Zambrana (2009) state that we should

> treat intersectionality as an analytical strategy—a systematic approach to understanding human life and behavior that is rooted in the experiences and struggles of marginalized people . . . inequalities derived from race, ethnicity, class, gender, and their intersections place specific groups of the population in a privileged position with respect to other groups and offer individuals unearned benefits based solely on group membership. (p. 4)

This theoretical framework has pushed me to consider ways to ensure that the mathematics classroom is a place that is diverse and inclusive. This includes using a range of assessment and teaching tools to meet students where they are as they strive for success.

Intersectionality and Mathematics: Making the Case

Intersectional analysis and its focus on structural change support the case for access to quantitative literacy in the United States. Quantitative literacy is described as the ability to interpret, argue, and reason while using quantitative information (Bennett & Briggs, 2008). While this numerate disposition is essential for understanding and problem solving in facets of personal, civic, and professional life, "illiteracy in math is acceptable the way illiteracy in reading and writing is unacceptable. Failure is tolerated in math but not in English" (Moses & Cobb, 2001, p. 9). It is widely agreed that imparting quantitative literacy is best accomplished when incorporating mathematics and its tools within a context and a discipline—a strategy completely counter to historic ways of teaching and learning mathematics. "Few can doubt that the tradition of decontextualized mathematics instruction has failed many students, including large numbers of women and minorities, who leave high school with neither the numeracy skills nor the quantitative confidence required in contemporary society" (Steen, 2001, p. 5). The link between quantitative literacy and these intersecting identities is quite clear. Given encouragement, innovative contextual pedagogy, and undergraduate research in quantitative fields, the population of underrepresented groups in mathematics and related STEM fields will continue to increase. "Consider the role of mathematicians here. There is nothing in the training of mathematicians that prepares them to lead in such a literacy effort. Yet the literacy effort really cannot succeed unless it enlists the active participation of some critical mass of the mathematical community" (Moses & Cobb, 2001, p. 16).

Colleges and universities in the United States enroll students from diverse intellectual, social, racial, and multiethnic backgrounds. Simply said, given the range of identities students embody and the resulting privilege and oppression that occur in their intersections, some students are better prepared to study collegiate mathematics than others. Unfortunately, this lack of preparation is read as individual deficiency and less often connected to systemic inequality stemming from the consequences of intersectional oppression, like economic disparity in communities of color, which leads to an unequal distribution of educational resources (Gutstein, 2006). The mathematics professor who has a goal of equitable access must have the desire and then develop the ability to navigate students' diverse mathematical skills while also traversing a set, standard curriculum. This is a complicated terrain. Given complex mathematics concepts that must be covered in the collegiate classroom, the question becomes, how can a mathematics faculty member become equipped to deal with each student's lived experiences and the subsequent impact of those experiences in the classroom? Dill and Zambrana (2009) state: "Teaching is one of the primary modes of dissemination of these ideas and people engaged in this work express considerable engagement in finding innovative and creative ways to teach about power, inequality, and social justice" (p. 249). If the mathematics classroom only focuses its content on mathematics wherein power, inequality, and social justice are neither inherent nor obvious contextual concepts, it becomes necessary to have a broad and dynamic understanding of the students in the class and the ways power, inequality, and social justice impact their ability to learn mathematics. It also makes it necessary to embed the mathematical theory, concept, and practice into contexts that reflect these concepts as will be shown later.

Models That Challenge Inequities in Mathematics

As mentioned, there is an inherent disregard for the underprepared student (of which there are many) in mathematics. "Large disparities between whites and students of color, and between well-off and low-income students exist in . . . membership in mathematical (and scientific) fields . . . measures of achievement and learning. Some may argue about the size of, and trends in, the gaps, but the travesty of unequal experiences, opportunities, and outcomes between rich and poor and between whites and students of color is unarguable—equity is not here" (Gutstein, 2006, pp. 11–12). Underrepresented groups such as females, students of color, or students with learning disabilities experience very real "stereotype threat" in mathematics classrooms. In math this threat is "a standard predicament of life . . . [which] springs from our human powers of intersubjectivity" (Steele, 2010, p. 5). Students' sense of underlying stereotypes and expectations from the human experience of their identity and this pressure manifest in a classroom situation in negative ways. Traditional mathematics pedagogy focuses its efforts on exclusive and exhaustive independent work. Absent in its day-to-day class work is a community of mathematical learners, a community of identities that can shape mathematics instruction. I contend that conventional methods exclude and prove ineffective for a vital number of students in diverse classroom settings.

When a graduate student in mathematics at Berkeley in the mid-1970s, Uri Treisman developed a philosophy of instruction he terms an "Emerging Scholars Program" (ESP). Treisman had witnessed and was motivated by a striking failure rate in calculus for Black and Latino/a students at Berkeley. "Calculus was then, and remains today, a major barrier for minority students seeking to enter careers that depend in an essential way on mathematics" (Treisman, 1992, p. 362). Attempting to list reasons for the disparity in student learning, he and his colleagues hypothesized motivation gap, poor basic mathematics training, lack of family support, and income (Treisman, 1992). Not one reason alone explained the discrepancy in calculus performance, but rather a deep and intersectional examination of students' identities both inside and outside the classroom was the answer. Because of the inherent "vertical" nature of mathematics, in that, new mathematical topics depend directly on a student's preceding courses, students who fare poorly in introductory courses invariably labor in subsequent intermediate and advanced courses. When students fall behind early, they tend to remain behind or drop out of mathematics classes in the future. Students in Treisman's (1992) experimental instruction participated in "workshops," and his goal was to "construct an anti-remedial program for students who saw themselves as well prepared. . . . [It] emphasized group learning and community life focused on a shared interest in mathematics" (p. 368). His initial inquiry was focused on comparison groups of Black and Chinese students at his northern California institution. Each of these groups had distinct approaches to mathematics at the university level. In general, Black students studied in solitude, infrequently taking advantage of academic and social resources, while Chinese students depended on classmates and each other for mathematical comprehension and learning. Inspired by their observations, Treisman and his colleagues "did not question that minority students could excel" (1992, p. 368). In fact, Treisman did not merely want students to pass calculus at a basic level, but rather, he aimed for students to acquire the skills to pursue research-level mathematics. In no way could his program be construed as remedial. In particular, introductory calculus students work in supportive small groups with the intent to solve difficult problems they have not yet seen before, usually in the form of exercises distinct from a customary textbook. Meeting in supplemental class sessions the students succeeded mathematically like never before. Treisman's success over the past 30 years shows early intersectional foundations in mathematics instruction.

Corner University's[1] Mathematics department developed a similar program in 2001, leaving the invitation open to students from all backgrounds. As a graduate instructor in this program for two years, I created Emerging Scholars Program–inspired worksheets that students collaborated on in extended 120-minute class sessions. Developing worksheets, to distribute in laboratory-style conditions, proved invaluable for a diverse range of mathematical abilities. Students who struggle benefit from their peers in a low-stress and low-stakes environment, while those who are particularly mathematically successful are challenged further by math problems that extend their knowledge. There is a "social construction of mathematics. Students learn that math is the creation of people—people working together and depending on one another. Interaction, cooperation, and group communication, therefore, are key components of this process" (Moses & Cobb, 2001, p. 120). In this class the community that struggled together, mathematically speaking, came together as a support network for one another both inside and outside of calculus class.

Emerging Scholars Program–type work sets the groundwork for improved, innovative mathematics instruction in the 21st century. Both Treisman's work and my own Corner experience show that the intersectional framework can be learned and applied effectively. It requires an understanding of social constructs that may prohibit student learning and most important, it makes a call for the change in these power dynamics. Treisman's work illustrates that a lack of understanding about student learning differences can lead to a remedial approach that obliquely blames the students. An intersectional lens encourages educators to learn their students' styles and cultural approaches to learning and reshape their own pedagogy accordingly.

It is clear that intersectionality is an appropriate framework with which to view and permeate mathematics instruction in American higher education. This chapter will examine my own day-to-day practices and strategies in my mathematics classroom. This account is certainly not complete and is continuously refined each academic year. Much work still remains in collegiate mathematics pedagogy to ensure learning equity.

Teaching and Learning

My location as a teacher

As an undergraduate in 1996, I was a participant in River College's[2] Summer Program for Women (SPW). The four-week-long summer program has female undergraduates live and learn in community for a concentrated mathematical experience, including two upper-level mathematics classes, seminars, problem solving, and panels dedicated to answering the question, "What's next in mathematics?" Funded by the National Science Foundation, participants complete two courses, honing mathematical reasoning, proof writing, problem solving, and presentation skills while building self-confidence. As a participant in the program, I was forced to draw upon my SPW community of learners for constructing and completing complex homework assignments and making mathematical connections. It was simultaneously apparent that this community environment was inaccessible to me at my home institution. Not all undergraduate women believe they can succeed at the advanced mathematics level, especially as female mathematical role models are few and far between. I completed the program and returned to college as an empowered junior-level mathematics major with a clearer vision of the mathematical community available (and unavailable) to me.

In 2003, as a graduate student, I rejoined the program as a Teaching Assistant, affording me the opportunity to live alongside the students in dormitories, help with homework, but also serve as a mathematical role model—a woman in the midst of her graduate work in mathematics and eager to share excitement about research-level mathematics. In subsequent years, I have traveled back to the program for reunions and two-week-long stays for my own personal mathematical research as a mathematician-in-residence. As a result, participants start to build a larger mathematical community parallel to and intersecting my own network of women in mathematics that informs my own teaching and learning each semester.

My own experience in mathematics is complicated; as a successful white female undergraduate mathematics student, I worked many hours during my undergraduate and graduate years tutoring NCAA Division I athletes. This student-athlete population was often male, Black, and poor with inadequate high school preparation for mathematics. Many of these students struggled daily to find a niche at their largely white privileged universities but were willing to learn from me. I come from a white, privileged, and suburban family in the Mid-Atlantic region, and daily involvement with such a diverse student-athlete population confirmed my intent to become an accessible and equitable collegiate mathematics professor, someone these students did not always experience. However, to date I am also an untenured female mathematics professor at a small liberal arts college in the Midwest. My own research area is in pure mathematics, an area historically known for being dominated by white men. I, too, struggle finding my position within these male power dynamics. The supremacy of white male privilege in mathematics renders us both subordinate in the field. However, Black male student athletes experience an oppression that I do not because of master narratives about race and class and their location in the U.S. social structure. Experiencing my own oppression in the professional field as a woman makes me an empathetic instructor, channeling these incidents for change in my mathematics classroom.

Practices and strategies

Often, the best place to witness a wide variety of student academic skills, mathematical fears, and confidence is a general education math course (for non-majors) that fulfills a college's quantitative reasoning or quantitative literacy requirement; many small liberal arts colleges have this structure. Mathematics in Contemporary Society is my institution's answer for the terminal liberal arts mathematics class that serves students who are non-majors seeking to fulfill their "Quantitative Reasoning" requirement for graduation. Colloquially, colleagues of mine call it "Math for Poets," and one even once said, "Isn't that where you teach students to balance their checkbooks?" The course content is extremely flexible; a professor can cover anything from voting theory and fair division to basic logic, set theory, introductory graph theory, and financial mathematics but *not* checkbook balancing. When teaching this course, I view the module featuring financial mathematics material as most important for undergraduates; it includes one common element for everyone in the world: money. Many mathematicians look down upon social quantitative literacy efforts in higher education, but I believe it is important. The following section contains a few examples of innovation, engaged learning practices, and success that can exist in today's mathematics field. The use of intersectionality gives educators a natural foundation from which to understand and enhance mathematics instruction, learning, and quantitative literacy at the collegiate level.

Strategy one: Collective learning

Traditionally speaking, most mathematical instruction in higher education is based in lecture style. Some instructors are known for mathematical instruction in the "Discovery" or "Inquiry-Based Learning" approach. For this method to succeed, students are given basic guidance about mathematical principles but let loose on their own to "discover" the rest of the course material. At the heart of this instruction is a belief whereby the brightest students will develop creative, original mathematics independently, with very little, if any, instruction. Such a professor might present to a class basic definitions of mathematical concepts but very few results and theorems. Students are expected to put these definitions together independently and creatively to determine the trajectory of material for the term. This practice lends credibility to Moses and Cobb's (founders of The Algebra Project) assertion that the "traditional role of science and math education has been to train an elite, create a priesthood, find a few bright students and bring them into university research. It hasn't been a literacy effort" (2001, p. 16).

To channel a collective, not elite spirit in my class, each syllabus includes this recommendation: "Mathematics is inherently a community-oriented discipline." This sentiment is contrary to the societal loner mathematician stereotype. Within every community, there is a gatekeeper; we know that mathematics is historically guarded by white men, introducing an foundational power dynamic that makes learning and doing mathematics a complex social and emotional endeavor for anyone who is ethnically or gender distinct. To achieve accessibility in learning mathematics, students are encouraged to form homework groups to complete assignments, help each other, and check their work. Classroom morale is high; students report an open space for inquiry, knowing they are not alone in their struggle, questions, or success.

Strategy two: Knowing your students

In order to immediately engage students as a community of learners each semester, I ask students to write about their own *mathematical experiences* as their first assignment. These are valuable examinations of the students. Asking students to answer the question "Why are you taking this mathematics course?" has them evaluate their motivations at the outset of the semester. Other important questions are: "What are your favorite and least favorite memories of mathematics?" "Will you be a major in mathematics? If not, can I convince you?" and "How do you define mathematics?" Given rampant math anxiety in the United States, this is an effective way to rate the class's emotional quotient. Asking students about their goals, aspirations, and history with the upcoming mathematical content allows an instructor to gauge classroom response, often before introducing a certain topic or chapter. If, for instance, my Multivariate Calculus class has many physics majors, spending more time on real-world application problems is necessary to enrich their experience with the theoretical mathematics. Autobiographies give the professor insight into the students' values and identities. In general, mathematics instructors have infrequently, if ever, asked about a student's personal educational history. Students want to give you the full story of their journey through mathematical education. It is intriguing that students, with little prompting, give these identity-based intersectional responses about the unique ways they connect themselves to mathematics. They connect identity to mathematics beyond deficit models that blame students for their social location, focusing on larger issues of environment, institution, or instructional practice. Interestingly, while I do not ask specific questions that address race, class, gender, and ability, students often respond to the autobiographical questions from this perspective. For me, students have written about estranged parents and strained socioeconomic conditions, how their at-home situation affects their learning, and what they hope to do with their undergraduate degree, oftentimes on behalf of the family they have left behind. One student wrote about his personal identity: "I am known as what people now call an ethnic mutt because I am mixed with Jamaican, Trinidad, Chinese, Barbadian, Panamanian, Scottish, Welsh, Spanish, English and Puerto Rican." This student went on to write about the most significant event for him during high school: "It was the day my father told me, 'I don't want to talk to you or see you anymore.'" In another instance, a student from Africa wrote about wanting to get a college education in the United States so that he might cure HIV, a disease that had hurt his village's population and his own close relatives. Other students have written about incarcerated parents and their own personal goals for a college education.

Often in these writings, students identify themselves as the product of a weak secondary school mathematics background, and implicit in their response have been their economic and social locations. When students write about lack of textbooks and mathematical technology in their high school classroom, this is an enormous challenge for me as the professor. Teaching simultaneously students who have experience using graphing calculators and taking Advanced Placement (AP)[3] courses and those who have not even used technology or had AP opportunities is a complicated intersectional classroom matter. In this case, ESP methods are particularly effective in small groups to give a weaker student more practice, while simultaneously challenging a well-prepared student with creative problem solving. The students' lived experiences frame how I approach mathematical content and context throughout any semester.

For those mathematics faculty members who might claim these autobiographies are secondary to conveying content in the mathematics classroom, I would argue that they inform and shape my pedagogy on a continuous basis. These personal student narratives inform my teaching and practice, reminding me that every student comes to the mathematical table with an extremely variable degree of content and confidence. I look back on these narratives continuously throughout the semester and throughout the students' collegiate work. They are valuable instruments with which to measure identity, growth, and experience. For example, during a class discussion of interest-only mortgages, I was well aware of the range of students' social locations in part because of these autobiographical narratives. Despite this, I was still caught off-guard by student comments and judgments about the financial and social implications of common mortgage options at the time, which I will return to later in this chapter.

While not directly shaping mathematical course content, these autobiographies build *context*. Those who are struggling emotionally with the transition to college or otherwise are identified more quickly in my classroom. If necessary, I am able to reach out and put them in touch with the college's resources for wellness, well-being, and academic engagement, all of which impact their ability to learn math. In the future, with upper-level students, I plan to ask: "What have your opinions been about mathematics? and How have they changed over time?" There is value in self-reflection about participation in mathematics; by reading and identifying the students' lived experiences, both mathematical and non-mathematical, the classroom becomes a richer community.

Strategy three: Small group learning in mathematics

As shown, autobiographies provide instructors with useful information about their students. A few years ago, a Black female, first-year student wrote about her apprehension of starting at a primarily white and coeducational college, the first coeducational learning environment in her life. She had up until that point attended an all-girls private school. Her classrooms at college were about to change drastically, and she was uneasy about how she would fit in, both socially and educationally in this setting. This was important information for me to have because in each of my classes, students complete at least one group project. Engendered power dynamics make the mathematical classroom a demanding and stressful place for women in mathematics.

An intersectional framework helps an instructor understand that the power dynamics regarding gender and math are not static but are continually reinforced when race, class, and ability, to name a few factors, are also a part of the classroom community. Jackson (2004) explained that "women usually do not engage in the aggressive, highly competitive sparring that sometimes prevails in mathematical conversations among men" (p. 783). In general, it is found that female mathematicians work on mathematics in groups using a conversational approach. As a result, when I assign groups in my classroom, I am mindful of gender and racial balance. I was particularly attuned to the gender balance of the group to which the young woman described above was assigned that semester. I try to form groups of three students, either made up of solely men or women, or one man and two women, as I find these arrangements diffuse the male mathematical power dynamic in these small groupings each semester. I want mathematical group projects to be a positive learning experience for all students and a unique way to be evaluated. Response from students on groupings has been positive; they are asked (as part of their rubric) to honestly evaluate their group members on contribution, creativity, and collegiality. Students report overall satisfaction with team members and the experience. My use of an intersectional lens allows me to interrupt what has traditionally been a male-dominated field with broader ways of teaching and learning.

Strategy four: Using features of the Emerging Scholars Program as instructional tools

As an ESP instructor in graduate school, I was a mentor and monitor and not a solutions manual, as so many mathematics teachers tend to be at the introductory level. Students were forced into consulting with one another for problem solutions while also encouraging each other as they worked. As a result of ESP methods, my students became tremendous mathematical communicators; they had to explain their calculations and logic to each other, with solid reasoning and confidence. I continue the practice of problem-solving workshops with my students currently, particularly in an introductory-level calculus course. This gives students the unique opportunity to see intensely challenging mathematics at a basic level (outside the realm of a textbook). As a professional discipline, mathematics is a community of practice and the ESP methods reinforce this philosophy to students in a unique way. Mathematics is not so much a "right" or "wrong" answer for ESP students.

Treisman (1992) wrote that "the time has come to reexamine undergraduate instruction and to make it more responsive to the needs of today's students. We can no longer offer courses that half of our students fail, nor can we lower our standards" (p. 372). Using my experience with ESP, I infuse my classroom approach with open conversation and problem solving. Students work their own examples in class and report their findings to the whole group. Often in my introductory courses, students work on an ongoing "open-ended" mathematical problem. For instance, one semester, my students worked on computing the volume of snow that would fill the arch of a campus building. The task came with few instructions; students were encouraged to use any creative strategy and write a final report with their results. Projects that were submitted included straightforward measurements, but also photos of students accompanied with angle computations, calculus, and the chemistry of snow. Students get a lot out of small group, ongoing projects in classes, learning not only mathematics but also collaboration and good communication. One student recounted, "I thought my team was all over the place, but we combined efforts to produce this report." Their final summary was creative, professional, and reflected each team member's unique strengths. This group in particular was a perfect example of intersectional context creating excellent mathematics.

Strategy five: Responsive pedagogy

Teaching with an intersectional lens requires an educator to be responsive in the classroom but also recognizes that learning to respond is ongoing. It is not necessary to have every answer at every moment but rather, knowing how to access, find information, and return to a topic. As mentioned earlier, in the spring of 2008, my class and I had just completed our discussion of how to calculate monthly mortgage payments when a hand rose in the very back of the room. The student inquired, "Can you explain the mortgage crisis to us?!!" The following class meeting, I arrived armed with worksheets to calculate varying term and interest rate loan payments, including an "interest-only" loan computation. (Interest-only loans are based on the premise that the borrower only pays the interest on the principal balance of their loan each month.) The students worked for about 20 minutes on their calculations and we checked our work together. When closing our discussion for the day, I asked for any further questions. Another student inquired, "Why would a person get an interest-only loan? The people who get them must be stupid!" I was caught off-guard and not prepared for a social discussion about the philosophy of procuring interest-only loans. Nonetheless, we brainstormed as a class for a few minutes about reasons that the public would be attracted to interest-only loans; in fact, they had a difficult time thinking of motivation, focusing mainly on the "stupid" Americans who were now in foreclosure (a common media stereotype at the time). Finally, our discussion yielded the idea that some Americans would be interested in short-term, interest-only loans as a viable option to be located somewhere temporarily with the plan that they will either sell or refinance the terms of the loan in the near future. In retrospect, I could have dealt with this mortgage discussion with more thought and more social context, including comprehensive examples using race, gender, and class.

For the future, a discussion of predatory lenders is in order. For example, we could discuss that in the United States owning a home is held out as part of the American Dream, a master narrative that frames both individual and collective self-worth. However, the reality is that many people, due to economic structures, cannot or do not own a home. Approaching this topic from a case study perspective, examining gainfully employed American borrowers, mostly people of color and people of all races with low incomes who were caught in tangles of loans and deceptive corporate financial practices, would be appropriate. In this classroom, I was well aware of a student audience from the most needy to affluent of home lives. It pained me to think that the mathematical example at hand could be a very real experience for some students and so unfamiliar and foreign to others. The social construction of this mathematical problem in class reinforced my students' identities of class and race. This experience also reaffirmed my commitment to financial and quanti-tative literacy.

Reflections and next steps

As an educator, my instructional practice is continually evolving with each academic year. I have given thought to refining my mathematical autobiography assignment, having students share their narratives with the whole class. This would have students get to know one another quickly, have a good sense of others in the classroom, and promote classroom citizenship. Perhaps small group interactions would be a particularly appropriate way of sharing their histories. To further develop my own responsive pedagogy, I hope to prepare case studies of real-world quantitative accounts to add to the mathematical conversation in the classroom, particularly at the non-majors' level. Conceivably for instance, the sociological and intersectional discussion that is relevant to financial mathematics would then be an invitation for students, not a surprise for the professor.

My own understanding of intersectionality and teaching and learning is ongoing. I participate in sociological reading and associated book groups and discussions. Since intersectionality is distinct from my own discipline, I must reach out for this context, engaging with researchers and other faculty in relevant work in various disciplinary areas. At my home institution, a col-league and I convened a cross-disciplinary Quantitative Literacy Faculty Learn-ing Community to discuss and learn definition and methodology, and strategize together. I seek out my own community of faculty and confidantes who represent a continuum of intersecting identities and intersectional lived experiences. Certainly, crafting this chapter has contributed to my personal intersectional reflection as a teacher.

Active mathematics recruiting

As continued community outreach, I participate in the Expanding Your Horizons (EYH) workshop program for sixth grade girls. The EYH program "nurture[s] girls' interest in science and math courses to encourage them to consider careers in science, technology, engineering, and math" (Expanding Your Horizons Network, 2010). In spring 2009, I had a white female student struggling to fit in. She was high achieving mathematically in her first year, but found herself unhappy with her college choice and had decided to transfer to another school. I selected her to be my workshop assistant for EYH, wanting to encourage her to stick with mathematics, even if it happened at another institution. She and I had great success sharing our enthusiasm for mathematics with nearly 40 sixth grade girls. I heard from her recently and she wrote, "While I probably won't be further pursuing math after undergrad, I have stuck with it because I enjoy it so much and have had so many positive experiences (including your class!) I'm sure you also agree that whatever I decide to do in the future, my interest and background in math will be helpful. Thank you again for your inspiration to pursue math (even as a girl!!)." I am careful in my classroom to mention relevant mathematical research (even in an introductory-level course). There are numerous enrichment and research opportunities available for undergraduates in mathematics, and I am watchful to point these out to students, recommending that they apply and examine creative ways to find their mathematical path. My role as an instructor is greater than defining concepts and applications; more so, it is about linking the mathematics to the real-life and real-world experiences.

Perhaps inspired by then president of Harvard University Lawrence H. Summers's 2005 controversial remarks about women not having the aptitude for high-end scientific professions, the American Association of University Women (AAUW)[4] recently published a report entitled "Why So Few? Women in Science, Technology, Engineering, and Mathematics" (2010). In their study, they conclude that stereotypes are still hard at work throughout primary education well into colleges and universities. "Most people associate science and math fields with 'male' and humanities and arts fields with 'female.' . . . Implicit bias is common, even among individuals who actively reject these stereotypes" (Hill et al., 2010, p. xvi). Many women and students of color in the United States do not pursue mathematics because of a lack of outside encouragement and doubts about being successful. AAUW gives recommendations for females in STEM fields that are directly applicable and successful for any cross-section of student population: cultivate a culture of respect in any classroom, send an inclusive message about descriptors of a good student, broaden the scope of early course work with real-world applications, and actively recruit students into a STEM major (Hill et al., 2010). Eric Gutstein (2006) writes that "limited mathematical understanding can prevent students from more fully grasping important political ideas . . . issues of academic achievement are concrete, and the barriers are real" (pp. 29–30). With a renewed effort to impart quantitative literacy to our students (across all levels), engaging and including other populations, educators create an informed citizenry, able to meet Barack Obama's recent call for excellence in STEM fields.

Stereotypical images of what makes a mathematician and elite gatekeeping in the discipline counteract intersectional work in the classroom. Faculty need to strive on a daily basis, with their students' identities and experiences in mind, to improve collegiate mathematics and the mathematics field for the future. To start, faculty must do a careful examination of quantitative literacy with the goal of creating an informed democracy. Banks adds in her book *Black Women Undergraduates, Cultural Capital, and College Success* (2009) that "implementation of strategy and policy that promotes and promulgates equity requires bringing the need for it to a high level of consciousness" (p. 125). Despite mathematics' perceptible disconnect with intersectionality, the use of the theory is an appropriate and indispensable framework from which mathematics faculty should perform their practice for the future.

Notes

[1] The institutions mentioned in this chapter are referred to using pseudonyms. Corner University is a large, public 4-year research institution located in a Mid-Atlantic state. The university is made up of 10 professional colleges from which students can earn undergraduate and graduate degrees. Corner University has a student body of 20,000 (approximately 13,000 are undergraduates). The African American student population makes up approximately 9.4% of the total student population, the Asian and Asian Pacific American percentage is 11% and Hispanic/Latino students account for 4.5%. Overall, approximately 30% of the total student population is from underrepresented groups in higher education.

[2] River College is a 4-year small liberal arts college located in the Midwest. The college enrolls 2,000 undergraduates in an isolated small town with a population of less than 17,000.

[3] The Advanced Placement program offers standardized college-level course work in high schools in the United States and Canada. Participating colleges and universities offer college credit to students who score well on exams.

[4] The AAUW is an advocacy group designed to promote education and equity for women and girls in the United States.

References

Banks, C. A. (2009). *Black women undergraduates, cultural capital, and college success.* New York: Peter Lang.

Bennett, J., & Briggs, W. (2008). *Understanding and using mathematics: A quantitative reasoning approach* (4th ed.). New York: Addison-Wesley.

Dill, B. T., & Zambrana, R. E. (Eds.). (2009). *Emerging intersections: Race, class, and gender in theory, policy, and practice.* New Brunswick, NJ: Rutgers University Press.

Expanding Your Horizons Network. (2010). About us. Retrieved from http://www.expand ingyourhorizons.org

Gutstein, E. (2006). *Reading and writing the world with mathematics: Toward a pedagogy for social justice.* New York: Routledge, Taylor & Francis Group.

Henrion, C. (1997). *Women in mathematics: The addition of difference.* Bloomington: Indiana University Press.

Hill, C., Corbett, C., & St. Rose, A. (2010). *Why so few? Women in science, technology, engineering, and mathematics.* Washington, DC: American Association of University Women.

Jackson, A. (2004) Has the women-in-mathematics problem been solved? *Notices of the AMS,* 51(7), 776-783.

Moses, R. P., & Cobb, Jr., C. E. (2001). *Radical equations: Math literacy and civil rights.* Boston: Beacon Press.

Steele, C. M. (2010). *Whistling Vivaldi: And other clues to how stereotypes affect us.* New York: W. W. Norton & Co.

Steen, L. A. (2001). *Mathematics and democracy.* Washington, DC: National Council on Education and the Disciplines.

Summers, L. H. (2005). Remarks at NBER conference on diversifying the science and engineering workforce. Retrieved from http://www.president.harvard.edu/speeches/ summers_2005/nber.php

Treisman, U. (1992). Studying students studying calculus: A look at the lives of minority mathematics students in college. *The College Mathematics Journal,* 23(5), 362-372.

Daring Pedagogy
Dialoguing about Intersectionality
and Social Justice

Julia R. Johnson, Mary González, Cris Ray, Jessica Hager,
Diana Leon, Sally Spalding, and Tiffany Brigham

As Dill (2009) contends, "Intersectional scholarship is the intellectual and scholarly manifestation of diversity. It is an outgrowth of the struggles of oppressed people to end oppression and achieve social justice" (p. 248). In our work as social justice educators and/or advocates, we concur with Dill's position that "[t]eaching is one of the primary modes of dissemination of intersectional thinking" that requires "innovative and creative ways to teach about power, inequality, and social justice" (p. 249). The purpose of this essay is to examine the pedagogical interventions that are necessary to do intersectional analysis as part of social justice pedagogy. As social justice educators, Julia and Mary regularly teach about identity, power, and oppression in college classrooms, student development workshops, and faculty development programs.[1] In all of these contexts, we have learned that teaching the theory of intersectionality and social justice is complex. What makes this teaching complex is not the concept of intersectionality or its constituent parts. Rather, what is most challenging is the work that must be done to engage in the complicated, nuanced, and rigorous analysis of selfhood, relationships, power, and privilege that trenchant intersectional analysis demands.

While we collaborated to write this book chapter, we were reminded of how difficult it can be to move beyond surface-level theoretical conversations about intersections of identity. Teachers and students[2] must be willing to engage (daring) pedagogical interventions that will create space and opportunity for students to develop their grammars for talking about identity and power. Power is a part of every pedagogical process, and addressing power dynamics within the pedagogical relationship is imperative for productive teaching and learning to occur generally and is particularly important to examine when one teachers about privilege and oppression. In this chapter, we share our attempts to dialogue about intersectionality, the pedagogical interventions we implemented, and how our student coauthors responded to that process.[3]

The authors of this chapter embody a constellation of intersecting experiences and identities. We are positioned in various institutional locations at our university and within social hierarchies. We connected through our work at a private, liberal arts, Methodist-affiliated, undergraduate university located in Texas. We speak from positions as staff, faculty, undergraduate students, business professionals, nonprofit professionals, and/or graduate students. We represent disciplinary and interdisciplinary spaces such as Communication Studies, Education, Business, English, and Feminist Studies. We also identify as Chicana, queer, disabled, Latina, white, TLGBPAAIQTS,[4] working class, middle class, disabled, African American, heterosexual, (Protestant) Christian, atheist, formerly Catholic, biracial South Asian, and more. Some of us know each other through formal contexts such as the college classroom or campus offices, and others of us met for the first time through this project. Our intention was to bring together faculty, staff, and students committed to intersectionality and social justice. Although classroom teaching is one important space intersectionality is addressed, there are many student affairs staff who dedicate themselves to social justice pedagogy in their daily work outside the formal classroom. By bringing together faculty, staff, and students—some of whom have worked together in classrooms, workshops, or through student activities—we hoped to disrupt the artificial (and yet real) barriers that often divide academic affairs and student affairs and to enhance interdisciplinary exchange. We believe that intersectionality is the purview of us all and should be addressed at all organizational levels and through all educational activities. As colleagues who regularly teach social justice courses, Julia and Mary constructed the framework for the project, and our student coauthors agreed to explore intersectionality therein. Our interdisciplinary backgrounds lead us to use a pedagogical model that foregrounded dialogic process, examination of privilege and oppression, and collaboration among all participants.

In this chapter, we offer a pedagogical strategy for teaching intersectionality that emerged from our work together. In order to collaboratively generate this book chapter, our group dialogued online and in person over a five-month period and explored how intersectionality shapes our self-understandings, educational experiences, pedagogical choices, and relationships within higher education. A core assumption that guided our collaboration was that intersectional analysis requires a nuanced examination of how identities are shaped by privilege and oppression. As we have learned through this project and others, it takes time and practice to generate nuanced intersectional analysis. In this project, we regularly attempted nuanced analyses but often found our language and analytic skills wanting. Thus, we were collectively prompted to identify more effective pedagogical strategies to develop our skills to this end. We begin this chapter by first contextualizing our study in relevant literature about intersectionality in higher education. Second, we explain how we dialogued about intersectionality and the pedagogical interventions we used to that end. Finally, we explore the challenges and barriers that emerged during our process and provide suggestions for navigating those challenges for teacher-practitioner-scholars.

Intersectionality in Theoretical Context

In an effort to promote social justice, activists and academics have developed theories and pedagogies that address the importance of identity in social life. As a result of this theoretical and political work, women's/gender studies and ethnic studies programs were created and numerous advances in educational policy and equal access emerged (Cory, 2008; Elenes, 2001). At the same time, essentialist conceptions of identity have perpetuated the invisibility of individuals who fall outside clearly defined identity frameworks (Kumashiro, 2001b). Understanding and incorporating intersectionality have been critical in overcoming some of the limitations of singular identity models (Crenshaw, 1989; Dhamoon, 2011; Jordan-Zachery, 2007), including moving individuals beyond choosing one salient identity (Cory, 2008; Pearson, 2010; Samuels & Ross-Sheriff, 2008) and understanding how to address personal experiences while simultaneously examining social and structural dynamics (Dill & Zambrana, 2009).

As the dominant model for addressing social justice issues, identity politics has been a practical instrument to examine issues impacting historically oppressed groups. At the core of identity politics is binary logic that positions an "us" against a "them" (Cole, 2008; Young, 1986). One of the consequences of this binary duality has been the promotion of homogeneous understandings of identity (Cole, 2008; Crenshaw, 1995) and the disenfranchisement of nondominant groups. This fundamental flaw of identity politics was the catalyst for an urgent incorporation of intersectional frameworks (Cole, 2008; Shields, 2008).

Intersectionality pedagogy is not neutral. Not only do intersectional frameworks recognize multiple identities (Brown, 1997; McCall, 2005), this type of theoretical framework promotes exploring how oppressions overlap, are perpetuated, and how oppression and privilege exist simultaneously (Collins, 2004; Dill, McLaughlin, & Nieves, 2007; Dill & Zambrana, 2009; Elenes, 2001; Jones, 2009; Pearson, 2010; Shields, 2008). As Freire (1970) explains, "naming" (identifying and labeling oppression) is central to its deconstruction. An intersectional position encourages "naming" oppression and identifying privilege, which creates opportunity for greater self-consciousness, ally formation, coalition building, and an overall stronger social justice movement (Knight, 2002; Pearson, 2010; Shields, 2008).

Furthermore, intersectionality is an important element of social justice education, and social justice education has always been grounded in an understanding of selfhood. As González-Lopez (2006) asserts, "My own self in the process of intellectual growth is becoming part of a larger process of social transformation" (p. 24). Self-examination that serves the interests of social transformation and justice requires awareness of multiple identities as well as more complex understandings of the interconnections between personal identity, structures, communities, and relationships (Baxter Magolda, 2001; Jones, 1997, 2009; Kegan, 1994). Considering the significant role that relationships and coalitions have played in the social justice movement, intersectionality provides an opportunity to strengthen these connections by promoting visibility of those in the most marginalized spaces (Cole, 2008; Crenshaw, 1995).

Although intersectionality has been a powerful response to identity politics, the structures that support identity politics and essentialist[5] frameworks in mainstream society are pervasive. Harris and Ordona (1990) express the frustration of the system by stating, "Clearly, shared oppression by itself does not override the forces that keep us apart" (p. 304). At the foundation of social justice is the desire to create a world that allows individuals to recognize their full humanity (Freire, 1970) as well as a consciousness of all forms of oppression (Dei, 2007; Pearson, 2010). As the social justice movement continues to evolve, intersectional pedagogy offers frameworks that could potentially move the movement forward by addressing some of the limitations of identity politics and by highlighting the intimate connection between individual experience and structures of power (Johnson, Bhatt, & Patton, 2007). As Pearson (2010) contends, "[W]e are all ensnared in this process of constructing/deconstructing oppression" (p. 341), or at least we should be.

Intersectional Pedagogy in Action

As a group, we embarked on this project outside of a formal classroom to develop our understandings of intersectionality and social justice. Mary and Julia created the framework for our process that included face-to-face interactions and e-mail exchanges. The (current or former) student coauthors were invited to participate in this project because of their commitment to social justice. Either Julia or Mary knew the students and had spoken with each of them about intersectionality in classrooms, through informal conversations, and/or through campus activism. We explained that they were chosen because of their social justice work and that the process would be the basis for a book chapter about intersectionality in higher education.[6]

Between May and September 2010, we engaged in several e-mail exchanges and two face-to-face dialogues. Our face-to-face meetings took place in a campus building dedicated to student services, including the Office of Diversity Education under Mary's direction. All of our meetings were videorecorded and subsequently transcribed by Cris. We compiled e-mail responses and transcripts and have used excerpts from both to conceptualize and present our learning about the implications of intersectional pedagogy.

We blended face-to-face and online dialogues for two primary reasons. First, Julia and Mary wanted to ensure that we all had time to critically reflect on the ways intersectionality impacts our lives and the ideas that arose during group interactions. While face-to-face dialogue creates space for ideas to emerge organically, many students need additional time to process ideas. As Maher and Hoon (2008) argue, online exchanges "give students a chance to interact more thoughtfully with each other without the constraints of time inherent in classroom-based discussions" (p. 205). Furthermore, online learning is increasingly used to address questions of identity and difference (Rasmussen, Nichols, & Ferguson, 2006; Wang, 2007). Second, many of us were in different geographical spaces during the five months we worked together. Because all authors had access to computers, we were able to blend learning modes and to maintain momentum with group dialogue.

To prepare for our first meeting, we asked our coauthors to read Berger and Guidroz's (2009) introductory chapter from *The Intersectional Approach: Transforming the Academy through Race, Class, and Gender* and Dill and Zambrana's (2009) chapter "Critical Thinking about Inequality: An Emerging Lens." The coauthors were also asked to journal about the connection between their most and least salient identities. At our first meeting, we gathered around a conference table and introduced ourselves, briefly described our identities, described our working style in groups, and explained our under-

standings of intersectionality. In addition, we established guidelines for interacting (triggers, how to keep a conversation going when we are trigged, our
commitment to listening to others). After our first meeting, the students
continued the conversation online by answering the following questions: How
have intersections been addressed in your teaching and learning (curriculum,
student activities programming, and so forth)? How have intersectional dynamics played out in your relationships with staff, students, and teachers?
How does academic discourse about diversity inform and/or disrupt analysis
of identity intersections? What is the relationship between intersectionality,
power, and social justice? We also asked that the students recount specific
experiences they have had in which their intersecting identities were acknowledged and erased or ignored. Using their own experiences as a point of reference, we then asked our coauthors to answer this question: How did these
situations impact your understandings of who you are and what identities are
valued and/or devalued in higher education? Students addressed these questions over e-mail and replied to the entire group when submitting their responses. In order to assess how comfortable students were with discussing
intersectionality and to minimize influencing students' responses, Mary and
Julia did not answer these questions.

Based on the responses students shared, it became clear that the students
had difficulty addressing intersectionality complexly. They were able to talk
about one or two identities independently, but they struggled to examine their
interdependence and how identity intersections were connected to privilege
and oppression. To help move the conversation forward, Julia and Mary e-
mailed the students and asked questions designed to prompt elaboration of
their analyses. Although most coauthors demonstrated an interest in developing their responses, they struggled with how to do so. As one student commented later, "I think communicating via e-mail was more difficult than I had
anticipated" and being together in person provided more of a "safe space" to
share and unpack identity. Based on the e-mail exchanges, Mary and Julia
knew the group was at an analytic impasse.

Julia and Mary strategized about how to advance the group's work in our
second face-to-face meeting. As we brainstormed, we sought to identify narratives that would fill the specific analytic gaps we identified in the e-mail responses, including our coming out stories and how race and class impact our
understanding of queer identity and interactions we've had with co-workers
about religious identity and sexual orientation. We continually returned to the
possibility of analyzing our respective childhood sexual abuse. We returned to
this topic for several reasons. First, childhood sexual abuse is often seen as a
solely personal phenomenon; however, it is a manifestation of structural

inequality. We believed that addressing such a "personal" issue[7] would be important to push our coauthors into analyzing how power and ideology manifest in their own lives/relationships. Second, by analyzing how we made intersectional sense of the abuse perpetuated against us, we hoped to illustrate that the personal can be pedagogical, particularly when the personal is contexualized within discussion of ideologies/master narratives. Finally, we hoped that by sharing our own experiences with each other, we might, in one sense, disrupt our privileged position as facilitators by demonstrating a willingness to make ourselves vulnerable to the group.

Mary and Julia began the second face-to-face meeting by talking with the group about how we might deepen our collective analysis of intersectionality in general, followed by an explanation of how we imagined achieving that goal through a fishbowl dialogue.[8] We faced each other as the students sat around us in a semicircle. Both of us began our narratives with a direct statement about being abused. For Mary, this statement was, "When I was four to eight years old my stepdad abused me" and for Julia, "I'm also a survivor of sexual abuse. My [genetic] father was my abuser." Beyond these statements, we offered no specifics about the nature of the abuse. The purpose and function of the story were to talk about how the abuse had impacted our understanding of identity, how intersectionality worked in our experience, and how our identities were impacted by dominant ideologies (including the interconnections of privilege and oppression). We discussed topics such as: The connection between identifying as queer and the dominant culture's assumption that to be TLGBPAAIQTS is a byproduct of abuse; how the patriarchy of Catholicism intersects with the patriarchy of (white and Mexican) working-class identity which requires women and girls to engender silence, even about sexual abuse; the ways sexual abuse and sexual assault are mechanisms of patriarchy used to control women's bodies generally; the role whiteness plays in facilitating women's ability to address abuse, particularly if the women's social class and ability status give them access to support services and cultural legitimacy; and the ways that colonizers utilized rape to control indigenous women's bodies (including how that history is differentially written on our bodies and positions us against each other in contemporary culture). We connected historical events and cultural dynamics to our "personal" experiences. We also examined how we simultaneously experience privilege and oppression in relationship to abuse and the ways that our respective identities (Latina and white, queer femme and gender queer, and so forth) might be positioned against each other. By comparing our different social positions, we were careful to talk about how we were structurally advantaged and/or oppressed in relationship to ideologies such as white supremacy, sexism, and ableism. We specifically discussed how we learned to think about the structural nature of abuse. When Mary asked Julia, "At what point do you feel like you started making it more structural" ze[9] talked about learning to think about it structurally from a friend: "Once I had the realization that it was structural, I could then starting taking what I knew about . . . sexism, about race, about class, about nationality and layer by layer . . . take . . . a personal example and go [through it] discourse by discourse." As our dialogue ended, we checked in with each other and also checked in with our coauthors to discern how they were doing. We reassured them that we were fine and explained that we did not need them to care-take us.

Engaging intersectional analysis of childhood sexual abuse was a daring, but necessary, pedagogical choice. First, this pedagogical choice is risky because it requires the use of personal narrative which can be misinterpreted as narcissistic; however, effective social justice pedagogy requires self-analysis and analyzing the self in relationship to structures of power (including institutional forces and ideologies/master narratives). Second, by analyzing the structural nature of the "personal," we intended to model both intersectionality and vulnerability: We wanted to run risks similar to those run by our student coauthors and to help them analyze their own identities as well as the identities of others. We were not asking them to share traumatic experiences. In fact, we do not believe intersectional analysis requires analysis of trauma and we emphasized such to students. Finally, sharing our experiences allowed Mary and Julia to analyze how our particular bodies were positioned similarly and differently in power hierarchies and to model how collaborative exploration of multiple positionalities is critical for forming alliances across lines of difference. Through that exercise and its subsequent unpacking with students, our collective understanding of identity intersections began in earnest. We also reinforced and challenged particular student-teacher power dynamics, which we address below.

Student responses and challenges

Immediately following our dialogue, we asked how the group was doing and what they needed. At first, our coauthors had difficulty responding to this question, which is not uncommon when students process emotionally and intellectually difficult material. To help them process their responses, we asked them to free-write. When they finished, we asked each person to share their thoughts, if they so desired. As one might expect, their feedback varied greatly and reflected various degrees of intellectual and emotional struggle. Below, we share some of their comments. To protect student anonymity, we've assigned each respondent a pseudonym.

The first respondent, Morgan, expressed confusion about how to contribute to our conversation and with naming an event that prompts intersectional analysis. In addition, hir comments illustrate struggles with privilege and its role in impeding critical reflection:

> I feel like I don't really know how to contribute to like the discussion, because I don't really feel like there's one lynch-pin moment that I can filter discussion through. And I think part of that is because in most circumstances I've always sat in a privileged position so I never really had to investigate anything. Um so I don't really know like if I can sit here and tell you about my intersectionalities from one experience or anything like that. Um, so I don't really know where to start to contribute.

The second speaker, Guadalupe, blamed hirself and feared perpetuating privilege—both of which appeared to be manifestations of internalized oppression. In the example below, ze took a comment from the dialogue and described feelings of self-judgment. Significantly, ze also came out as an abuse survivor:

> I actually feel kind of shitty. . . . I think it was you Julia who said, "When you don't look for these patterns you're perpetuating privilege." And I have a very similar situation that I've never shared with anyone but my girlfriend. Just thinking about all these things and actually seeing how I can bring the experience into a structural level, which is something I've never done, just kind of makes me feel really crappy about myself that by like never having . . . actually focused on how these things intersect, that I've been somehow perpetuating this system of privilege. And even how you guys were going through your stories, I was like, "Well mine . . . it doesn't fit here and it doesn't fit here." But taking the time to journal about it and actually like think about the ways in which it could fit into these categories, it does. . . . I guess just the words perpetuating privilege were really strong.

Understandably, Guadalupe experienced vulnerability as a result of audiencing our conversation, primarily because ze simultaneously identified as an abuse survivor and as privileged. As is frequently the case during dialogues detailing the personal effects of structural power, students' vulnerability and resulting anxiety can shift into personal blame.[10] When students internalize blame, we work with them to understand how these feelings are a response to new awarenesses of structural power and not an example of their "deficiency."

Sammi built on the comments provided by Morgan and added a layer of analysis questioning the development of hir intersectional thinking. Like Morgan, Sammi commented about the energy required to conduct intersectional analysis:

> I was just going to add to [Morgan] like what you said about not really being able to think of like a certain event or experience or even like assimilate all these things. I feel the same way . . . like I'm not in a place where I can do that yet. . . . [W]atching y'all working through that was pretty amazing because the level of analysis that your discussion was at was, I don't know, kind of mind-blowing. So I'm kind of wondering if I'm just not there to see things in that way and if like I could find something. I also feel like that would take a lot.

Importantly, Morgan felt confirmed by this response. As is often the case as students are learning new theoretical vocabularies, they compare their current levels of understanding against each other and against faculty. Certainly, one of the risks a faculty member takes when modeling analysis is placing themselves as an analytic standard, an issue we return to in our analysis.

Immediately following the post-free-writing conversation, we asked students to review the writing they completed in preparation for our meeting and to reflect more fully about the intersectional implications of their theorizing. This exercise offered them the opportunity to develop their analytic skills and to explore the value of their own narration. We talked about their analyses during the remainder of our second meeting.

As the conversation continued, the fourth co-author, Jariah, explicitly addressed the emotional energy required in conversations about intersectionality and noted the differences between face-to-face dialogue and e-mail exchanges:

> One thing [Morgan] and I were talking about . . . was that it's just very difficult to write in an e-mail what you're going through or thinking. So for me, like um, for years I've been trying to like figure out myself and all these intersecting identities. . . . I started seeing all the intersections and I just like what you're saying. It's amazing hearing other people's stories and at the same time it's like I'm in a place, I've gotten to a place where I can see the connections, but it's such a spaced out story. . . . I think for me it's just like the exhaustion of it all but also being able to sit in a room and feel the safety and like, I think it's an awesome experience to be able to have this moment. I was thinking I could go home and talk to [my partner] about it but I almost wish, like, she had this space as well for her. You know, like you wish it for other people. Because even though it's so hard, it's really amazing process to go through.

Analyzing the dialectic tensions between the personal and structural requires emotional energy as well as intellectual effort. As our coauthors commented, there is great value to be derived from this work, but one has to be willing to integrate various types of learning, including emotions that cannot be predicted or controlled. Importantly, the students built community with one another (and with us) by virtue of conducting the affectively charged analysis. While the work was "exhausting," Jariah felt that this kind of experience would also be valuable for others, including hir partner. Emotional expression was even a source of community building amongst the students—two students spoke openly about the role of crying in their learning.

The fifth student, Rory, contributed little to our group conversation. When we asked Rory if ze wanted to say something, ze stated, "Not right now. I really don't know what to contribute I guess to the whole thing." Initially, Mary and Julia assumed this co-author needed more time to process the fishbowl activity; however, this particular coauthor demonstrated great difficulty or unwillingness to share in general. We contemplated whether Rory did not feel safe or was triggered by some aspects of the dialogue. We employed multiple strategies to encourage hir participation but were only successful soliciting feedback when Rory was questioned directly. Even in those situations, ze resisted discussing identity intersections.

Pedagogy and power

Traditionally, institutional power is bequeathed to a teacher and students are expected to perform as receptacles for teachers' knowledge (Freire, 1970). Of course, critical and/or feminist pedagogies have challenged these oppressive dynamics, repugning hegemonic authority and questioning how identities are navigated in the classroom. Julia and Mary deliberately attempted to disrupt our authority even as we structured the group interactions and discussions of intersectionality. We navigated this authority-disruption dialectic in a variety of ways. We presented discussion questions but created space for students to respond to each other before interjecting. When the group dialogue stagnated, we posed questions to move the conversation forward and we also made ourselves vulnerable to the group. Our decision to analyze our personal experience illustrates well the dialectic of power disruption. We wanted to model the vulnerability we were asking of students, but in sharing our stories and analyzing it as we did, we also set a standard for intersectional analysis that felt intimidating to some coauthors.

Following our workshop, our coauthors commented (free-form) about their experience of the day. In general, they stated that the fishbowl was useful and stated that it "was the clarifying element" of the day. Subsequently, several coauthors shared additional feedback about the fishbowl exercise. Guadalupe stated:

> I didn't initially realize what an impact the exercise . . . would mean for me. When thinking back it really helped me to break down the "them" and "us" relationship and to also see an example of what intersectionality *can* look like. . . . The majority of my comfort came from the fishbowl. . . . That is where I gathered the courage to examine my own experiences.

In contrast, Morgan felt that we "exposed [ourselves] in a way that promoted inclusivity" but also commented that the fishbowl "positioned [us] as experienced participants in this sort of work. So, while it maybe engendered a feeling of community and openness on a personal level, I don't know to what extent it worked to dispel my own fears . . . that we were out of our depth." Sammi contended that ze

> felt like some of the power structures . . . broke down when you and Mary had the conversation with each other   , It was a time when the tables were turned and we heard from the facilitators. I thought it was a very beneficial move   , , It helped though since the same was being asked of the students.

As these comments illustrate, our attempt to disrupt power by analyzing our own experiences both facilitated our coauthors' intersectional understandings while simultaneously creating anxiety for Morgan about being "out of our depth" to produce similar analyses.

In general, our coauthors were attuned to power dynamics and commented that they knew the "bulk of the power resided with the . . . people who set up the meetings/asked the questions/got it all rolling." Sammi noted that power dynamics were "at play for each individual in a different way depending on their relationships (or lack thereof) with the other participants, and the level of relationship that they shared with each person." Morgan felt pressure in the process as a result of hir relationship with Julia: "I was not necessarily her student anymore, the dialogue was open and I had to deviate from my expectation of there being a 'right answer'" and to confront hir role as a "people pleaser" to move the dialogue forward. Importantly, the e-mail exchanges were important to some of our coauthors. Online communication was the space in which they "shared the most" and where power hierarchies were interrupted. Sammi commented, "Once our dialogue moved to an online setting the power seemed to shift . . . we were the ones in control of what would be said and how we would answer the questions."

The entire pedagogical process has served as an important reminder that power dynamics are inevitable, but our agency as facilitator-educators should be used to mitigate pedagogical hegemony. Additionally, our students can and do push us to create pedagogical spaces that are more empowering for them and that enhance their ability to be critical agents of social change.

Potholes, Barriers, and Hurdles

At the beginning of this chapter, we asserted that intersectional and social justice pedagogies require a different kind of work from teachers and students because complicated examinations of selfhood and power demand critical reflection about the connections between the personal and structural, a willingness to be vulnerable, and the release of foundational assumptions about who we are and how the world works. It is not surprising that social justice educators face many institutional and personal hurdles with intersectional pedagogy, including challenging perceived "objectivity" and traditional curricular content as well as disrupting the "norms about the teacher-student relationship" (Bell, Love, Washington, & Weinstein, 2007, pp. 392–393). As we reviewed the transcripts of our dialogues and e-mail exchanges, familiar barriers emerged. We identified several hindrances to addressing the structural inequalities that undergird intersectional analysis.

Emotional Intensity and Deflection

Emotional intensity is intrinsic to social justice pedagogy. When one addresses privilege and oppression, emotions surface and take the form of feelings like anger directed toward social groups or instructors, resistance to unpacking topics such as racism or Christian supremacy, fear of offending others, or grief about one's experience of oppression or complicity with dominance. As Griffin and Ouellett (2007) continue, "[P]articipants who feel overwhelmed by new feelings and information in reaction to what they are learning in social justice education courses often feel immobilized and powerless to change oppression, withdraw from participating in group dialogue, and/or fear being perceived as a bigot (among other dynamics)" (p. 110).

Many teachers and students are uncomfortable with the affective dimension of social justice. Although teachers should not act as therapists, we contend that the majority of discomfort expressed about emotion in the classroom is the result of a deep-seated investment in traditional epistemologies. As Simpson (2003) states, "Traditional epistemologies often assert that knowledge is pure, abstract, rational, universal, dispassionate, and entirely disconnected from the knower" (p. 73)—a perspective that has long been critiqued by feminist scholars. As academics, we often fetishize control and *feel* much more comfortable imagining ourselves as talking heads instead of emotionally charged bodies.

> Whenever emotional responses erupt [in the classroom], many of us believe our academic purpose has been diminished. To me this is a really distorted notion of intellectual practice, since the underlying assumption is that to be truly intellectual we must be cut off from our emotions. (hooks, 1994, p. 155)

We concur with Simpson (2003): "[A]ffective reflection and critical analy-sis . . . [are] required for social change" (p. 190).

As teachers, we can assist our students in navigating emotions in the class-room and also direct students to trained support providers when they demon-strate that need. When our coauthors cried or felt guilt—and before it emerged—we discussed the role of guilt in social justice work. During our first meeting, Julia explicitly stated: "Guilt is going to come up because it does in these conversations. . . . You feel guilty because you said something someone's offended by . . . because you perpetuated oppression. You feel guilty because you critiqued oppression . . . we are all going to experience feelings of guilt." We also explained that guilt is a manifestation of structural power—it is one of the ways dominant discourses work on and through us, including those of us (like Mary and Julia) who have been doing this work for a long time.

Guilt did emerge in our work together. As one coauthor stated:

> I feel shame because I feel guilt, I feel guilt because of past practices of homophobia, sexism, racism, etc. I feel guilt because I didn't recognize, understand, or criticize the privilege and power accorded my body. . . . I saw how my position as a white, middle-class, Christian, able-bodied person affected my growth. . . . Before I simply was those things and practiced my power in oppressive ways. Now I still grapple with those privileges, but am often burdened by guilt and shame which prevent me from growing and actively combating those privileges. I've made the oppression all about me and my guilt and not addressing the current structural issues I perpetuate.

As this coauthor asserts, guilt individualizes structural oppression and di-rects one's attention to the feeling itself instead of the source of the feeling which exists in the structure. Furthermore, guilt often leads to feelings of shame, resentment, and defensiveness. Culturally, we have learned to purge ourselves of guilt by deflecting blame or scapegoating others and/or we have learned to blame ourselves for the oppression we experience. Dominant ideologies/master narratives are sustained through guilt and scapegoating. In all its manifestations, guilt is a hindrance to social justice pedagogy because it obfuscates the analysis of how power functions at a structural level, thereby supporting status quo power relations. Importantly, the coauthor's comment illustrates hir awareness of how guilt works, which creates the possibility to move through the feeling.

Also, guilt and other emotions are problematic when they are used to di-vert conversations from a focus on privilege and oppression. As Johnson, Rich, and Cargile (2008) argue, diversion strategies often result from students' discomfort thinking about identities that are regularly treated as the "invisible" norm against which others are measured. The hegemony that accompanies privilege also results in a lack of awareness of dominance or a lack of experience discussing the meaning of identity. One coauthor commented that "it is much more difficult to confront the ways you perpetuate oppression the more privileged identities you hold." As a teacher, one must continually guide discussions toward analysis of structural oppression, addressing deflective acts that blame the oppressed for their own oppression (Johnson, Rich, & Cargile, 2008, p. 127). We also need to address our own privilege and oppression inside (and outside) the classroom. Faculty often desire to or are expected to take care of students and are swept into supporting a student's feelings rather than addressing *the structural role of the feeling*. It is important to both acknowledge the discomfort guilt creates while also talking about the ways a feeling like guilt can inhibit justice and create barriers to connecting across lines of difference.

Christian privilege

Christian privilege regularly presents itself as one of the most challenging barriers we confront. Because Christianity is the dominant religious discourse in the United States, cultural belonging is entrenched in Christian practices and morality. As Accapadi (2009) contends, "At its very core, morality, goodness, and ultimately the right for humanity is grounded in Christian dominance" (p. 113). More locally, our institution is affiliated with a Protestant denomination and is located in the South, a geographic region where Christian ideology is made more visible by its overt performance in daily life, although it remains hegemonic for many. Because many of our students were raised in Christian traditions, coupled with the erasure of other spiritual and religious practices on campus, our working group struggled with Christianity.

Two of our group members grappled with recognizing or disrupting their Christian privilege. They navigated balancing religiosity with a commitment to social justice, particularly in relationship to sexuality and gender:

> [T]he thing that struck me most was my struggle with religion. Religion was always a part of my life and one of my identities, and I never realized it. . . . My parents' views of religion and sexuality are different from mine. They believe homosexuality is immoral and I am completely on the fence about it. . . . I felt like there was a battle going on in my head, and . . . I am still working on it.

One must challenge personal beliefs about faith and morality to disrupt institutional Christianity and privilege. Assumptions that religion is "good" or that "having faith" is a gateway to "salvation" make questioning Christian supremacy extremely difficult, particularly when preserving heterosexism is fundamental to one's understanding of religious identity. The respondent quoted above, Rory, engaged in group conversations and presented superficial analysis of identity intersections. Ze was most adept at talking about race and racism but consistently demonstrated difficulty providing substantive intersectional analysis. The group regularly attempted to bring Rory into our group dialogue but was rarely successful to that end. The quotation above was the first explicit indication that Rory was grappling with the relationship between religious identity and sexuality, although the statement that ze is "on the fence about it" signals difficulty claiming a social justice identification. Ze resisted working through the interconnections of heterosexism, homophobia, and Christian supremacy. Accapadi (2009) contends, "[I]t is difficult for one to acknowledge the power that comes with their dominant identities, when that same individual is trying to survive the oppression experienced by one's subordinate identity" (p. 123). For some people of color, religious identity has been integral to their resistance of racism. Accapadi continues:

> [I]t would not be surprising for Christian people of color to recognize their Christian identity as a dominant identity, because they rely on that dominant identity for strength to overcome the racism associated with their subordinated identities as people of color. Yet it is important to consider that Christianity, and emulation of physical representations of Christianity, religious or secular, itself offers access and entry to mainstream societal norms in a way that no other religious identity can ever rival. (p. 123)

Conclusion

A primary goal of intersectional pedagogy should be to promote relationships based in social justice. Intersectionality enables coalitional work and community building (Cole, 2008). To build relationships grounded in social justice requires moving beyond one's own experience and working toward understanding the lived realities of those vastly different from us. As one coauthor stated, "That was a sort of revelation to me—to do this work you have to be willing to step outside of yourself or your comfort identities in order to truly examine how intersectionality influences your experience." To "step outside of yourself" requires self-awareness as well as a willingness to be changed by others. Some people are not willing or able to transform their understandings, perhaps because the fear and pain of change are too much or because one's attachment to a particular identity consumes all other sensibilities.

The willingness to be moved demonstrated by many of our coauthors prompted us, as teachers, to be more daring and vulnerable. They also pushed our collective understanding of the positive power of affect and the challenges of deflection and Christian supremacy. As teachers, our responsibility is to engage the difficult dialogues we want our students to have (Kumashiro, 2001a) and to humbly learn from/with them as they resist, confront, and labor with us.

For educators interested in doing the kind of pedagogical work we explore in this chapter, we offer several specific suggestions for teaching intersectionality. We offer these suggestions with the recognition that there is no easy formula for teaching about intersectionality and social justice. We also recognize that there are specific, contextual issues instructors will face in terms of hir comfort addressing power and oppression, specific institutional dynamics that inform what one can do in a classroom, as well as the climate of each classroom. With these complexities in mind, we believe that the following three suggestions are general starting points for intersectional pedagogy.

First, it is important for faculty to provide students with a clear theoretical framework for critically reflecting about identity and power. While this may seem an obvious recommendation, when students are asked to examine their personal relationships to structures of power, they often resist "self-exploration" and claim that reflexivity diverges from the "appropriate" academic work one should do in a classroom. By providing literature that presents (a) the theoretical perspective of intersectionality, (b) examples of how specific persons examine the connection between "personal" experiences and structures of power, and (c) readings that explore how privilege and oppression work independently and in connection with each other, faculty can establish foundational knowledge to which they and students can refer when classroom dialogues become emotionally charged and unproductively centered on any one person's experience. Critical self-reflection is imperative to intersectional pedagogy and requires that faculty continually point to this work as theoretically grounded and informed.

Second, we have found it invaluable to collaborate with students to create the space for critical engagement and reflection. In part, this suggestion involves creating a "safe" environment for dealing with intellectually and emotionally intense material. It also involves creating guidelines for communication and interaction that establish expectations for self-examination, analysis of relational dynamics, and commitment to working through difficult feelings and conversations. By collaborating to create guidelines for engagement, everyone has the opportunity to develop ownership of the conversation and their agency as members of the classroom community. The process of "creating space" helps students develop greater understandings of communal learning and solidarity. It also allows everyone to practically apply and reflect on social justice principles and to decide how those principles might be operationalized.

Finally, carefully examining one's own identity assists instructors in leading students through doing the same. By examining one's own identity we mean that teachers have dedicated significant time and energy to understanding hir own identities, how they intersect, and how dynamics of privilege and oppression work through and on those identifications. This kind of work is important for several reasons. It assists faculty in having an operational understanding of intersectionality and social justice theories; it exposes instructors to a repertoire of thoughts, feelings, and beliefs that students will likely encounter when doing similar work; and it results in faculty accumulating lived experiences that they can share with students facing similar issues. Teaching intersectionality and social justice well requires embodied knowledge in addition to command of theory. Most important, deep understanding of selfhood and power is integral to the possibility of liberation. As Lorde (1995) argued,

> My fullest concentration of energy is available to me only when I integrate all the parts of who I am, openly, allowing power from particular sources of my living to flow back and forth freely through all my different selves, without the restriction of externally imposed definition. Only then can I bring myself and my energies as a whole to the service of those struggles I embrace as a part of my living. (p. 289)

Notes

1   Julia and Mary assumed responsibility for framing the research process and for writing this chapter. Cris, Jessica, Diana, Sally, and Tiffany were actively involved as research participants. In addition, the nature of their participation with Mary and Julia and with one another pushed us all to deeper reflection and analysis. From our first meeting as a group, Cris, Jessica, Diana, Sally, and Tiffany knew they would be included as coauthors of this chapter and that their responses would be integrated into the chapter. Because they were not actively involved in the writing process and because they are student co-researchers, their anonymity is honored herein.

2   We use the words "teachers" and "students" broadly to mean people who are teaching and learning about intersectionality. Intersectional analysis is relevant to any life or organizational context and needs to be explored broadly to transform how identity is engaged.

3   Cris, Jessica, Diana, Sally, and Tiffany have all been students enrolled in classes taught by Julia and/or students who have worked with Mary through the Office of Diversity Education. Jessica, Diana, and Sally are currently working and/or attending graduate school (or are working toward that goal). Our use of the word "student" references our initial relationships but is not intended to erase their agency within or beyond this role.

4   Transgender, lesbian, gay, bisexual, pansexual, allies, asexual, intersex, questioning, Two Spirit.

[5]   As Fuss (1989) explains, "Essentialism is most commonly understood as a belief in the real, true essence of things, the invariable and fixed properties which define the 'whatness' of a given entity" (p. xi). Essentialist frameworks define identity as some kind of "transhistorical, eternal, immutable" (p. xi) essence. In this chapter, we subscribe to a social constructionist perspective, which postulates that identity is a construction of human action, such as language use and other behaviors.

[6]   It is important to acknowledge that Mary and Julia had institutional power throughout this pedagogical process. As faculty and staff, we navigated our differential positions explicitly, and collaboratively made pedagogical choices that positioned the two of us as "in charge" of the group dialogue. We also deliberately disrupted the power hierarchy in various ways.

[7]   Identity is always simultaneously personal and structural. We place "personal" in quotations to highlight the interdependence of the personal, relational, and structural, recognizing that the existence of each is dependent on another. Furthermore, in the context of teaching, students will attribute personal motives to our teaching critically about identity, even in cases where we do not necessarily share personal stories (Johnson-Bailey, 2002; Moule, 2005).

[8]   A fishbowl dialogue involves several people sitting in the center of a circle where they discuss a critical issue and are surrounded by people who listen quietly to the conversation taking place. Generally, the conversation opens up to people outside the circle as the exercise progresses.

[9]   In this essay, we intentionally use ze as a gender neutral pronoun to replace she, he, or s/he and hir to replace his or hers. Not all authors identify as gender nonconforming, although Julia does identify as transgender, specifically gender queer.

[10] Although the kind of social justice pedagogy we practice creates powerful emotional responses for students, we work carefully not to act as therapists. We have learned that it is imperative to appropriately follow up with students and ensure that they are provided contact information with qualified professionals who can assist them as needed. During class, we address student feelings, but make sure to direct the conversation to course concepts and goals.

References

Accapadi, M. M. (2009). When a safe space becomes an oppressive space: Christmas in a cultural center. In. W. J. Blumenfeld, K.Y. Joshi, & E. E. Fairchild (Eds.), *Investigating Christian privilege and religious oppression in the United States* (pp. 113–131). Rotterdam, the Netherlands: Sense Publishers.

Baxter Magolda, M. B. (2001). *Making their own way: Narratives from transforming higher education to promote self-development.* Sterling, VA: Stylus.

Bell, L. A., Love, B. J., Washington, S., & Weinstein, G. (2007). Knowing ourselves as social justice educators. In M. Adams, L. A. Bell, & P. Griffin (Eds.), *Teaching for diversity and social justice* (2nd ed.) (pp. 381–393). New York: Routledge.

Berger, M. T., & Guidroz, K. (Eds.). (2009). *The intersectional approach: Transforming the academy through race, class, and gender.* Chapel Hill: University of North Carolina Press.

Brown, W. (1997). The impossibility of women's studies. *difference: A Journal of Feminist Cultural*

Studies, 9(3), 79–101.

Cole, E. R. (2008). Coalitions as a model for intersectionality: From practice to theory. Sex Roles, 59, 443–453.

Collins, P. H. (2004). Toward a new vision: Race, class, and gender as categories of analysis and connection. In L. M. Heldke & P. O'Connor (Eds.), Oppression, privilege, and resistance (pp. 529–543). Boston: McGraw-Hill.

Cory, R. (2008, May 31). Towards an intersectional and relational model for social justice education. In Thinking beyond borders: Global ideas, global values. Symposium conducted at the University of British Columbia, Vancouver, British Columbia. Retrieved from http://www.oise.utoronto.ca/////Cory.pdf

Crenshaw, K. (1989). Demarginalizing the intersection of race and sex: A black feminist critique of antidiscrimination doctrine, feminist theory and antiracist politics. University of Chicago Legal Forum, 4, 139–167.

Crenshaw, K. (1995). Mapping the margins: Intersectionality, identity politics, and violence against women of color. In K. Crenshaw, N. Gotanda, G. Peller, & K. Thomas (Eds.), Critical race theory: The key writings that formed the movement (pp. 357–384). New York: New Press.

Dei, G. J. (2007). The denial of difference: Reframing anti-racist praxis. In T. D. Gupta, C. E. James, R. C. Maaka, G. E. Galabuzi, & C. Anderson (Eds.), Race and racialization: Essential readings (pp. 188–201). Toronto: Canadian Scholars Press, Inc.

Dhamoon, R. K. (2011). Considerations on mainstreaming intersectionality. Political Research Quarterly, 64(1), 230–243.

Dill, B. T. (2009). Intersections, identities, and inequalities in higher education. In B. T. Dill & R. E. Zambrana (Eds.), Emerging intersections: Race, class, and gender in theory, policy, and practice (pp. 229–252). New Brunswick, NJ: Rutgers University Press.

Dill, B. T., McLaughlin, A. E., & Nieves, A. D. (2007). Future directions of feminist research: Intersectionality. In S. H. Hesse-Biber (Ed.), Handbook of feminist research (pp. 629–637). Thousand Oaks, CA: Sage.

Dill, B. T., & Zambrana, R. E. (2009). Critical thinking about inequality: An emerging lens. In B. T. Dill & R. E. Zambrana (Eds.), Emerging intersections: Race, class, and gender in theory, policy, and practice (pp. 1–21). New Brunswick, NJ: Rutgers University Press.

Elenes, C. A. (2001). Transformando fronteras: Chicana feminist transformative pedagogies. Qualitative Studies in Education, 14(5), 689–702.

Freire, P. (1970). Pedagogy of the oppressed. New York: Continuum.

Fuss, D. (1989). Essentially speaking: Feminism, nature and difference. New York: Routledge.

González-Lopez, G. (2006). Epistemologies of the wound: Anzaldúan theories and sociological research on incest in Mexican society. Human Architecture: Journal of the Sociology of Self-Knowledge, IV (Special Issue), 17–24.

Griffin, P., & Ouellett, M. L. (2007). Facilitating social justice education courses. In M. Adams, L. A. Bell, & P. Griffin (Eds.), Teaching for diversity and social justice (2nd ed.) (pp. 89–113). New York: Routledge.

Harris, V. R., & Ordona, T. A. (1990). Developing unity among women of color: Crossing the barriers of internalized racism and cross-racial hostility. In G. E. Anzaldúa (Ed.), Making face, making soul/Haciendo caras (pp. 304–316). San Francisco, CA: Aunt Lute Publishing.

hooks, b. (1994). Teaching to transgress: Education as the practice of freedom. New York: Routledge.

Johnson, J. R., Bhatt, A. P., & Patton, T. O. (2007). Dismantling essentialisms in academic organizations: Intersectional articulation and possibilities for alliance formation. In B. J. Allen, L. A. Flores, & M. P. Orbe (Eds.), *International and Intercultural Communication Annual XXX* (pp. 21-50). Washington, DC: National Communication Association.

Johnson, J. R., Rich, M., & Cargile, A. C. (2008). "Why are you shoving this stuff down our throats?" Preparing intercultural educators to challenge performances of white racism. *Journal of International and Intercultural Communication, 1*(2), 113-135.

Johnson-Bailey, J. (2002). Race matters: The unspoken variable in the teaching-learning transaction. *New Directions for Adult and Continuing Education, 93,* 39-49.

Jones, S. R. (1997). Voices of identity and difference: A qualitative exploration of the multiple dimensions of identity development in women college students. *Journal of College Student Development, 38,* 376-386.

Jones, S. R. (2009). Constructing identities at the intersections: An autoethnographic exploration of multiple dimensions of identity. *Journal of College Student Development, 50*(3), 287-304.

Jordan-Zachery, J. S. (2007). Am I a black woman or a woman who is black? A few thoughts on the meaning of intersectionality. *Politics & Gender, 3*(2), 254-263.

Kegan, R. (1994). *In over our heads: The mental demands of modern life.* Cambridge, MA: Harvard University Press.

Knight, M. G. (2002).The intersections of race, class, and gender in the teacher preparation of an African American social justice educator. *Equity & Excellence in Education, 34*(3), 212–224.

Kumashiro, K. K. (2001a). *Troubling intersections of race and sexuality: Queer students of color and anti-oppressive education.* Boulder, CO: Rowman & Littlefield Publishers.

Kumashiro, K. K. (2001b). "Posts" perspectives on anti-oppressive education in social studies, English, mathematics, and science classrooms. *Educational Researcher, 30*(3), 3-12.

Lorde, A. (1995). Age, race, class and sex: Women redefining difference. In B. Guy-Sheftall (Ed.), *Words of fire: An anthology of African American feminist thought* (pp. 284-292). New York: The New Press.

Maher, J., & Hoon, C. H. (2008). Gender, space, and discourse across borders: Talking gender in cyberspace. *Feminist Teacher, 18*(3), 202-215.

McCall, L. (2005). The complexity of intersectionality. *Signs: Journal of Women in Culture and Society, 30*(3), 1771-1800.

Moule, J. (2005). Implementing a social justice perspective in teacher education: Invisible burden for faculty of color. *Teacher Education Quarterly, 32*(4), 23-42.

Pearson, H. (2010). Complicating intersectionality through the identities of a hard of hearing Korean adoptee: An autoethnography. *Equity & Excellence in Education, 43*(3), 341-356.

Rasmussen, K. L., Nichols, J. C., & Ferguson, F. (2006). It's a new world: Multiculturalism in a virtual environment. *Distance Education, 27*(2), 265-278.

Samuels, G. M., & Ross-Sheriff, F. (2008). Identity, oppression, and power: Feminisms and intersectionality theory. *Journal of Women and Social Work, 23*(1), 5-9.

Shields, S. A. (2008). Gender: An intersectionality perspective. *Sex Roles, 59,* 301-311.

Simpson, J. S. (2003). *I have been waiting: Race and U. S. higher education.* Toronto: University of Toronto Press.

Wang, M. (2007). Designing online courses that effectively engage learners from diverse cultural backgrounds. *British Journal of Educational Technology, 38*(2), 294–311.

Young, I. M. (1986). The ideal of community and the politics of difference. *Social Theory and Practice, 12,* 1–26.

Reframing "Diversity" in Higher Education

An Argument for an Intersectional Approach

Liz Braun

Introduction

Most colleges and universities in the United States today claim that "diversity" is an important institutional value, but it is not always clear what they mean by this term. Within the higher education setting the term "diversity" is often utilized as an indirect way of talking about race, and it is also meant to simultaneously encompass a broad array of identities including class, gender, nationality, religion, ability, and sexuality. In her linguistic anthropological analysis of the usage of "multiculturalism" and "diversity" in higher education, Urciuoli (1999) notes that terms like these are problematic specifically because "what they actually signify may seem vague, underspecified, wobbly, even within a given field," and yet these terms are usually deployed with a sense that the meanings are "obvious and unproblematic" (p. 289). Since the emergence of the term and concept of "diversity" in higher education in the 1990s, "diversity" has evolved over time to refer to a range of topics including demographics and inequality and also social identities like race, class, gender, sexuality, and ability. "Diversity" has also become a commodity that many colleges sell along with "leadership" and "global citizenry" as a marketable skill that can be obtained through higher education (Urciuoli, 1999, 2009).

Colleges and universities have made progress in creating more diverse and inclusive learning environments in terms of increases in underrepresented populations amongst students, faculty, and staff; changes in the curriculum; and increases in programmatic support for a range of diversity initiatives, but there is still much work that could and should be done. Embracing an inter-sectional approach both inside and outside the classroom is a particularly critical shift that could dramatically impact the experience of individual students and the culture of higher education as a whole. In this chapter I will show some of the limitations that exist in the way that "diversity" is currently conceptualized and understood within higher education and how these limitations impact students. I will also illustrate the possibilities that exist for reframing "diversity" and shifting towards an intersectional approach.

Intersectionality, Categorization, and Subjectivity

As mentioned, the definition of "diversity" has evolved in its usage within higher education to become an umbrella term for a range of different social identities. These social identities still are held apart from one another as discreet categories with no expectation that there is any connection or linkages between them. When taken in isolation from each other, these overly simplistic categories perpetuate a less nuanced understanding for students about the complex ways that power and privilege operate. One result of this conceptualization is that students may feel forced to choose a single identity category that will define them and their college experience. Lowe (1996) argues for the importance of understanding an individual position within multiple strands of power using the experience of Asian immigrant women as an example, "The particular location of racialized women at an intersection where the contradiction of racism and patriarchy, and capitalism converge produces a subject that cannot be determined along a single axis of power or by a single apparatus, on the one hand, or contained within a single narrative of oppositional political formation on the other" (p. 164). Using the current "diversity" framework with its reliance on monolithic categories denies the complexity of students' individual identities, the ways they intersect, and the impact of difference on a student's experience of an institution. In a larger sense when race becomes equated with diversity, there is a loss of analysis of class, gender, sexuality, religion, ability, and the resulting consequences when these power dynamics intersect.

The separation of students by colleges and universities into discreet categories, particularly racial categories, closes off opportunities for students to understand themselves and others in terms of differences between and among the varying groups that they identify with, an understanding that Brewer (1999) identifies as a feature of intersectionality. I do agree with Spivak that there are times when "strategic essentialism" is an important and valid political strategy, but I also agree with her concerns about its theoretical limitations, for example, the way that the category of "women" can reinscribe a particular view of "women," or more specifically "Third World women," that does a disservice to women as a whole (Spivak, Landry, & MacLean, 1996).

Many researchers have noted the importance of utilizing an intersectional approach, particularly race, class, and gender intersections, when analyzing educational environments (Bettie, 2003; Diamond, Randolph, & Spillane, 2004; Flores-Gonzalez, 1999; Fordham, 2008; Horvat & Antonio, 1999; Hubbard, 1999; Shaw & Coleman, 2000). Bettie's (2003) ethnographic study of working-class white and Mexican American high school senior girls set in a rural school in California's Central Valley is a particularly compelling example of the need for a more intersectional approach. Her goal

> was to learn how these young women experience and understand class differences in their peer culture and how their and their parents' class location and racial/ethnic identity shaped the girls' perceptions of social differences at school and the possibilities for their futures. (p. 7)

Bettie identifies and analyzes the "common sense categories" the girls used to describe their class differences and in particular looks at how these "common sense" class categories intersect with race and gender.

Bettie's (2003) theoretical approach reflects her focus on intersections of class, race, and gender. She identifies several key issues: how class/race analyses have often focused on men, leaving women untheorized; how conflating race and class or using class as a solution to identity politics issues should be avoided; and class as relational and constructed rather than a category that is simply there. She notes the relevance of "subcultures" in understanding identity categories and formation, for example, she observes that "[c]lass and racial/ethnic signifiers are melded together in such a way that 'authentic' black, and sometimes brown identity is imagined as lower-class, urban, and often violent—and male as well" (p. 48).

An intersectional approach embraces the complexity of identity and subjectivity by examining how different social identities interact with each other to influence and shape our understandings of who we are in relation to others. The challenge is to analyze these intersections without conflating or overly simplifying how these categories relate to one another.

Dexter College: A Case Study

The examples used throughout this chapter come from an ethnographic study that I conducted at a predominantly white small northeastern women's liberal arts college in New England, which I will refer to by the pseudonym of Dexter College. The population at Dexter is approximately 2,200 undergraduate students. At the time of my research the demographics of the college were as follows: the domestic student population was approximately 69% white, 8% Asian American, 4% Latina, and 4% African American, and the international student population was roughly 15%. At the time of this study, students who identified as multiracial were not broken out into a separate category but folded into the other existing categories. The student population comes from 48 states and 70 countries. The campus is primarily residential with approximately 95% of all students living in on-campus housing. The college was known for its "diverse" population of students, particularly for a college of its size.

My study addressed three areas of inquiry: the experience of students attending a predominantly white institution in relation to issues of race and racial identity; institutional practices related to race, "diversity," and "culture"; and examples of "white cultural practices" within the institution. I was particularly interested in looking at the circulation of discourses and narratives related to race, diversity, and culture—including, when, how, and by whom are race and racism talked about on a college campus? How does this "talk" or discourse shape the culture of higher education and the educational experience for students, specifically students of color? What linguistic strategies are used to create and sustain understandings about race within colleges and universities? How do these discourses reinforce the majority culture, which is white culture?

My place in the research

First, I began to think more deeply about the uses of "diversity" and its implications for higher education after spending several years working as an administrator at Dexter College. Like many colleges and universities, Dexter College clearly articulated the importance of racial and ethnic "diversity" to its mission and emphasized that it should be cultivated and celebrated. It gives institutional support for student cultural organizations, cultural houses, and other programs and organizations for African American, Latina, Asian American, and Native American students. The college website and publications feature photos from cultural shows and events as points of pride and as evidence of thriving campus "diversity."

I was trying to understand why domestic students of color on my campus continued to express dissatisfaction and frustration with their overall college experience, despite the college's expressed "commitment to diversity" and the things the college had put in place to support students of color. What caused the disconnect between our institutional intentions and the lived experience for many domestic students of color? In my role as a student affairs profes-sional, primarily at small private liberal arts colleges, I have been both an observer and a participant in these discourses of race and "diversity." My professional experiences combined with a growing awareness of my own racial identity as a white woman led me to pursue this area of research. This research focuses mostly on issues of race and whiteness related to diversity; however, the work helps inform the broader issues related to the framing of "diversity" and the importance of embracing an intersectional approach both in and outside of the classroom.

Conceptualizations of "Diversity" at Dexter College

At Dexter College student definitions and institutional representations of "diversity" typically focused on race and "culture" versus other facets of diversity such as class, religion, disability, sexuality, religion, and gender. Further, when other facets of diversity were referenced, it was most often as stand-alone categories rather than a discussion of the intersections between them. During the college admissions process, students received the message that "diversity" was an important aspect of the college, but in many ways they were left to create their own interpretation of what "diversity" means and how it will actually impact their college experience. The institutional clues that are given to them include not only statements from the website and viewbook but also photographs that depict students with a range of different skin colors engaged in a variety of activities. These photos show students in groups interacting across racial lines. There are also pictures of more racially homogenous groups of students. Skillfully combined, these photos serve to project several key images related to the manifestation of a "diverse community," including harmonious cross- and intra-racial friendships.

When asked about diversity, students at Dexter College frequently refer-ence the memorable "1 in 3" statistic, namely: "Approximately one in every three students is an international citizen or African American, Asian Ameri-can, Latina, Native American, or multiracial" as evidence. Camille, a white senior from San Francisco, told me that she felt that Dexter College presented itself very well in terms of diversity. When I asked her what specific things stuck out to her she explained,

> I mean part of it was numbers, just looking at the, "one out of every three students is"–that whole thing really. And then I think also when you look at the brochures or the [viewbook], just seeing all the actual images of people–it's such a diverse population.

As Urciuoli (2009) argues, "Higher education promotional practices depend heavily on the deployment of such categories, most directly in the advertisement of diversity numbers" (p. 22). Lindsey, a white first year from upstate New York, offered a different perspective and critique of the way that "diversity" is framed in the United States college admissions process:

> It seems like that diversity is based more on your outward appearance or, "I'm from Zimbabwe, so I'm obviously diverse," or "I'm from Vietnam, so I'm obviously diverse," which, is so weird to me, I mean, anyone can be diverse based on how they look on the outside, but [the college] might want to maintain a certain quota and the outward appearance of having a certain amount of students that they have to do that, but it's just always weird to me, cause anyone can be as diverse as the next person or not as diverse as the next person.

Presenting these numbers and statistics is a way to provide countable, quantifiable evidence of "diversity." This focus on numbers places students into easily identifiable categorical groups. This in turn, emphasizes a singular aspect of a student's identity. This reductionist approach may translate into a sense that Dexter College views this fraction of who they are as most important.

Students often noted that one of the main things that attracted them to apply to (and eventually attend) Dexter College is the campus "diversity." How they conceptualized "diversity" varied broadly, but most often they referred to international diversity and/or racial and ethnic diversity. This growing trend toward linking "diversity" with international or "global" allows for colleges to further distance themselves from the messy complications of domestic racial issues. This characterization of global citizenship in the college admissions process does not take into consideration the complexities of international conflicts but rather focuses on international harmony. One student told me that she often heard Dexter College described as a "mini United Nations." The frequent conflation of race, ethnicity, and nationality also undercuts the complexity of the relationships between these categories in terms of the lived experiences of today's college students. For example, there is a growing percentage of U.S.-born students who have grown up in multiple countries and have a very complicated relationship to concepts like nationality. There are also increasing numbers of first- or second-generation immigrant students who have a distinctive relationship to their parents' country of birth versus their relationship to the United States. These intricacies are lost or masked when using terminology such as "international students."

In general, college applicants see "diversity" as a desirable concept and characteristic. When white students equate "diversity" with "difference," this points to an underlying notion that people from different racial groups are all the same. While for many white students there is excitement about "diversity" as a desirable attribute along with academic excellence and student-faculty ratio, the issue of "diversity," and specifically racial diversity, is more complex for students who fall under the large and institutionally constructed category of "students of color." White students conceive of "diversity" as something outside of themselves. For those who are placed under the umbrella of "students of color," "diversity" becomes an integral part of how they are viewed by their peers and the institution as a whole.

These comments from white students are congruent with what Bush (2004) found in her study on student attitudes about identity, privilege, and intergroup relations at a large urban public university. Bush identified that white students often took pride in being part of a "diverse" community and that this helped them claim to be "colorblind, multiculturally oriented, and nonracist" (p. 86). Bush further argues that this "type of identification allows whites to deny how they are perceived while receiving the privileges of that perception" (p. 87). So while students describe feeling excited to be part of a "diverse community," from the beginning their vantage point is as an observer, viewing "diversity" as an antidote to what many students described as "boring" all-white environments. In this dynamic, white students do not see themselves as adding to the "diversity" of the community. "Diversity" is an external element separate from them, an exotic commodity that they can consume as a cultural tourist. This is another example of where "diversity" can be reframed using an intersectional approach. Intersectionality explains that all students, even those with dominant social identities, are included in the concept of "diversity." This reframing of "diversity" sets the expectation at colleges and universities that all students would need to grapple with the true complexity of "diversity" as a community.

Student Talk and Intersectionality at Dexter College

Many of the comments that I heard from students highlight the institutional tensions that exist between common notions of "diversity" that promotes an image of global diverse citizenship and the expectations for students who are institutionally categorized as "students of color." Within the institutional definitions of "diversity," there is a real danger of trapping or directing students toward a particular presentation of self that limits their possibilities for multifaceted identity expression and exploration. Minh-ha (1989) writes at length about the limitations of being placed into a "special" category; in her case she is speaking to the category of Third World women, "Difference or uniqueness or special identity is both limiting and deceiving" (p. 95). She further comments, "It seems quite content with reforms that, at best, contribute to the improvement and/or entanglement of the identity enclosure, but do not, in any way, attempt to remove its fence" (p. 96). The current master narratives of "diversity" within higher education do not promote fluidity and intersectionality. Rather, the current models of categorization reify a monolithic homogenized sense of identity that not only negatively impacts a student's personal identity development but limits their ability to bring a deep critical analysis of this type of socially constructed categorization into the classroom. In the following section I will analyze four examples of student talk about race and the impact of the lack of an intersectional approach.

"Experience Diversity" program

When asked to reflect on their own racial identities, many students talked about a student program, "Experience Diversity," that up until recently was specifically for students who identified as "students of color." Many students of color described feelings of discomfort that the college was defining them based on their race. Catherine, a first-year multiracial student who grew up in San Francisco and attended a racially diverse high school, told me that she attended Experience Diversity, but that she thought it was really strange. When I asked her why, she responded,

> I just thought it was weird because it was like let's invite all of the not-white students this weekend. Yeah, it, I don't know, I kind of feel like race here is a lot, it's paid attention to a lot more and it's like a bigger deal and that's kind of weird for me.

Catherine went on to describe growing up surrounded by many Asian Americans and some white people: "So, being Asian was never like a big deal. I don't know. And then coming here where people are like, 'You're Asian, yay!'"

Catherine's experience growing up in a predominantly Asian neighborhood made Dexter College's emphasis on race seem odd and created discomfort for her. For many years, much of the thinking behind these types of programs at the institution was based on the assumption that for a student of color or multiracial student entering a predominantly white institution, race would be their most salient identity and their biggest transitional issue. But what I found in my interviews and conversations with students is that the saliency of race and racial identity for incoming students depended on a range of variables including where they grew up, their class background, ethnicity, religion, and many other factors.

Analyzing the student response to this program from an intersectional approach, examining race and class intersections, is also revealing. The majority of students who felt that the Experience Diversity program was unnecessary tended to come from middle-class or upper-middle-class backgrounds like Catherine. Whereas other students from lower socioeconomic classes emphasized how critical this program was to their transition into the college environment. For example, Maria, a senior from the Bronx and first-generation immigrant from a poor background, talked about how important this program was for her as someone who was navigating the college admissions process very much on her own:

> I think that I felt comfortable knowing that there were other girls in the same . . . situation as I was, that they didn't know which college they were gonna pick and everything. So I was asking, "So are you gonna choose [this college]?" trying to get as many opinions as I could. But I think it was the team-based activities that we did a lot that actually kind of made me feel more comfortable. Because when I came, and I saw how fancy it was and everything . . . the whole environment it's so different. It's a small town, and I was like oh, wow, you know.

For Maria, the program gave her an opportunity to get support from other students whom she felt were like her. Even though class is clearly a salient issue for many first-generation students of color from low-income backgrounds, Dexter College does not focus on or name socioeconomic class in relation to this program. This is an excellent example of how colleges and universities could benefit from an intersectional approach. An intersectional framework can help institutions identify students in need of additional support and guidance in making the transition to college based on a variety of factors, not just race and ethnicity. This will not undercut the very real issues that many students of color face while attending college as a numeric minority on a predominantly white campus. An intersectional approach has the potential to simultaneously focus on issues related to specific identities and backgrounds while also helping students understand how their individual identities interact with one another and affect the unique way that they will experience the college environment.

Cultural organizations

The way that students of color understood or related to campus "cultural organizations," student-run clubs that typically are organized around a racial or ethnic grouping, is another example that illustrates missed opportunities in not pursuing an intersectional approach. Devaki, a junior who is multiracial with a white mother and a father who is a first-generation immigrant from India, was most frustrated by other students' assumptions and subtle pressure that she should be involved in a cultural organization.

> People who I vaguely knew would try to get me involved in that, because they knew I was involved in other things and we all kind of were in the same involved-people group. And I kind of would be polite, but I wouldn't take them up on it, ever, because I just felt there was this idea of what it was, what I was supposed to be doing. They were saying, "Oh, you need to be more involved in your culture," and stuff like that. And I'm . . . my culture is not this idea of . . . wearing saris and stuff like that. And also, why is it . . . it would seem like really false to me to overly embrace one side of my race versus the other.

Based on her phenotypical appearance and her name, other students might not even realize that Devaki was multiracial; for her, participating in the cultural organizations would have felt like an implicit denial of her mother's racial heritage as a white woman. She went on to further describe this sense that other students wanted to define her by her Indian background, which she saw as just one aspect of who she was:

> I feel like, I guess one of the main reasons why I was so hesitant to be involved in any of those things in the past was because I didn't, I felt that's what people were trying to do, they were trying to isolate this one experience that seems bigger to them, and I didn't want. . . . I don't know, I didn't want to say like, all right, well this is the most important part of me, or something like that, or this is more than just one nuance of my experience.

Even though she did not use the word "intersectional," Devaki's understanding of self reflected the "overlapping and simultaneous" nature of identity, further highlighting the need for colleges and universities that categorize along race and ethnicity to use a more intersectional approach (Brewer, 1999). This includes taking into consideration all features of student identity, particularly when designing policy and practices aimed at student support.

Similar to the example of the admitted student program, cultural organizations still serve a critical purpose for many students of color as a place for forming community, for managing the stress and strain of attending a predominantly white campus, and as places for identity exploration and growth. Even so, colleges and universities need to play an intentional role in articulating the relevance and importance of these types of cultural organizations. They must create a space where students do not feel obligated to participate. It must be clear that choosing a cultural organization does not mean that they are choosing to only celebrate or contemplate one aspect of their identity. If Dexter College placed as much emphasis on intersectionality as it does on discrete social identity categories it would open up a space where students would feel empowered and affirmed in exploring multiple facets of their identity rather than just having to choose one.

The equestrian team

Students consistently conflated social identity categories when I asked them to describe "white culture" or examples of whiteness. For example, when I asked students to give examples of "white culture" on campus, without fail the most common response was "the equestrian team." Their answers reflect the way many people conflate whiteness and wealth. Within the Dexter College community, the equestrian program represents that conflation. Charlotte, a white junior, participated in the equestrian team during her first year at Dexter College but then stopped because she did not like the culture:

> I never wanted to be part of the culture because it was just so irritating to me, cause I feel when you get to that level it's all about the money and winning and it's so white and moneyed and privileged and for me, that just kind of kills the fun that I have riding. . . . I can give you an unofficial uniform for them, a lot of them, of course with any stereotype it doesn't apply to all of them, but many of them have a lot of money and they wear it, be it with most of them wear pearl earrings, they'll wear their riding pants and boots or like their socks and like tennis shoes or something around. They'll have really nice polo shirts, just like the brand names. You can see the nice brand names on them.

Maria gave the equestrian team as an example of how often felt that she did not quite fit in at Dexter College.

> There were a lot of girls from the equestrian team in my hall, and I was [wondering] why are they dressed like that? [*laughter*] "Dressage," I said, "What is dressage?" I would always hear that word, and I was like what? And then I looked it up on YouTube, and I [thought] this is it. But I encountered things that I didn't really know, and I didn't know existed. I don't know how to explain it. Those little things, I guess that's when I really started to realize that I hadn't been exposed to a lot of things.

When I asked Maria what about the equestrian team felt white to her, she mentioned that first of all there were no (phenotypically visible) students of color on the team. She then went on to comment:

> Yeah. And the outrageous fees that you need to have. And also you know that if these girls do equestrian, it's probably because they own a horse, so their family has had the opportunity to put them into like horseback riding classes, and they're pretty expensive, I'm guessing. So that also creates a divide, like the social, and I guess the costumes they wear. I don't know, I found it very strange. For me, that was one of the signs, I think, of white culture.

For Maria the equestrian team was emblematic of white culture. It was striking to me how consistently the equestrian team came up as an example of white culture from a variety of students from different backgrounds, including many white students. One factor in the students' identification of the equestrian team with whiteness may be a recognition that whiteness is about exclusion and property (Harris, 1993). Another possible hypothesis for this is that they are an easy target; as Charlotte mentioned, they have a clearly identifiable "uniform," and there is a clear understanding about the elite nature and expense that go into participating in the equestrian team. They are also a group made up overwhelmingly of white students and, perhaps in part due to the riding pants and boots, they become one of the few instances where the "whiteness" of a white group of students is visible within the college community.

The equestrian team is clearly viewed not only as white but white and privileged in a way that sets them up in opposition to other white students. This is another example of how critical it is to consider intersecting identities within the culture of higher education. Conflating whiteness with wealth erases the experience of poor white students at Dexter College. Analyzing the role of the equestrian program within the campus community as both a marker of whiteness and socioeconomic class creates an opportunity for students to grapple with the complicated interplay between these specific identities.

Sexuality and the social scene

Students also frequently discussed how they saw race with sexuality intersections when they were trying to articulate examples of whiteness. Gloria, a black senior who was a first-generation immigrant, talked about how she felt that there were clear cultural messages about how to be "gay" at Dexter College and that these images were linked specifically to whiteness,

> When I first got here it was like this is how you're gay: you have short hair, you play rugby, you dress like a guy, and you're really cool, a hipster, and you're funny. And you're white—yeah, okay. And I was, okay, that's weird.

Eleanor, a white junior, had a similar perspective:

> I think what I notice the most is in terms of race and sexuality intersections, in terms of what people [chuckle]—some student used the analogy of big ants and little ants on this campus, and use that analogy to talk about the cool gays and people who identify as queer, but people don't believe them, or for all the stuff that goes along with that. And that has—there's a certain dress code here that's very white, preppy, certain brand names.

As Gloria and Eleanor both point out, within the context of Dexter College there is a particular brand of white culture linked to being gay or lesbian that is expressed through dress, attitude, and even activities, such as the rugby and crew teams. As these students point out when a gay or lesbian identity is considered to be inherently linked to whiteness without a deeper analysis of intersections of race and sexuality, what options does that leave for a student of color who also identifies as gay or lesbian? Within this framework a student of color in this situation could choose to try and fit into the prescribed cultural model for being gay or lesbian that is seen as a white model, or they could decide to focus solely on their racial identity or perhaps try and avoid contemplating identity issues at all. An intersectional approach would allow for this student to embrace both of these pieces of her identity and to consider the unique elements of her specific combination of identities, for example, grappling with the fact that homosexuality is still a taboo in some communities of color. The larger point I want to make here is that exploring race, class, and gender intersectionally is also pivotal to understanding discourses of whiteness (which are present but often unnamed) and the way that students "perform whiteness" within a predominantly white institution.

Diverse, Inclusive, Learning Environments and Intersecting Identities

I would argue that to make real progress in the creation of diverse and inclusive learning environments, we need to first make visible and then reframe the discourses in higher education that lead to silence and "misrecognition" (Bourdieu, 1977) related to race, "diversity," "culture," and whiteness. This would include integrating the academic mission of the college more closely with the goals of diversity and inclusion and providing more opportunities for white students to view themselves as having a pivotal role in conversations about race. Thus, shifting to a model of "diversity" that truly embraces analyzing the intersectionality of social identities. In her study of race and class intersections at a small New England liberal arts college, Aries (2008) raises the question of institutional responsibility, "While students are being asked to adjust to the culture of an elite college, are there adjustments that the college must make to incorporate a more diverse student body?" (p. 12). Aries makes the critical point about the role that the institution needs to play in providing structured opportunities for students to talk across lines of race and class and to develop a critical analytic framework for understanding race and class. As Aries underscores, having a diverse student population will give students the opportunity to learn about the lives and experiences of students from very different backgrounds but will not give them the tools to critically think about how these social hierarchies are formed, maintained, and the ways in which they intersect.

The current structures of higher education mark "students of color" in such a way that assumes that race will be the most salient part of their identity, and the corresponding assumption is that race will not be salient at all for white students. Tabitha, an African American student affairs administrator, mentioned this dynamic during our interview,

> And I hear students so often say, I came to Dexter College and all of a sudden I'm now just this student of color. Which I think is important because it is so visual and people are going to treat you a certain way based on that, but you get to be that and all of these other things.

As Tabitha underscores, race does still matter, but anyone who falls under the "student of color" category should be actively encouraged (and given the opportunity) to examine their multiple identities and learn about the ways they connect and inform one another. It became clear to me how much *all* students crave this opportunity to explore and share the complexity of their social identities while watching them participate in an activity called "Strands of Identity" during an orientation leader training.

In this activity, there are signs posted around the room; each sign has a different social identity written on it (e.g., class, gender, race, religion, et cetera). During the activity the facilitator reads out a statement such as, "This is the identity that is most salient for me today" or "This is an identity that I would like to learn more about." Students go to the piece of paper with the relevant identity and then engage in conversation with the other students standing there about why they chose that identity. Simply put, the students loved this activity. Several days after the training, students were still talking to me about it and reflecting on the conversations they had with other students. The activity clearly struck a chord. Gloria reflected on doing this activity during our interview,

> And so [it was] me seeing that and being exposed to that and realizing that there's all these characteristics and identities within me, and how all of them are connected . . . and that it's okay, you don't have to go around carrying one identity.

Listening to Gloria describe what she had taken away from the activity brought home for me the fact that so much of education—and society in general—places students into categories of one type or another and then often expects them to be some sort of "representative" for that category. Giving students the opportunity to see themselves as whole and multifaceted is not only better for their overall development but also creates enhanced possibilities for connections across lines of difference by accenting the similarities that students share as well as their differences. When we do not help students think critically about both individual social identities and how they intersect, students will often conflate issues like race and class (Bettie, 2003). I frequently saw this play out when white students from lower socioeconomic backgrounds would have a difficult time grasping a sense of their own white privilege since they already felt so disadvantaged by their class background. Using an "intersectionality" approach would allow those same students to hold these things together in tension and dialogue with each other.

I also want to underscore that critical thinking about identity development and social constructions of identity should not solely be relegated to the co-curricular realm. This was another clear theme that emerged from my research. One African American staff member with whom I spoke explained it this way, "As much as we talk about pulling diversity and inclusion to the center, it's still separate. And so I think institutionally it's still an add-on I think because of . . . what gets credited and what doesn't get credited." The institutional goals for diversity and inclusion should always be connected to and reinforced by the academic mission. Many white students described to me that they were too overwhelmed by their academics and other commitments to consider participating in a program or a workshop; in stark contrast, many students of color talked about how their academics had suffered because of the responsibility they felt to support cultural programming and events. I would argue that there should be more of a synthesis between the "diverse community" and the "learning environment" or the out-of-classroom and in-classroom experiences of students. This change would have significant impact in shifting the current dynamics that can end up negatively impacting all students and prevent higher education communities from reaping the full potential benefits of a diverse learning environment. Over time the concept of and framework for "diversity" have continued to evolve and expand, and with the growing complexity of identity found within our student populations, higher education is at a critical juncture where it is time for a thorough re-evaluation of the current model. This reframing should consider a shift away from monolithic categories toward an intersectional approach that embraces the complex, and often messy, facets of identity formation, subjectivity, and power. If we do not model this approach within higher education, how can we expect our students to work toward creating a world that fosters inclusivity, equity, and social justice?

References

Aries, E. (2008). *Race and class matters at an elite college*. Philadelphia: Temple University Press.

Bettie, J. (2003). *Women without class: Girls, race, and identity*. Berkeley/Los Angeles: University of California Press.

Bourdieu, P. (1977). *Outline of a theory of practice*. (Cambridge Studies in Social and Cultural Anthropology). New York: Cambridge University Press.

Brewer, R. M. (1999). Theorizing race, class, and gender: The new scholarship of black feminist intellectuals and black women's labor. *Race, Class, and Gender*, 6(2), 29–47.

Bush, M. (2004). *Breaking the code of good intentions: Everyday forms of whiteness*. Lanham, MD: Rowman and Littlefield Publishers.

Diamond, J. B., Randolph, A., & Spillane, J. P. (2004). Teachers' expectations and sense of responsibility for student learning: The importance of race, class, and organizational habitus. *Anthropology and Education Quarterly*, 35(1), 75–98.

Flores-Gonzalez, N. (1999). Puerto Rican high achievers: An example of ethnic and academic identity compatibility. *Anthropology and Education Quarterly*, 30(3), 343–362.

Fordham, S. (2008). Beyond capital high: On dual citizenship and the strange career of "acting white." *Anthropology and Education Quarterly*, 39(3), 227–246.

Harris, C. I. (1993). Whiteness as property. *Harvard Law Review*, 106(8), 1707–1791. Retrieved from http://ssrn.com/paper=927850

Horvat, E. M., & Antonio, A. L. (1999). "Hey, those shoes are out of uniform": African American girls in an elite high school and the importance of habitus. *Anthropology and Education Quarterly*, 30(3), 317–342.

Hubbard, L. (1999). College aspirations among low-income African American high school students: Gendered strategies for success. *Anthropology and Education Quarterly*, 30(3), 363–383.

Lowe, L. (1996). *Immigrant acts: On Asian American cultural politics*. Durham, NC: Duke University Press.

Minh-ha, T. T. (1989). *Woman, native, other: Writing postcoloniality and feminism*. Bloomington: Indiana University Press.

Shaw, K. M., & Coleman, A. B. (2000). Humble on Sundays: Family, friends, and faculty in the upward mobility experiences of African American females. *Anthropology and Education Quarterly*, 31(4), 449–470.

Spivak, G. C., Landry, D., & MacLean, G. M. (1996). *The Spivak reader: Selected works of Gayatri Chakravorty Spivak*. New York: Routledge.

Urciuoli, B. (1999). Producing multiculturalism in higher education: Who's producing what for whom? *Qualitative Studies in Education*, 12(3), 287–298.

Urciuoli, B. (2009). Talking/not talking about race: The enregisterments of culture in higher education discourses. *Journal of Linguistic Anthropology*, 19(1), 21–39.

Afterword

Final Thoughts

Cerri A. Banks and Susan M. Pliner

In this text we have shown a range of ways that the theory of intersectionality informs the processes of teaching and learning. The chapters demonstrate how intersectional pedagogy enhances the student-teacher relationship and campus interactions, and, most important, how it deepens student learning. The contributors have demonstrated the impact that intersectional pedagogy has had in their schooling experiences including: (a) grappling with multiple identities and the relationship of those identities to power, (b) creating meaningful experiential and co-curricular learning to enhance student engagement, and (c) making choices about content, curriculum, and classroom strategies that provide theoretical knowledge and that represent intersectional methods. In our focus on teaching and learning, we have been transparent about our broader agenda, that is, to facilitate a social justice mission in our pedagogy that empowers students with the knowledge and skills necessary to take up this work, if they so choose.

We are committed to our stance that our world with its economic, social, and political challenges needs academic scholarship firmly grounded in theory and practical application. One of the goals of the text was to reinforce the ways theory can and should inform practice. We believe, and the student authors have told us, that using intersectional theory to drive pedagogy helps them better understand the world and their place in it. It helps them expand content knowledge in practical ways. It allows them to form alliances on campus and motivates them to create change.

Academic disciplines in higher education are broad and often changing, and we recognize we have not covered them all in this text. We do believe that much of the discussion about "good teaching" resulting from intersectional pedagogy is transferable in a way that any field or discipline can apply the theory, methods, and strategies. In the landscape of U.S. higher education, colleges and universities are being called to task on the increasing costs of earning a degree. There is a call for institutions to identify and articulate evidence of student learning, not just of content but also of skills that will allow them to work and function in a global, diverse, and connected world. We believe intersectional pedagogy represents a response to that call. In addition, at its core, intersectional pedagogy promotes equitable access to knowledge and learning and ultimately supports the goal of living to our full humanity.

Contributors

REINA APRAEZ is a recent Studio Art graduate of William Smith College, currently pursuing her NYS teacher's certificate in K-12 Art. She is a young woman of Colombian descent from a multiracial family. She is also a student of public-city education as well as a number of different streets, families, and environments. Because of this, understanding privilege, identity, home, experience, expression, utility, agency, and perseverance have all been focuses of her art and mission in education. She is an abstract painter and space-constructor, a performer, a poet, a feminist, a teaching artist, a void-eater, a part-hippie-punk, and hopefully, one day, she'll kick the bottom out of her childhood and become a revolutionary (oh, and also an MFA graduate exhibiting in contemporary galleries).

CERRI A. BANKS is the Vice President for Student Affairs and Dean of the College at Mt. Holyoke College. Banks received her Ph.D. in Cultural Foundations of Education from Syracuse University. Banks specializes in sociology of education, cultural studies, multicultural education, and qualitative research. Committed to educational reform and issues of inclusion, Banks draws from educational theory, feminist theory, and critical race theory in her work as the dean and in her teaching, research, and writing.

NEETA BHASIN is Assistant Professor of Writing and Rhetoric at Hobart and William Smith Colleges. She received her Ph.D. in 2007 from the department of English at Carnegie Mellon University. Her areas of specialization include discourse analysis, sociolinguistics, and rhetorical studies. Her research and pedagogical interests focus on the intersections of language and identity, with special emphasis on migrant and diasporic identities, the relationship between language and culture, race and ethnic studies, and nationalisms. Additional interests coalesce around intercultural communication, ethnography of communication, world Englishes, globalization studies, media studies, popular culture, and immigrant literature.

LESLEY BOGAD is an Associate Professor of Educational Studies and Women's Studies at Rhode Island College and the founding director of the A.L.L.I.E.D. mentoring initiative. She received her undergraduate degree in English and Education from Barnard College at Columbia University and her Master's and Ph.D. in Cultural Foundations of Education from Syracuse University. She teaches undergraduate and graduate courses in sociology of education, multiculturalism, qualitative research methods, and popular culture. Her research interests include youth culture, schooling for social justice, and media literacy. Lesley tries to work every day to contribute to a more socially just world, but sometimes she gets distracted by working in her garden, cooking interesting meals, blogging, or watching *Glee*.

JENNIFER BOWEN is Assistant Professor of Mathematics at The College of Wooster. Her mathematical research lies in the field of nonassociative algebra, Jordan algebras, and matrix rings. She is passionate about all things mathematical in a liberal arts environment, specifically opportunities for underrepresented groups in mathematics, summer experiences for undergraduates, and equity and accessibility for all students in mathematics.

LIZ BRAUN is a cultural anthropologist and a student affairs administrator. Her current position is as dean of students at Swarthmore College. Her research focuses on higher education and the creation of diverse inclusive and engaged learning environments with a particular focus on issues of race and whiteness.

TIFFANY BRIGHAM is a recent Communication Studies graduate from Southwestern University. While studying at Southwestern she was involved in two diversity student groups: Encouraging Blacks and Others to Never Yield (E.B.O.N.Y.) and the Coalition for Diversity and Social Justice (CDSJ). She and members of E.B.O.N.Y. organized a lecture series during Black History Month that surrounded the theme of celebrating Black media. As co-director of CDSJ she supported the campus diversity and social justice groups by offering advice and help as a mediator and by helping groups prepare for campus events. Currently, Tiffany plans to attend graduate school for a degree in Student Affairs Administration in Higher Education. Her aim is to guide student organizations in their efforts to reach all of their goals.

KIM A. CASE, Ph.D., is Associate Professor of Women's Studies and Psychology and Director of the Teaching-Learning Enhancement Center at the University of Houston–Clear Lake. Her research on prejudice confrontation and ally behavior focuses on dominant group responses to prejudice in social contexts. She also studies strategies for raising awareness of male, white, heterosexual, and gender-conforming privilege in educational and community settings.

ANNA CREADICK is Associate Professor of English at Hobart and William Smith Colleges, where she teaches courses in twentieth-century American literature, cultural studies, and women's studies. Her book *Perfectly Average: The Pursuit of Normality in Postwar America* was recently published by the University of Massachusetts Press.

JENNIFER ESPOSITO teaches qualitative research methods and social foundations of education at Georgia State University. Her research interests include the study of race, class, gender, and sexual orientation representations in popular culture texts, feminist qualitative methods, and urban education. In addition to book chapters, recent publications include articles in *Gender and Education*, *Journal of Educational Foundations*, and *Educational Studies*.

MARY GONZÁLEZ has dedicated her life to promoting social change through her community engagement, professional experiences, and academic background. Currently, she is pursuing her doctoral degree in Curriculum and Instruction–Cultural Studies at the University of Texas at Austin, focusing on social justice education research. Mary received her bachelor degrees in History and Mexican American Studies from the University of Texas at Austin and a Master of Liberal Arts with a concentration in Social Justice from St. Edward's University. She has previously served as program coordinator in the Multicultural Engagement Center at the University of Texas at Austin and as assistant dean for student multicultural affairs at Southwestern University. Currently she is a graduate research assistant at the University of Texas at Austin, where she develops curriculum for the UT Outreach Centers in San Antonio and the Rio Grande Valley. She is also forming her own consulting company, Izel Consulting.

JESSICA HAGER is currently working toward her Master of Arts in Social Service Administration at the University of Chicago. She has spent her professional career in the nonprofit sector, primarily working with communities who lack access and/or abilities to meet their basic needs. Jessica hopes to continue her education and career by working to develop effective and efficient programs that recognize and promote change surrounding the systemic problems which face communities daily.

ALISON HAPPEL is a doctoral student in Educational Policy Studies, and her concentration is in Social Foundations of Education. Her research interests include feminist theory and pedagogy, neoliberalism in education, and feminist qualitative research methods. Her dissertation is a feminist ethnography that explores how girlness was conceptualized and constructed in an all-girls middle school club. Her recent publications include two media reviews in the journal *Educational Studies*.

IBILOLIA HOLDER is an elementary teacher and the State Coordinator for Family, Career and Community Leaders of America (F.C.C.L.A.) in Rhode Island. She received her undergraduate degree at Rhode Island College and was an original member of the A.L.L.I.E.D. group. She currently is a Learning Support teacher in Townville, Australia. Her research interests include education and social justice, dual-language education, and media literacy.

KHURAM HUSSAIN is a former New York City schoolteacher who currently serves as Assistant Professor of Education at Hobart and William Smith Colleges. He received his Ph.D. in 2010 from Syracuse University's Cultural Foundations of Education. His scholarly inquiry focuses on the capacity of public schooling to both reproduce social inequality and democratize educational opportunity. His current research agenda includes the social history of grassroots school reform movements and the intellectual history of multiculturalism. In his work with pre-service and in-service teachers, he aims to inspire educators to integrate culturally relevant pedagogy within their repertoire of best practices and develop a personal understanding of the significance that difference plays in the classroom.

AMBER JACKSON was born in Syracuse, New York but now resides in Geneva, New York, where she is a junior at Hobart and William Smith Colleges. She is majoring in English and Media and Society but is currently studying abroad in Galway, Ireland, for the semester. Her interests are creative writing, music, community service, and rugby.

SHAPRIE BAMBACIGNO JACKSON is a graduate student in the Psychology master's program at the University of Houston–Clear Lake with an emphasis on social issues and women's studies. Her research investigates biracial and multiracial identity development among children and adolescents.

JULIA R. JOHNSON is Associate Professor of Communication, Associate Dean in the College of Liberal Studies, and Director of the School of Art and Communication at the University of Wisconsin, La Crosse. In her teaching and research she emphasizes critical approaches to the study of communication and culture, including navigating difficult dialogues about difference, transgendered approaches to gender, social justice education, and transracial feminist alliances. She has been teaching communication principles and practices in corporate and nonprofit settings since 1989. Some of her recent publications appear in journals such as the *Journal of International and Intercultural Communication* as well as edited volumes such as *Border Rhetorics: Charting Enactments of Citizenship and Identity on the U.S.-Mexico Frontier.*

LAURA M. LARSON is Instructor of Human Services at Holyoke Community College in Holyoke, MA. She holds a Master's degree in Social Justice Education from the University of Massachusetts and a B.A. in Women Studies from the University of Colorado.

DIANA LEON is a queer Latina scholar interested in exploring the representation of underrepresented groups in the media. Within communication research, she focuses on critical race theory, critical cultural theory, and intersectionality. Her current research explores audience responses to the representation of Latina bodies in the media. By using audience response case studies, she attempts to shine light on what audiences, particularly Latina/os, are asking the media to do in terms of their representations. After having received her Bachelor of Arts in Communication Studies she went on to pursue her Master's degree in Intercultural Communication at the University of New Mexico, where she is currently enrolled. Diana ultimately wishes to receive her Ph.D. in Communication and spend the rest of her days teaching and researching in the world of academia, specializing in Latina/o media studies.

LINDA MCCARTHY is Professor of Sociology at Greenfield Community College in Greenfield, MA. She has a doctorate in Social Justice Education from the University of Massachusetts and a Master's degree in Sociology from the University of New Hampshire.

ANGELA R. MILLER is currently earning her Master's degree in Sociology and certificate in Women's Studies at the University of Houston–Clear Lake. Her current research interests include examination of social, religious, and economic factors that differentially impact women's informed decision making with regard to health and pregnancy.

JUANITA MONTES DE OCA is an undergraduate student at Rhode Island College. Her major is Elementary and Middle School Education with a concentration in Social Studies. Her 5-year-old daughter drives her continued love of education and work for social justice.

SUSAN M. PLINER is the Associate Dean for Teaching, Learning, and Assessment; Director of the Center for Teaching and Learning; and Director of the Centennial Center for Leadership at Hobart and William Smith Colleges. In addition, she holds an assistant professor position in the Education Department. Susan has a B.A. in Secondary Social Studies Education, an M.Ed. in Special Education, a CAGS in Social Justice Education, and an Ed.D. in Human Development. Her areas of specialty include multicultural and social justice education, universal instructional design, disability studies, and special education.

MARTIN QUIGLEY is a member of the class of 2013 at Hobart College. He is majoring in Media Studies and minoring in Political Science and Sociology. Martin's interests are music, hiking, and skiing. He is actively engaged in various departments on campus and has been involved with the orientation program.

ANDRES RAMIREZ is Assistant Professor in the Educational Studies Department and Coordinator of the Intensive English as a Second Language Program for Adults at Rhode Island College. Andres has taught ESL/EFL and graduate and undergraduate teacher education courses in adult education and higher education institutions both in his native Colombia and the United States. He holds a B.A. in Spanish and English from Universidad de Antioquia, an M.A. in Teaching English as a Second Language from West Chester University, and graduated from the Language, Literacy, and Culture doctoral program at UMass-Amherst, Massachusetts. His scholarly interests and expertise are in the development of academic literacy for language minority students through methodologies associated with dual-language education, English as a Second/Foreign Language, Systemic Functional Linguistics, and Critical Literacy.

CRIS RAY graduated from Southwestern University in 2011 with a bachelor's degree in English Literature and a minor in Feminist Studies. Outside of the classroom, he was a founder and co-director of the Coalition for Diversity and Social Justice and a member of the Diversity Enrichment Committee and SU Allies. He currently lives in New York City and plans to begin the study of law in the next couple of years.

SALLY SPALDING received her B.A. in Communication Studies at Southwestern University and is currently working toward an M.A. in Communication and Rhetorical Studies and a Certificate of Advanced Study in Women's and Gender Studies at Syracuse University. While at Southwestern Sally was exposed to theories central to critical cultural studies that truly reframed her understanding of the world around her. She owes a large debt to Dr. Julia Johnson for turning her into an anti-racist feminist and helping her set the course for a future in the Critical Cultural field. Under Dr. Johnson's tutelage Sally developed a profound passion for critical pedagogy and the use of academic inquiry and writing as a form of activism which she carries with her as she pursues her advanced degrees. Ultimately, she hopes to receive a Ph.D. in Communication Studies with an emphasis in critical pedagogy and gender studies and continue inspiring a new generation of students to think critically about the world around them.

CHRIS SUSI is a graduate student in an Individualized Master's in Race, Class, Gender and Sexual Orientation at Rhode Island College, after completing a Bachelor's of Art in Women's Studies in 2010. S/he is currently working on incorporating a nonprofit organization focused on providing safe housing for homeless LGBTQ youth. Ultimately, s/he aims to teach cultural/women's studies at the collegiate level. Sociopolitical interests include unifying and advancing the queer community, the impact of government in/on education, and the role of media in shaping social discourse. In rare "quiet" time, Chris enjoys playing multiple musical instruments and spending time with family and friends.

ASHLEY M. TAPSCOTT is a high school English teacher at Penn Yan Academy. She graduated from William Smith College with an undergraduate degree in English. She also received a Master's of Arts in Teaching from Hobart and William Smith Colleges, during which time she completed a Master's thesis entitled "Cultural Relevancy in the Secondary English Classroom: Gender, Power, and Perspective in Classic British Fiction." Ashley is also an adjunct instructor of English at Finger Lakes Community College. Her work as an educator revolves around the social, cultural, and historical implications set forth by classic and contemporary literature.

PATRICE THOMAS was born and raised in Port-Au-Prince, Haiti, and immigrated with his two siblings to the United States when he was eleven. He is a junior at Hobart and William Smith Colleges, majoring in Sociology and French. After traveling abroad in Senegal for the spring 2012, he plans to pursue a career in a humanitarian field. Eventually, he plans to get a law degree and work towards reforming schools for youths in his homeland of Haiti.

JALISA WHITLEY recently graduated from Hobart and William Smith Colleges with a B.A. in Public Policy Studies and Sociology and a double minor in Political Science and Peer Education in Human Relations. Her experiences as an upper-middle-class individual in one of the poorest cities in Ontario County, NY, and her subsequent experiences as a downwardly mobile student on an affluent, racially homogenous campus provided the foundation for her exploration into the intersectionality between race, class, and gender issues. These experiences were built upon as she studied and taught courses in the Peer Education in Human Relations program and investigated race and ethnic relations in Central Europe for a summer. Jalisa currently lives in the D.C. metro area working at Alliances for Quality Education, Inc., a consulting firm focused on eliminating educational and health disparities in disadvantaged communities.

LEAH WING has been active in the conflict resolution field since 1983 and is a senior lecturer in the Legal Studies Program, Political Science Department, University of Massachusetts at Amherst. She is co-director of the National (U.S.) Center for Technology and Dispute Resolution and founding director of the Social Justice Mediation Institute.

KATY WOLFE graduated from Hobart and William Smith Colleges in 2011. She majored in Africana Studies and English and minored in Peace Studies and Political Science. Katy studied abroad in Ghana for a semester and in Egypt for a summer. She moved around the United States throughout her childhood, which allowed for her to understand and appreciate the importance of different lifestyles. Cultural awareness and tolerance continue to be of high ethical importance in her life. Katy currently resides in Waterloo, NY, where she works as a Youth Care Professional at a children's residential treatment center. Katy plans on returning to school to obtain a Master's in Social Work.

Index

Questions about the
Purpose(s) of Colleges
and Universities

Norm Denzin,
Shirley R. Steinberg
General Editors

What are the purposes of higher education? When undergraduates "declare their majors," they agree to enter into a world defined by the parameters of a particular academic discourse—a discipline. But who decides those parameters? How do they come about? What are the discussions and proposed outcomes of disciplined inquiry? What should an undergraduate know to be considered educated in a discipline? How does the disciplinary knowledge base inform its pedagogy? Why are there different disciplines? When has a discipline "run its course"? Where do new disciplines come from? Where do old ones go? How does a discipline produce its knowledge? What are the meanings and purposes of disciplinary research and teaching? What are the key questions of disciplined inquiry? What questions are taboo within a discipline? What can the disciplines learn from one another? What might they not want to learn and why?

Once we begin asking these kinds of questions, positionality becomes a key issue. One reason why there aren't many books on the meaning and purpose of higher education is that once such questions are opened for discussion, one's subjectivity becomes an issue with respect to the presumed objective stances of Western higher education. Academics don't have positions because positions are "biased," "subjective," "slanted," and therefore somehow invalid. So the first thing to do is to provide a sense—however broad and general—of what kinds of positionalities will inform the books and chapters on the above questions. Certainly the questions themselves, and any others we might ask, are already suggesting a particular "bent," but as the series takes shape, the authors we engage will no doubt have positions on these questions.

From the stance of interdisciplinary, multidisciplinary, or transdisciplinary practitioners, will the chapters and books we solicit solidify disciplinary discourses, or liquefy them? Depending on who is asked, interdisciplinary inquiry is either a polite collaboration among scholars firmly situated in their own particular discourses, or it is a blurring of the restrictive parameters that define the very notion of disciplinary discourse. So will the series have a stance on the meaning and purpose of interdisciplinary inquiry and teaching? This can possibly be finessed by attracting thinkers from disciplines that are already multidisciplinary, for example, the various kinds of "studies" programs (women's, Islamic, American, cultural, etc.), or the hybrid disciplines like ethnomusicology (musicology, folklore, anthropology). But by including people from these fields (areas? disciplines?) in our series, we are already taking a stand on disciplined inquiry. A question on the comprehensive exam for the Columbia University Ethnomusicology Program was to defend ethnomusicology as a "field" or a "discipline." One's answer determined one's future, at least to the extent that the gatekeepers had a say in such matters. So, in the end, what we are proposing will no doubt involve political struggles.

For additional information about this series or for the submission of manuscripts, please contact Joe L. Kincheloe, joe.kincheloe@mcgill.ca. To order other books in this series, please contact our Customer Service Department at: (800) 770-LANG (within the U.S.), (212) 647-7706 (outside the U.S.), (212) 647-7707 FAX, or browse online by series at: www.peterlang.com.